DIGITAL MARKETING MADE SIMPLE

A Jargon Free Review of
Theory, Tools &
Leveraging Human
Psychology to
SELL MORE

ISBN : 978-1-9996225-3-4
eISBN: 978-1-9996225-2-7

CONTENTS

*Dedicated to my wonderful wife Diana, who bravely
endured my manic schedule for too many years. And
to my daughter Beatrice...without you, this book
would have been completed a year earlier.
I love you both.*

FOREWORD

I have started to write this book out of the desire to help business owners, entrepreneurs and marketers to take command of their digital marketing strategies, demystify the aura of magic surrounding the concept of digital growth hacking, and help them to improve their businesses. The book is the result of over 200 interviews with business owners, entrepreneurs, non-technical managers, experienced and novice digital marketers, and students in digital marketing, who over a period of six months have unconditionally provided insights into the challenges, successes, failures, anxieties and frustrations they have faced while working with digital marketing agencies or consultants to grow their businesses online. It is also, in part, the result of self-reflection on my own challenges, perceptions, and gaps of knowledge, both prior to embarking on and throughout my journey into the digital marketing field. The decision to trade the comfort of a successful career as a hotel general manager for a field that I perceived as highly technical, specialized, and exclusive, was not an easy one to make. In spite of my successful professional record and academic background—an MBA and an MA in Marketing and Innovation—following the 2007 meltdown of the global economy I often found myself wrestling with the idea of starting a new career in a more technical field that besides being exciting would have a greater likelihood of being future proof. Like most industries, after 2007 hospitality has faithfully followed the trend of increased efficiency at the expense of employee motivation and quality of service. Hotel owners came to realize that their efforts to build customer loyalty through great customer service were fruitless, as the prospect of better service was overshadowed by price sensitivity in those very same customers. Understandably, they then saw reducing the wage bill as a priority in increasing efficiency, acknowledging that, given the precarious state of the economy, customers would trade service quality for price savings. Organizations restructured themselves, flattened their reporting structures, and in many cases centralized their operations. Jobs were lost; roles were combined or eliminated altogether. There was still the problem of reducing salaries and wages though, and owners achieved this goal by systematically deskilling their workforce and shifting the bargaining power from the professional hotelier to the owner. This outcome was achieved through leveraging two particular trends: outsourcing and automation. One example that underlines the impact of outsourcing in hotels concerns the housekeeping teams of many branded hotels, such as Hilton or Holiday Inn. Previously, the typical hotel had employed housekeeping team members directly. However, the need for increased efficiency meant that that system gave way to a new business model; third party companies were formed with the objective of convincing hotels that it was cheaper to outsource than to manage the housekeeping function in-house. How was better efficiency achieved? The catch is that most often the very same housekeeping team members that were employed by the hotel directly were now being forced to choose between losing their income through being made redundant by the hotel or working for the agency. We now have the same team, in the same hotel, working for lower wages and under increased strain to increase productivity. Hotel owners had to either continue their commitment to employee and customer satisfaction, or make employees redundant, enjoy services of similar quality from an agency that re-employed their former employees, and save both on wages and on the financial responsibilities associated with employing housekeepers directly. Of course, the only person disadvantaged was the housekeeper, who now experienced increased workload and lower wages. An identical trend is being noticed in the translation and interpreting field. Previously, experienced linguists worked directly with various government institutions, such as tribunals, police forces, and crown courts. In a drastic attempt to reduce costs, consequently at the expense of quality, the government organized a bidding process and granted contracts for these services to the third party companies that promised the highest savings, with no consideration of how the savings were to be achieved. How did these companies achieve the savings? By forcing professional translators and interpreters to make a choice: work for them at dramatically reduced rates and disadvantageous conditions, or be replaced by lower skilled, inexperienced people who often had no prior knowledge or understanding of the field, let alone the legal implications and obligations involved. Many experienced linguists resisted, and many gave in. Regardless of their choice, the results were mainly felt by the experienced linguists, who saw their income drastically reduced, and by defendants, who saw their right to accurate and professional language services diminished. Many other examples exist that underline the trend that sees experienced professionals being irremediably impacted by outsourcing, and in many cases by offshoring as well.

Regarding automation, one example that comes to mind in hospitality is the testing and adoption of self-check-in/check-out stations in many branded hotels. Now, the witty, smart and educated front desk receptionist was being replaced with lower-skilled hostesses, who now attended to multiple check-in/check-out machines simultaneously. This certainly achieved the goal of reducing both staffing levels and wages at the same time. The situation is symptomatic of most industries I can think of. Only last week I entered my local Morrisons store to find that one more human-manned check-out stations had been removed, bringing the number of self-check-out points to 10, against eight human-manned check-outs. Of course, one visibly worn down member of staff was managing the whole 10 self-check-out machines. Similarly, my local Tesco Express boasts two human-manned check-out points vs. three self-check-outs, and my local Sainsbury's has two human-manned check-outs vs. four self-check-outs. The ultimate example is provided by the launch of the Amazon Go stores in US: simply check-in with your mobile phone at the entrance, pick up your groceries and go – no staff required at all. Digital marketing is no exception to this trend; we will see later in the book how platforms such as Copify, PeoplebyHour, Freelancer and SEOClerks have shifted the balance of power away from experienced digital marketers, who are now faced with the options of accepting a significantly reduced income or joining these platforms on lower rates of pay. And, things will only get worse for these experienced professionals. I will later argue that outsourcing most often precedes automation, and that it is only a matter of time until technological advances further reduce the pool of jobs available, increase competition for lower paid positions, and ultimately leave candidates with no other alternative than to accept further decreases in wages. Perhaps Uber, a company that succeeded in leveraging technology to make the expensive taxi trip in London more affordable, provides the best example of how the outsourcing–automation trend unfolds. You can easily argue that Uber successfully reduced trip fares by outsourcing their services to taxi drivers who owned their own car; in fact, to the best of my knowledge, Uber owns no cabs at all. Various scandals over the years have pointed to the fact that savings in fares come at the expense of lower incomes for drivers, who seem to have resigned themselves to earning less than in their pre-Uber life. However, Uber's well-known venture into developing autonomous self-driving taxis leaves no doubts about what their long-term ambitions are. In fact, taxi-drivers cannot assume their jobs to be safe in the long run. They find themselves one step away from being made redundant by technology. That is outsourcing followed by automation.

Back to my idea of leaving the comfort of an established career in hospitality: in light of the trends I've described, I have come to the realization that my need to make a decision was no dilemma after all, and that I simply couldn't have afforded not to board the digital marketing train. The alternative would have been far more daunting: complacency in a role that was slowly being commodified. I did not want to be that general manager, that check-out point operator, that front desk assistant or that taxi-driver. With these things in mind, I decided to make the move. But I was anxious, and I was worried about the prospect of getting up to speed with the skills required to start afresh in a field that seemed so technical and exclusivist. The very name search engine optimization seemed to imply that graduating with a degree in computer science was essential for operating in the field. Similarly, terms such as growth hacking raised in my mind images of genius geeks who had gotten into programming at a very young age, subsequently hacking their way into NASA's computers. And the term digital marketing seemed to conjure up the image of the MIT graduate we often see in Hollywood movies. Because of such images, many bright but anxious entrepreneurs, business owners, and marketers employ the expensive services of digital marketing agencies and consultants. And, when they do, they are often met with lots of technical jargon, which further reinforces the idea that they made the right decision in employing professional support. Indeed, the idea of DIY was a fantasy, they reason; after all, they could never perform the complicated tasks described in this technical jargon.

I assure you that every digital marketing task can be, and will be, learned by you, the savvy entrepreneur, business owner or non-technical marketer. You will, sooner or later, realize that you are better off managing your digital marketing campaign with little or no support from professional digital marketers. Indeed, you will make professional and expensive digital marketers a commodity. As hotels did, you too will achieve this outcome by leveraging the rise of outsourcing and advances in technology. You will also gain a far better understanding of human behavior than most of the digital marketers you have been employing or working with. If, for whatever reason, you decide against a DIY approach, you will find yourself in a far better position to challenge your digital marketing agency or consultant to do better. However, as a digital marketer I must emphasize the futility of relying on the aura of wizardry created around the profession to maintain, let alone grow, your business. By understanding the trends defining the future of the digital marketing profession, as described in my book HACKING DIGITAL GROWTH 2025: Exploiting Human Biases, Tools of the Trade & The Disturbing Future of Digital Marketing, you will find yourself in a better position to upgrade your skills in the right areas. Whether a novice or an experienced digital marketer, you will find the section on psychology beneficial in improving the performance of your digital marketing efforts, generating more conversions and ultimately more leads. And, if you ever wondered what kinds of tools a growth hacker uses behind the scenes, the chapter on the tools of the trade will provide a short overview of some of these tools.

When I started to write this book, I did not imagine that it would take ten months and fill 350 pages. I initially intended to write a practical book about the tools, practices and principles of growth hacking. However, I quickly understood that I could not simply explain the working of these tools and practices without diving deep into the psychological principles they leveraged. After all, it is important that people understand why these tools succeed if they are to best leverage the power of them. So I decided to write a section on consumer psychology as well. Over time, I have witnessed the major changes that have occurred in the digital marketing industry. Google is a prime example of how advances in machine learning technologies have shifted the bargaining power away from SEOs. The idea of a section on the future of digital marketing and SEO seemed natural. I now had over 350 pages in the cloud, separated into a section on the future, one on psychology, and another, highly practical section. It became clear to me that the type of audience that might enjoy the first two chapters might not enjoy the more practical part of the book. Similarly, the busy business owner or marketer who wants to learn hands-on the tools and practices, would not necessarily enjoy the section on the future. So, I decided to split my book into two separate books, which would best address the different proclivities of the audiences I had in mind. After some reflection, I decided to include the section on psychology in both books, as it is relevant both to experienced marketers who want to improve their existing skills, and to the novice business owner or entrepreneur who wants to understand how to get into their clients' minds. My first book, HACKING DIGITAL GROWTH 2025: Exploiting Human Biases, Tools of the Trade & The Disturbing Future of Digital Marketing included an extensive conversation on the technological forces impacting the proffesion of Digital Marketing, and the furture of this profession. By contrast, the book you are reading has a more practical feel, where concepts are described and explained in straightforward language, with a minimum of jargon, the purpose being to demystify digital marketing and make it more accessible to the business owner, to the entrepreneur, and to anyone not a digital marketing professional. This second book comprises an extensive list of digital marketing tools, beyond the ones described in my first book. In fact, this second book is aimed at giving business owners and non-technical marketers the confidence that behind the jargon lies a very simple task, and provide them with an easy-to-use tool that can perform that task, with no engagement of a website developer or digital marketer. In a nutshell, when writing this second book I went to great lengths to imagine every potential digital marketing task that you might need to perform as a budget-aware business owner or entrepreneur, and the tool you might be using to complete that task.

Enjoy!

PART 1.
THE PSYCHOLOGY

CHAPTER 1.
INTRODUCTION

Human psychology has always fascinated me, ever since I used to manage large hotel teams for brands such as Holiday Inn and Hilton. That being so, for years I have been reading every psychology, marketing, and leadership book I came across. I have done so because as a leader I have always thought that included in my personal development was a duty of care toward those I was in charge of; after all a good or a bad leader impacts directly on the happiness and effectiveness of his or her staff. Far too many leaders stopped learning a long time ago, and I often see demotivated staff, low customer satisfaction, and poor business performance for this reason alone. I apply the same line of thought in everything I do, and digital marketing is no exception to that rule. When I first started in digital marketing, one of the many areas I wanted to learn about was the behavior of customers online. Having worked in a more traditional bricks-and-mortar type of business, I was keen to learn more about the irrational behavior displayed by people while online, in relation to the more conventional leadership-focused psychology I had come to know over the years. So I started to read as many books as I could find on the subject of online psychology. I was both surprised and disappointed to realize that many promises made by these books were simply not met. Specifically, when discussing online psychology most SEO books focus on understanding the way people search, and on their intent as users. For example, in their landmark book The Art of SEO, Eric Enge and his associates discuss at length the types of search people perform, how visitors perform their searches, and how websites must be designed so that they are able to answer the queries they are intended to answer. (Enge, Spencer, Stricchiola, & Fishkin, 2013) Other books seem to convey the message that conversion optimization actions equate to psychology. Indeed, heat map studies and live behavior studies have been performed and have found that people spend more time in certain areas of the screen, click more on buttons of particular colors, and respond better to a "Buy Now" call to action than to "Learn More." The problem is that this kind of finding focuses on the effect rather than on the cause of that behavior, which provides little information on how successful the digital marketing strategies used really are. Sure, we know that red "Buy Now" buttons deliver more conversions, and that clean to-the-point landing pages perform better than "busy" pages. However, the right question to be asked is: "Could these pages perform even better?" The point is that, at the time of my investigations, I was less interested in the effects of human psychology and wanted to understand more about the reasons for these online behaviors—what was their cause? In a nutshell, these books were telling me that "X% of people click on the middle-size red button because...."— and the reason was missing. I was running out of ideas until I read one of Rand Fishkin's books, where he quotes from Robert Cialdini's book Influence: The Psychology of Persuasion. (Cialdini, 2007) As Cialdini's was one of my favorite books, I was surprised at what I found. It seemed that, after all, online psychology may have had a bit more in common with traditional psychology than I had initially assumed. Next, I reviewed all the psychology I had read over the years with a completely new mindset, trying to reconcile that psychology with the psychology of the online world. I have the habit of underlining all the interesting things I read directly on the book pages, and this allows me to read over and over again the same book in as little as one hour at times. It is strange to notice how the content of a paragraph on the page can have so many different applications, and how your mindset completely changes the meaning of the text. So, armed with this new mindset, coupled with a lot of self-reflection on my own online behavior, I was now noticing a lot of connections I had not seen before. But most importantly, I realized that I had been looking in the wrong place to receive answers to my questions—the same principles I had been forging throughout my hotel management career I could now extend, adapt, and apply in influencing people online as well. In this chapter I will share many of these principles in the hope that they will help you to further improve and grow your business online. In some cases, I attempt to provide examples of how traditional psychology can also be applied in digital marketing. In other situations, I have left to your imagination the multitude of applications you might find for the principles discussed. Finally, this is not a book that will serve it all up to you on a tray, it is not a to-do checklist either. Rather, I encourage a reflective approach—in what other ways can you apply these principles to improve your online results?

Let's get started!

The Nobel laureate Daniel Kahneman is one of the most often quoted psychologists alive. Kahneman has described the workings of the brain using the metaphor of two systems: a slower but more accurate one (System2), and a faster thinking but less accurate one (System 1). System 1 is in charge of automatic thinking and feelings, responses to various situations, such as unexpected emergencies, and is also responsible for the thing we call intuition. System 1 responses are based on familiarity with the situation at hand. The more familiar the situation the more System 1 one takes over, in preference to System 2, and responds in line with previous experience. In popular terms, System 1 is in charge of "jumping to conclusions," and is prone to many biases and errors that Kahneman refers to as heuristics. System 2 by contrast is the slower, more analytical and conscious part of the brain. System 2 is in charge of "conscious thoughts," monitoring our behavior and self-control, paying attention to our actions, and answering questions that cannot be answered by System 1. We all believe ourselves to be masters of our own decisions and actions, indeed that System 2 is in the driving seat of our behavior. We believe that we can access our consciousness at any time, make unbiased decisions and understand the reasoning behind those decisions. The truth is that most of the time our mental processes are operating outside of our consciousness, well beyond our awareness and deep in unconscious. The mistaken belief that we can access our conscious mind, understand how it works, and make decisions freely has been referred to as an "introspection illusion" by psychologist Tali Sharot. (Sharot, 2012) In fact, within the psychology field there is almost unanimous agreement that un-consciousness is in fact in the driving seat of our behavior. In a nutshell, the idea that we can access the processes that underlie our decisions, and the idea of conscious decision-making are mainly illusions. If in disbelief, or looking for proof, then read on. Throughout this chapter I will present a variety of studies, concepts, and psychology experiments revealing the multitude of biases and unconscious processes at work throughout our decision making activity. And, after a life of research in the field Kahneman explains that automatic decision making (System 1) can not be turned off at will, and biases are difficult if not impossible to prevent. Kahneman concludes that "...disbelief is not an option...you have no choice but to accept that the major conclusions of these studies are true...Priming phenomena arise in system 1, and you have no conscious access to them" (Kahneman, 2011, p. 57). Psychologist Claude M Steele also points out that: "One of the first things one learns as a social psychologist is that everyone is capable of bias. We simply are not, and cannot be...completely objective." (Steele, 2011, p. 13). Furthermore, Benjamin Franklin, quoted by Chabris & Simons, states in a very emphatic manner that, "There are three things extremely hard: steel, a diamond, and to know one's self." (Chabris & Simons, p. Intro). But my favorite statement is provided by Noah Yuval Harari who concludes that, "attributing free will to humans is not an ethical judgment." (Harari, 2015, p. 283)

CHAPTER 2.
PERCEPTIONS

One of the most misused Internet marketing techniques is promotion through special offers, free products, or various types of webpage content. Tools like Hello Bar or AddThis provide marketers with the ability to create pop-ups, sticky bars, and exit pop-ups, featuring various lead magnets offering something in exchange for giving contact details, sharing, liking, following, and other similar actions. Unfortunately, far too often webmasters offer stuff of no value to the user, ending up with sign-up rates below their expectations, a result easy to foresee. These disappointing results are often caused by a lack of understanding of the psychological principles that these tools are trying to leverage and build on. In fact, most marketers do not think of digital marketing tools as a way of leveraging human biases, but rather think of them in a simple transactional way: I give you this, but you need to give me that in return. So, without any further introduction, let us have a look at some well-founded psychology findings that digital marketers need to be aware of and to leverage online. First things first: the offer. I am afraid there is nothing new or exciting here, you must offer something of exceptional value to your website visitors. In simple terms, if you want to make an impression on your website visitors then your product or offer must stand out from the crowd. Psychologists refer to the human bias toward noticing and remembering the unusual as the Von Restorff effect. And marketing guru Seth Godin branded exceptional products as "Purple cows" when noticing that "services that are worth talking about get talked about...the lesson is simple—boring always leads to failure. Boring is always the most risky strategy." (Godin, 2005, p. 33, p. 50). The reality is that in a market that is well oversupplied, many marketers find it hard to come to terms with the situation: they create an OK product and focus most of their efforts on promoting it. Of course, this works less and less well, as most market leaders well understand. For example, Jeff Bezos, Amazon's founder pointed out that old models of companies spending 30 percent of their time on building a product and the remaining time on marketing is redundant, and points out the fact that those percentages have in fact inverted. Eric Schmidt, the former CEO of Google has described Google's intense focus on user experience, acknowledging that this focus has resulted in a significantly higher user base, which has naturally attracted more advertisers and increased revenue. (Schmidt & Rosenberg, 2014, p. 13:15) The moral of the story? Stop offering basic digital marketing guides to professional marketers! The same goes for your 10 percent off the first purchase, a free guide with every sign-up, and many other similar offers. One company I know, which offers high-cost services, went as far as dedicating an entire banner which said: " Free Gift with your First order. Fox's Fabulously Biscuit Selection (300 g)—Your gift will be added automatically to your first order". I looked up the cost of the Free Gift at my local supermarket—it was £3. Your visitors are being hit with these offers every day. In fact, a study carried out by the McKinsey Institute found that a typical American hears or reads in excess of one hundred thousand words a day, including emails, text, tweets, blog posts, and videos. (Pink, 2013, p. 159) This being so, it is easy to see that you must put real effort into ensuring that your offer is exceptional and of high value to your audience. To sum up, purple cows and purple cows alone will best leverage the unconscious biases and heuristics discussed throughout this chapter.

2.1 First impressions matter...

We all know that first impressions count, though we neither reflect on nor understand the real meaning and implications of the statement. Take an experiment conducted at Harvard. Students were presented with a two-second silent clip of a teacher they'd never seen before, and were asked to rate his effectiveness. The ratings were compared with the ratings provided by students who actually studied with the teacher for one semester. Findings? The ratings were identical. Yes, by simply looking at a two-second silent video students were able to correctly infer the level of professionalism of the teacher. (Cabane, 2012) In brief, within a split second we unconsciously apply a label to an experience, thing, performance or, yes, a website, page, product, or piece of content. Indeed, a very suggestive experiment concluded: "Attention web designers: You have 50 milliseconds to make a good first impression." (Krug, 2014, p. 90) And once we make up our mind, we filter out information that contradicts the opinion we now hold. It is what psychologists call a confirmation bias. In Kruger's experiment, the opinion formed within 50 milliseconds agreed with the judgements of the website made by people who spent more time on a website.

Another way of making a good first impression is by providing audiences with indicators of the legitimacy of your business. Eye-tracking studies have shown that while navigating your website people look for phone numbers at the top right hand side of the page, or scroll down the page and spend some time in the footer area where they would most often expect to find an email address. (Jones, 2014) Tools such as virtual numbers track both the number of calls generated by your website and inspire confidence in the legitimacy of your business. Google Reviews plugins and the availability of live chat are also tools that provide a sense of legitimacy.

2.2 ...but what you remember first matters as well

So, first impressions of your website matter. However, the most readily available impression, whatever that may be, is equally powerful. Psychologists labeled this effect the availability bias. A myriad of experiments confirm that people make decisions based on the most readily available information to hand, as opposed to the more logical approach of reviewing all available information. For example, various studies have found that 80 percent of us think accidental death is more likely than dying from a stroke, but strokes cause twice as many deaths as all accidents. Similarly, death by accident is perceived to be 300 times as likely as death by diabetes even though diabetes kills four times as many people as accidents do. (Kahneman, 2011) Moreover, after an aviation accident, the number of people traveling by plane decreases, even though statistics show that significantly more people die in car accidents. Ok, but why does a plane crash remain so strongly available in our memory? The answer is simple: it is mostly down to the media, which in turn are being influenced by the freshness of the news. There is no hiding from the fact that, just like Google, the news media also shape our thoughts and perceptions. Take the announcement of the engagement of Prince Harry of the UK to Meghan Markle, which was discussed in literally every UK media publication I laid my eyes on. In spite of finding the publicity of the event somewhat overdone, the wedding saga is probably one of the most available memories I have, far more available than starving children or human rights abuses in many underdeveloped countries. That being said, attributing the state of things to the media alone is far too convenient; after all, newspapers write about what is of interest to their audiences. In effect, we feed the media machine that molds our most recent perceptions. Imagine for a moment that some top newspapers had decided not to publish the Harry and Meghan story. How many people would have switched to a competitor in search of news about the royal engagement? The conclusion must be that the availability bias with respect to our memory of, and interest in an event grows in direct proportion to the amount of media coverage given to that event. But what does this have to do with digital marketing? Well, quite a lot actually. SEOs have known for a long time that Google prioritizes fresh, popular, and current affairs. If you are an SEO person you will remember one of Rand Fishkin's interesting experiments. In the middle of a conference, Rand asked participants to click on a certain search result that was ranking on the first page in Google. Google algorithms assumed that there was a sudden interest in the content and moved it up the website through the rankings. Similarly, popular news such as the royal engagement will rate higher in the rankings than other content. In fact, it seems that in the end both the news media and Google are shaped by what users want and like. The point is that as an SEO, content writer or business owner looking to engage audiences with your brand, product, or content, while also improving your SEO rankings, you must consider your audience's most available experience or piece of information, and build your strategy around it. Unfortunately, far too often content writers or bloggers write about stuff they like, as opposed to considering the likes and passions of their audience. This is a shame, as there are many tools that monitor current trends or hot subjects on social media, BuzzSumo being one that comes to mind. And yet, in my experience many but not all writers and SEOs put very little effort into using these out-of-the-box tools.

2.3 ...and don't forget the last impressions, either

Negative or extreme events have a strong impact on what we feel, and how we act by being more available to us in our memories. But what happens when no extreme events exist? What if we fail to make a great first impression on the audience? According to our prior discussion we must be doomed, and condemned to a life of blogging in anonymity, as people will most likely never return to our website. Or they may label our website as "bad" or "OK" and filter out any future appearances of it in line with this perception. And, if we made only an OK first impression, the experience will most likely be anything but available in our audience's mind. Availability to the rescue again, in the form of last impressions. In one study on perceptions of their holidays, the scores awarded by participants to their vacation experiences were determined by the final evaluation of their experiences. (Kahneman, 2011) A myriad of studies in various fields confirm that people use as their reference point, and attribute more value to, the last impressions held about a product or experience. Thus, if you have a great check-in into a hotel, receive great service throughout your stay but experience a bad check-out, you will most likely report the bad check-out disproportionately when reviewing the hotel. This in spite of the fact that your checkout experience represented only a very small percentage of the time you mostly enjoyed at the hotel. In this context, Neil Patel's advice on using exit pop-ups to boost conversion rates makes sense. Great "Thank you" pages or auto respondent Thank you emails served after the submitting of a contact form are yet another opportunity to keep in mind.

2.4 Relevant beats cool...

There are various reasons why your website's identity, imagery, general look, and feel must match the expectations of your target audience. Unfortunately, we humans have this tendency of extending our judgement of prevalent characteristics of a person to all their characteristics, which is referred to as the "halo effect". (Kahneman, 2011) For example, if I believe your website funnel or homepage to be bad, then I will most likely extend this perception to all other features of your website, products, and offers. While online, people associate the look and feel of your website with prices they expect to pay, or with the quality of your products. To begin with, your brand identity dictates the prices people have been primed to pay. For example, while navigating the website of Poundland people expect to pay lower prices than while navigating the website of Apple. (Jones, 2014) Being aware of this distinction makes all the difference between a high and a low conversion rate on your website. You would be surprised how many Poundland-like businesses build upmarket-looking websites, violating people's expectations of what "cheap" should look like. The same principle applies to products sold on your website, as well. Do you have a purple cow? Just don't sell it on a cheap-looking website, it will only devalue your product and reduce your margins. Conversely, if you have an expensive-looking website, put some effort into packaging your purple cow to look expensive. Take an experiment carried out by Dan Ariely , which found that people felt more energetic and less tired after drinking the same energy drink when it was presented at a higher price vs. when it was presented as discounted. (Ariely, 2009) Or the classic experiment of Joshua Bell, a top violinist, who played his 3.5 million-dollar Stradivarius violin in a Washington, D.C., subway station, just like a regular street artist. Throughout this experiment, when people did not know who he was, Bell raised only $32 through donations. (Bloom, 2011) A classic example of a great product (Joshua Bell's music) on the equivalent of a cheap-looking website (subway vs. concert hall).

Consider another implication of your website's consistency, look, and feel. Take people who visit an expensive site. By doing so they reinforce an ideal image of themselves; the website and its products say something about them, and the type of person they are or aspire to be. This ideal-self idea is powerful as most people generally purchase on websites that reinforce this ideal self-image. Thus, your website must reinforce and acknowledge the identity of your audience. The first way of achieving this is by labeling your audience in line with behaviors that correspond with their goals and desires. On one side, we fall prey to what psychologist Richard Wiseman labeled "the flattery effect" (Wiseman, 2007): we most often choose to believe cues that show us in a good, positive light and make us feel good about ourselves and our skills. Take LinkedIn's labeling of people as Influencers, which serves to generate more input from those contributors; or labeling your website visitor or forum member as a gold level contributor, which generates more contributions on their part, intended to maintain and improve their status. In the words of Dale Carnegie: "The deepest urge in human nature is the desire to be important." (Carnegie, 2006, p. 18) A second way of nurturing your audience's identity is to acknowledge that we are generally aware of how our perceptions of other people, products, or experiences are influenced by stereotypes. But at the same time, we often fail to consider the impact of stereotyping in changing the behavior of people who are being stereotyped. The fact is that the way people think about us will often impact on how we behave, a concept often referred to as a "self-fulfilling prophecy". For example, in one experiment people were primed into thinking about a football hooligan, and answered correctly to 46 percent of the questions presented to them, well below the 60 percent achieved by people primed into thinking about a professor. (Wiseman, 2010) Similarly, a platinum member on your website will most likely behave differently than a gold member who will behave differently to a silver member.

In conclusion, designing your website with the audience in mind will significantly improve your chances of generating consistent conversions and engagement. Of course, this seems quite intuitive and simplistic; after all we all know that. Right? In my experience, this is not often true. Particularly in the case of small and medium-size businesses, website designers tend to build beautiful-looking websites with little thought being put into sales funnels, SEO, brand identity or the target market. In fact, very often web designers build cool websites that say something about themselves and their skills, rather than saying more about the intended audience of the website.

2.5 Why do reviews work?

Entrepreneur Daniel Priestley once stated: "Most great businesses grow because of what others are saying about them" (Priestley, 2014, p. 178). We all know that reviews work on the principle of social proof: the more people believe my product is good the more people try and like my product, which in turn leads to more people purchasing and liking it, and so forth. "Wait a second," you may say; "I agree that reviews improve visibility to my product, but the suggestion that people will also like it is far off the mark." And you are right, up to a point. Yes, a bad product is a bad product and no reviews can change a person's experience of that product. However, the situation can be quite different in the case of average or good products. In these cases, reviews *can* change someone's perception of the product, make average products good, and good products great. Take an experiment in which students were questioned on the quality of two types of beer: a classic Budweiser beer and an MIT Brew that was contaminated with two drops of balsamic vinegar. When unaware about the vinegar, the MIT beer was most often chosen as the winner. Things changed when students were told in advance that the MIT beer contained two drops of vinegar. Now, after tasting the beers the Budweiser won. (Ariely, 2009, p. 157:159) What this ingenious experiment shows is that expectations have a direct influence on our perceptions. In simple terms, if we believe a product is good prior to trying it, we will be more likely to like it. (Ariely, 2009) Hence, prior to watching a movie you might increase people's enjoyment of the movie by pointing to the fact that the movie has great reviews. (Ariely, 2009) Reviews can therefore make an average movie better, and a good movie great. In the same manner, reviews can influence our perceptions of OK products, content, authors or experiences.

For a finer understanding of how reviews work, let us now consider a classical sidewalk experiment conducted by psychologist Stanley Milgram as long ago as 1968. Milgram monitored 1,424 pedestrians and their behavior while walking by various-size groups of Milgram's accomplices, who were looking up to the sixth floor of a building for one minute. At the sixth floor nothing special was happening. Milgram wanted to find out the size of groups that provided sufficient social proof to persuade pedestrians to stop and copy the behavior of his accomplices, i.e., look up at the sixth floor. The experiment found that only 4 percent of pedestrians stopped when only one person was looking up. By contrast, when the group was formed of fifteen accomplices, 40 percent of people stopped and looked up. Moreover, an extraordinary 82 percent of the people imitated the behavior of the larger group by looking up at the sixth floor but not stopping. (Christakis & Fowler, 2011) What can the reason be for this behavior? The answer is simple: people looked up under the assumption that as other people were looking up there must be a reason for it.

That insight explains many other riddles, such as why people are influenced by reviews, recommendations, social media, celebrity endorsement, and so forth. After all, if one book has lots of great reviews on Amazon or Google, or one article is the topic of many shares, there must be a reason for it. By the way, there are many creative ways in which sellers can manipulate the number and the quality of reviews. However, Taleb brilliantly argues that reviews from readers on websites such as Amazon are all about the persons themselves, in contrast to reviews by qualified people, when the reviews are all about the book. (Taleb, 2007) Yes, the logic says that we should take Amazon reviews with a pinch of salt, and yet our decisions are being shaped by these reviews. Of course, it does not stop here. Amazon then points out that "people who bought this also bought this". Amazon does not even have to pitch the book to me—if other people, people like me, bought a book, then surely I should also have a look. The canned laughter during TV comedy shows provides yet another, finer insight into the workings of social proof. Psychology experiments have found that the audience laughs more and finds the shows funnier than when presented without the background laughter. (Cialdini, 2007) Social proof fuels reviews and recommendations: most of us are aware that the laughter is artificial, and yet we find the relevant moments funnier and more engaging. Somehow, the social proof provided by canned laughter is likened to a favorable review: the more people laugh, the better the show must be.

If you are anything like me, whenever you are looking around for a book on Amazon you will pay little attention to books with no reviews or a low number of reviews. My default assumption is that lack of reviews means that not many people have been buying the book, hence the book must be no good. In contrast, I always choose the books with the largest number of reviews and ratings. After all, if a lot of people have been reviewing the book, there must be a reason for it; it must be a good book. So, the more people review a product positively, the more we infer that the product is more popular and of better quality. This is particularly important in cases of uncertainty, such as when we are unsure of the quality of a product, or have no experience of it. In these cases, we most often observe what other people are doing or buying; we study the number of stars and the reviews received by, say, a book, and very often replicate the behavior of the people who also bought that book. After all, if people who purchased a book that I have read and liked also bought another book, it must be that the recommended book is also good. Of course, this is a fallacy, as at this point the only information I have about the recommended book is that people with similar reading behavior have purchased it and reviewed it. By comparison, you may have a purple cow product, but if no one tries it, and no one reviews it, you will struggle. Back to my Amazon purchase of a book. After the number of reviews and the rating of a book have attracted my attention, I continue by reading some of the reviews. The reviews will most often confirm the overall ratings and my initial gut feeling about the book. And when a bad review comes up, I can easily explain it away: the guy who wrote it has no idea what he's talking about, he is not experienced enough, or he is not open-minded enough. In brief, I interpret that review as being about the person rather than about the book, which is exactly the approach I should take with the remaining reviews. In fact, our tendency to explain away things that don't fit in with our views has been widely documented and investigated in thousands of experiments. For example, during an experiment carried out at the University of Melbourne, subjects were provided with two sets of reviews of two fictional coffee brands, one negative and one positive. After they had read the reviews, the subjects were informed that a mistake was made and that in fact the negative reviews belonged to the company that was initially labeled as positive, and the positive reviews belonged to the company initially labeled as negative. Did the subjects change their minds? No, they still provided high ratings to the company that was erroneously labeled as positive. (Jones, 2014) In simple terms, people had made a decision about the company based on the initial reviews, and further information was made to match their first impressions. Reviews rule!

In another experiment, Salganik, Dodds, and Watts monitored people who were navigating a website where downloadable music was given away free. The study found that, for many songs the first review of an item influenced the whole trajectory of subsequent ratings. (Christakis & Fowler, 2011) We recognize at work here a principle that has been labeled "the anchoring effect": people evaluate things they are unsure about by attuning their judgement to evaluations already available. In the absence of other reviews, first reviews act as an anchor, set preconceptions about quality, and influence subsequent perceptions and reviews. Of course, the product plays a part and, as discussed earlier, no amount of favorable reviews can make a bad product seem good. To further understand how you can put the anchoring effect to work, reflect for a moment on your perception of what is the fair value of a product. If you think about it, your perception of a fair price is to some degree determined by the price the seller asks: the higher the price, the higher the perceived value of the product, and the more willing you are to pay a price in the range set by the seller. By contrast, if the same product is positioned at a lower price point, the lower price provides a cue, indicating a lower value, a value that you now assign to the item. Now, you will perceive any subsequent increases in price as unfair. Notice that the same product's value is being perceived differently based on the price point you have initially set as an anchor. Take a study carried out on people who were asked to contribute to an environmental cause. Initially, the team of researchers asked the participants an anchoring question: "Would you be willing to pay $5..." prior to asking them to contribute. When the request was served with no anchor, participants were willing to pay on average $64. However, when the $5 anchor was introduced participants were willing to pay on average only $20. And, when the anchor was set at $400 people were willing to pay on average $143. (Kahneman, 2011) Same request, different anchor price, significantly improved conversion. This example sheds some light on the main use that marketers find for the anchoring principle. Many marketers, though, miss the opportunity of leveraging the anchoring effect in the context of improving the reviews profile of their websites or products. In Salganik, Dodds and Watts's experiment the first review—the anchor—determined the trajectory of all subsequent reviews. Unfortunately, marketers and business owners often fail to make Google or Yelp reviews part of their website's core launch strategy. Of course, this may not present a problem when the first reviews are positive. However, when negative and allowed to stand, first reviews have the ability to kick-start a self-reinforcing spiral of negativity, damaging conversions, leads, sales, and ultimately your business. In fact, plenty of research indicates that negative emotions and bad feedback loom higher in people's minds than positive emotions and feedback, are quicker to form, and are much harder to dislodge. (Kahneman, 2011) People pay more attention to negative reviews than to positive reviews, and negative reviews have a stronger impact on purchasing behavior. If you think about it, how many times have you bought a book rated 2.5 out of 5 on Amazon? Not very often, I bet. And yet 2.5 out of 5 represents a 50–50 ratio. In fact, if you are like me, you will most likely try to maximize the use of your time and purchase books with reviews within the range of 4.5 and 5 stars. A rating of 3, 3.5 or 4 has a considerably higher number of positive reviews than a 2.5, and yet it is the lower number of negative reviews that looms higher.

So, we have not been paying attention to our Google Reviews score, ended up with low scores, and all is lost. Is that it? Not quite; as always there are ways you can improve conversion rates on your website by putting to good use various psychological concepts. Take the primacy effect as an example. The primacy effect refers to people's bias of interpreting later information based on earlier information about a product, event, person, content, and so forth. (Sutherland, 2007) Psychologist Solomon Ash conducted an experiment in which two groups of people were prompted to rate a person based on nothing more than a set of adjectives provided about the person. Both groups received the same adjectives, but for one of them the positive adjectives were presented before the negative words, while the other group received the negative words before the positives. For example, the first group was presented with adjectives such as *intelligent, industrious, impulsive, critical, stubborn, envious,* while the second group was presented with the same adjectives in the following order: *envious, stubborn, critical, impulsive, industrious, intelligent.* The group that received the positive adjectives first rated the person described as significantly more positive on attributes such as happiness or how sociable they were than the other group did. Hence, simply priming people with positive adjectives impacted their overall perception and rating of the person. (Sutherland, 2007) But what does this have to do with reviews? In Ash's experiment people made up their mind based on the first adjectives presented within the list. Your reviews work on the same principle; people most often scan the most recent reviews of the product and very rarely navigate to page two of the reviews. The obvious follow-up is that you should work hard on consistently building positive reviews. In this way, your product or website will benefit from a constant pool of positive adjectives on page one, and your audience will have the most accurate and recent feedback on your business, as well. This is particularly important on high-traffic third-party review websites like TripAdvisor. You can go a bit further by installing a Google Reviews plugin such as Rich Snippets, which provides the capability of displaying Google reviews on your website with a great deal of customization. For example, you can choose to display only reviews with higher ratings or only reviewers who have avatar images, you can change your business image or the number of characters to be displayed before the Read More button, and much more. In this way, you can screen out negative reviews by choosing to display only 4-star or higher reviews, and reviewers with avatar images—i.e., real people— and you can allow 155–200 characters before the Read More button, priming your audience with more-positive perceptions. You can also add a Write a Review button, encouraging more people to write reviews and hopefully improve your overall rating score.

Up to this point we have been discussing the effect of reviews. Yes, reviews work and they are powerful. But why are they working? Let's begin by briefly reviewing the process we go through when reading online reviews. We like to believe that we consciously read reviews, analyze the pros and cons they mention, and then make a conscious decision on whether to buy the product. Unfortunately, our assumption that we can compare reviews in an unbiased manner is an illusion. As the University of Melbourne experiment concerning the fictional coffee companies revealed, even after being informed about the reviews mix-up, people still rated higher the company that initially wrongly received the positive set of reviews. Thus, as we read reviews our brain makes its own decision about the product, well before our decision to "consciously" and "freely" assess the reviews. And, when we do make a decision, the decision is nothing but a confirmation of the decision our brain has already made beyond our awareness. It is a fact that our perceptions form outside our awareness well before we decide to consciously assess the reviews. In the words of psychologist Dan Ariely: "We usually think of ourselves as sitting in the driving seat, with ultimate control over the decisions we make...but this perception has more to do with our desires, with how we want to view ourselves than with reality" (Ariely, 2009, p. 243). As an example, consider the simple act of moving one of your fingers. If I asked you to move your finger, you consciously decide to move your finger and believe that YOU have taken the decision. And yet, fMRI studies have found that while you are still assessing whether to move your finger or not, your brain has already started the action, well before you consciously reached the decision of moving your finger. (Hood, 2009) Similarly, neuroscientists have found that when you take a conscious decision of throwing a ball, the part of the brain involved in performing the action is being activated half a second before you actually decide to perform the action. Not convinced yet? Consider another example: if you are presented with a choice between two switches, simply by monitoring your neural activity scientists can accurately tell you the switch you will eventually press, before you consciously decided to press it. (Harari, 2015) And in another 2008 fMRI study, researchers found the unaware to aware time gap to be as long as 10 seconds before participants formed a conscious intent of performing an action.

(Trivers, 2011) We like to believe that when making a decision we follow a logical and conscious process; we read reviews about the product, analyze the reviews, weigh up the reviews in an unbiased manner, and after a conscious and unbiased deliberation finally make up our mind. However, as we have seen, these "free will" decisions are illusions of control, being preceded by decisions taken well beyond awareness, and thus are simply manifestations of those unconscious decisions. That being so, reading one review, or no more than a couple, is all it takes for our website audiences, like us, to infer the quality of a product. An overly negative recent review will be hard to overturn with positive reviews. Similarly, a lot of positive reviews will be easily overturned by one negative comment. In fact, prior to reading any reviews the brain has already inferred the quality of a product based on the number of reviews and the overall rating. After this, reading reviews or assessing the quality of a product is a simple matter of fitting in the information at hand to the perceptions we have formed beyond awareness.

2.6 Reviews + Recommendations = Growth

Often, marketers miss the opportunity to grow their business because they focus too much on core products, centering their recommended products system and their marketing strategy entirely on those products. In fact, I often have to fight my clients' stubbornness and persistence in focusing on particular products that generally deliver higher margins in individual sales. The online competition for these products is often so high and the search volume so low that the results are just not there. I generally win by convincing them that often "the biggest money is in the smallest sales". (Laws quoted by Anderson, 2009, p. 23) The former Editor-in-Chief of *Wired* magazine, Chris Anderson, has written at length on this subject in his thought provoking book *The Long Tail*. Anderson provides a myriad of examples of online businesses such as Amazon, Jukebox, and Netflix to support his claim that large chunks of sales come not from the well-known products but rather from long tail products which are rarely sold. In brief, your business might be more profitable by recommending 1,000 rarely sold products than by pushing your main products, which in total sell less. Reed Hastings, CEO of Netflix:" About 30 percent of what we rent is new releases and about 70 percent is back catalogue...because we create demand for content and we help you find great movies that you'll really like. And we do it algorithmically with recommendations and ratings." (Anderson, 2009, p. 110) Of course, what is not being mentioned is the low cost associated with selling the 70 percent of the movies in the back catalogue vs. the 30 percent releases. The truth is that in reality the strategy is different for every business; your recommendation and ratings tools and filters need to be set to match your strategy.

CHAPTER 3.
IT'S ALL ABOUT THE FEELINGS

3.1 Introduction

Marketers have known for a long time that audiences are most vulnerable to their messages when they "feel". Thus, any marketing strategy must be construed around a thoroughly researched palette of emotions, emotions that are most likely to trigger the desired action. But how powerful are emotions really? We often consider the impact of emotions in relation to decisions made at an individual level: if a person feels a connection with us, then he or she is more likely to take act in the way we want. However, psychologists have been teaching us, and it has been confirmed through thousands of experiments, that we greatly miscalculate the reach and potential of emotions. Specifically, emotions, like things on social media, propagate to those around us in a process of emotional contagion in which "the emotions expressed by one individual are caught by another one." (Cabane, 2012, p.145) In simple terms, our emotions and moods are being influenced by the emotions and feelings of people around us. When you make me feel some emotion, people around me have a tendency to feel the same way. And, as I argued in the introductory part of this chapter, how we feel impacts directly on how we act. Take mood as an example. Numerous studies on athletes, nurses, and accountants have concluded that positive mood equals more-altruistic behavior. (Christakis & Fowler, 2011) Similarly, a negative mood increases the likelihood of people remembering negative events. (Wiseman, 2010) So what happens when people are in a good mood? They feel safe. And, as they feel safe they cede more responsibility for monitoring their environment to System 1, become more prone to biases and thus to influencing. Conversely, when in a bad mood, people put more effort into scrutinizing their environment, use

System 2 more, and are less prone to external influences. (Christakis & Fowler, 2011) The "mood heuristic," as referred to by Daniel Kahneman was demonstrated in an experiment in which people were asked to fill in a questionnaire rating the level of satisfaction with their lives. Before filing in the questionnaire though, the researcher asked a favor of each participant: make some copies on a nearby photocopier. In one situation, subjects found a coin on top of the photocopier. Compared with the control group that did not find a coin, the coin group reported a visibly higher satisfaction with life (Kahneman, 2011) Or take another interesting concept best demonstrated in a classic experiment where subjects were being asked to hold a simple crayon between their teeth, forcing participants to adopt a smiley expression. After the exercise, people found a set of cartoons funnier then another group that was forced into a frown by asking them to hold the pen in a different position. Moreover, the frowning group reacted more strongly to emotional images such as children starving or people arguing. (Kahneman, 2011) On the one hand these experiments reveal that how we feel and behave is influenced by external factors such as the weather or finding a coin. On the other hand, the last experiment teaches us that the process works in reverse, as well: how we behave impacts on how we feel. In the words of psychologist Daniel Gilbert , "Our brains are hell-bent on responding to current events, we mistakenly conclude that we will feel tomorrow as we feel today." (Gilbert, 2007, p. 123) Online, our feelings influence our perception of a website, the amount of attention we give it, and our attitude toward an offer, product, request, or call to action. Indeed, when life is good, we feel more altruistic; and sharing, liking, following or subscribing seems more natural. And when life is not so good, applying a strategy that makes people behave in a positive manner will most likely help them internalize the behavior, get them in a better mood, and bring you more leads or sales. For example, one clever strategy marketers leverage in improving the mood of their audience is the principle of associative activation. In this situation marketers promote ideas that are directly related to the feelings and emotions they are looking to trigger. (Kahneman, 2011) To see this principle in action you can review the myriad of commercials that teleport people back to their childhood, the smell of their mom's pastas, the happy feeling of sharing a meal with the whole family, or sharing sweets and other good things.

3.2 Power of feelings: a case study in fear

To illustrate the power of feelings let's consider one emotion that is often employed by marketers to trigger a particular behavior in the audience, such as buying the marketers' products. We fear rank losses and Google updates, we fear airplane crashes, we fear for our security, health, and so forth. But we are lucky, because marketers are always on hand with a solution to alleviate our fears: employ an SEO consultant; he has inside information, a broker to provide us with life insurance, or a security company to install an alarm system. Even when the probability of our fears coming true is low, we simply cannot stop fearing the future. For example, we have seen that the probability of dying in a car crash is much higher than that of dying in an airplane crash and yet after an airplane accident we suddenly stop flying and rush to the closest car-rental center. Another telling example of this is revealed by some interesting studies at the University of Chicago. Researchers used physiological measures such as heart rate to conclude that the mere potential of getting an electric shock triggered the same degree of fear in subjects as actually receiving the shock. (Kahneman, 2011) Simply exposing people to fear of a potential harm is sufficient to trigger the goal set by the marketer. So, if I manage to instill in you the fear of being robbed, I will improve my chances of selling you a security alarm, insurance, a self-defense course, and even a pepper spray. In the words of journalist Dan Gardner: "Fear sells. Fear makes money...The more fear, the better the sales. Fear is a fantastic marketing tool...We listen to iPods, read the newspaper, watch television, work on computers...The wonder is not that we sometimes make mistakes about risks. The wonder is that we sometimes get it right." (Gardner, 2009, p. 15, p. 354) Fear operates directly on our emotions, bypassing awareness, and focuses System 1 on responding to the threat. It may sound cynical, but start by understanding the fears of your audience, develop your website around the targeted emotion, make the emotion available (more on this later), and trigger the target behavior. In a nutshell: make people feel fear and provide them with the remedy.

3.3 Power of feelings: a case study in reciprocity

What happens when we are being offered purple cows in some shape or form? When we are being offered something of value to us, we feel an unconscious need and urge to reciprocate. The words "need" and "urge" are particularly important in distinguishing the strength of reciprocity from a simple feeling of polite appreciation. Psychologists have known for a very long time about the powerful effect elicited by what seem to be spontaneous favors. In fact, the unconscious pressure to reciprocate is so strong that often we are drawn into granting larger favors in return in order to re-establish psychological balance, and remove the pressure of being in debt. (Cialdini, 2007) An interesting experiment by Dennis Reagan gives us a glimpse in how reciprocity works. Volunteers each visited a gallery, ostensibly to rate various paintings. While at the gallery they met another person, who, unknown to them, was an accomplice of the experimenters. During their visit, the accomplice pretended that he had suddenly become thirsty, and offered to bring back a free cola to the unaware volunteer, as well as one for himself. When the tour ended the accomplice presented the volunteer with the chance to buy raffle tickets. The result? The small favor of bringing back the coke generated twice as many sales of raffle tickets compared with sales to volunteers who were not offered a drink. (Wiseman, 2010) Similarly, if people seem to make concessions to us we feel the urge to reciprocate by making a concession in return. (Cialdini, 2007) To further investigate the impact of concessions on decision-making, Robert Cialdini devised an experiment. Cialdini was looking to test college students on their willingness to accompany groups of young juveniles to the zoo, as volunteers. He initially asked the students for a larger favor, which was spending two hours a week as counselors to a juvenile delinquent for a minimum of two years. When this request was refused, as expected, he made a smaller request pitching the product he was actually intending to sell, the zoo trip. Now, given his perceived concession, three times as many students made a concession in return and agreed to volunteer for the zoo trip. (Cialdini, 2007) In this case the contrast principle was also employed, as the zoo trip was perceived as three times as acceptable as the larger request. Cialdini referred to the concession principle as "the door in the face" technique. Now, consider a situation in which your audience perceives your product as being too expensive. The intention to leave the website is signaled when the website visitor moves the cursor toward the "Close window" button. At this point, an exit pop-up appears offering a concession from the seller, such as a discount, a different package, similar but lower-priced products, and so forth. Because of your making a concession, your audience is now ready to make a concession in return. This further explains Neil Patel's advice on using exit pop-ups, and his findings that exit pop-ups have been greatly increasing his website conversions. OK, so to recap: reciprocity works by offering something of value to your audience. The principle works on us when we receive a gift we value. Now, without our being aware of the reason, a feeling of stress begins to form: we must reciprocate the gift. And how do we respond? One option is to sign up to the email database of the marketer who offers his gift in return for our details. Indeed, the Oxford Handbook of Internet Psychology explains that people are happy to share personal information if they perceive the benefits to be worth it. (Jones, 2014) Yes, the importance of your purple cow offer or product is being demonstrated yet again. However, in my experience things are never that easy. On reflection, I have often passed on offers for signing up, even when the offers or products were compelling. Occasionally, my decision has been a simple matter of not having the time, although I have come to realize that often egotism clearly played a part, as well. We make decisions that are consistent with the kind of person we are or aim to be, a principle referred to as self-affirmation. In my case, I felt too smart to get "trapped" into offering my details, and in an almost automatic manner I was looking to re-affirm the type of person I felt I was. And how do we go about that? We begin by devaluing the offer. In my case, I thought something along the lines of, "Yet another piece of research on SEO with a great title," or, "They give it for free, so it can't be that great." Furthermore, when the offer was highly compelling, and I could not refuse it, I'd been telling myself, "Ok, I'll sign up, as I have no choice, but I will unsubscribe when the newsletter comes." Have you ever been in this situation? And if you signed up, did you read the auto-responder emails that followed? If we are to go by MailChimp's research, only 34 percent of the auto-responder emails sent by online marketers are being opened. Moreover, email automation was also found to create negative perceptions of the brand. (Jones, 2014) Hence, if your pop-up tool is to help you meet your goals, a great offer is paramount but insufficient on its own. Yes, you want people to sign up because they want to, not because they feel forced to, and a transactional mindset is, more often than not, insufficient.

An unexpected ramification of reciprocity has been dubbed "the Franklin effect" by psychologists; it is a strange behavior noticed by the polymathic politician Benjamin Franklin: you can increase the likelihood of someone liking you simply by asking them to do you a favor. Apparently, Franklin needed the support of one very difficult and apathetic member of the Pennsylvania state legislature. Rather than offering something to him (and triggering reciprocity), Franklin simply asked his target to do him a favor, namely lend him a rare and unusual book from the target's private library. The person complied, and on subsequent visits he demonstrated an unusual willingness to help Franklin on various issues. A similar finding has since been demonstrated in various social psychology experiments. (Wiseman, 2010) So, next time you are looking to get people to take an action, i.e. share, like, follow, email, you may want to start by first asking for a favor. This will increase their willingness to help on your next request.

3.4 The world gets faster: a feeling of impatience

OK, so you perform a search, you are served with various results on the first page in Google, you click on a website link, and you wait. The very first impression you will get about this website is its speed. Research shows that improving your website's speed can increase your sales by two-thirds and your conversion rates by 15 percent. Conversely, a one-second delay in accessing a webpage will reduce your conversions by up to seven percent. Moreover, 79 percent of people that have visited a slow website will never visit that website again. (Jones, 2104) But what happens here? When did we become so impatient? I don't know about you, of course, but to me life seems to become faster by the day: news, updates, digital advancements, upgrades— they all happen so fast that I am barely able to keep up. Psychologist Robert Levine has studied the pace of life in 30 cities according to three measures: how fast people walk, how fast postal clerks work, and the accuracy of public clocks. The rankings are not important for our purpose, but the finding that most of the countries involved had experienced a significant increase in the pace of life over the last decade is. (Laham, 2012) Yes, we are busier than ever, and, by implication, our time is scarcer than ever, as well. We value scarce resources more highly, thus we place more value on our scarce time. Interestingly, several follow-ups to this study found that people in countries with a faster pace of life are less likely to help other people. (Laham, 2012) Making a parallel, these findings suggest that demands for higher page speed may be greater in industrialized, fast-paced countries than in slower-paced countries, and that the acceptable level of page speed may differ from country to country, based on pace of life. And the higher the gap between the pace of life and expected page speed, the less likely people will be to put up with it. Another common mistake I notice when working on clients' websites is accessibility. Examples include contact forms that are too long, complicated registration processes, complex sales funnels, and much more. Always remember, though, that your audience's time is a scarce resource. Follow the advice from Steve Krug's book *Don't Make Me Think*: keep it simple, easy, and, above all, don't waste my time. To sum up, obsess about speeding up your website and make it easy for people to access is, navigate it and get in touch.

3.5 Monkey see, monkey do

Emotional contagion is widely used by digital marketers, particularly with video content. Take the example of charities; often, horrific images are screened in an attempt to get people to sympathize, feel the pain of the victims, and take action. This works, as research has shown that beyond their awareness humans have an ability to read facial expressions, even when no explicit expression is being displayed. Moreover, as we read other people's emotions, we internalize their feelings and are more inclined to take the action triggered by that sympathetic feeling. Indeed, neuroscientists know that without being aware of the reason, humans mimic emotions displayed by other people. Research at the University of Parma for example, uncovered the existence of so-called mirror neurons in primates. In his experiments Giacomo Rizzolatti placed electrodes in the parts of primate brains associated with empathy, and monitored the nerve cells that fired both when the animals performed an action themselves and while observing other animals performing the action. (Baron-Cohen, 2012) These findings led to further investigation, and subsequently to confirmation of the existence of mirror neurons in humans, as well. For example, Tania Singer and her colleagues monitored people using fMRI technology and found that as people received a painful stimulus on their hand, one area of the brain associated with empathy, the middle cingulate cortex (MCC), also got activated. Interestingly, the same area of the brain also became activated when the participants observed their partners receiving the stimulus. Similarly, studies carried out by neuroscientist Jean Decety and his colleagues noticed that while watching someone's hand being caught in a door the MCC gets activated. The conclusion is that we are unconsciously placing ourselves in other people's shoes and internalizing their emotional states and feelings. In fact, rather than simply imagining the other person's pain, we somehow feel other people's sensations, as if they were our own. (Baron-Cohen, 2012) Furthermore, simply imagining ourselves performing an action, enjoying an experience, or using a product activates the parts of the brain that are engaged in actually performing that activity. For example, imagining yourself playing the piano, done alongside sufficient real practice, will most likely lead to an actual improvement in your performance. (Cabane, 2012) To conclude, our ability to empathize is often more of a liability than an asset, leaving us prey to expert marketers engineering their sales funnels to both trigger and cash in on our emotions. Conversely, as a marketer you can leverage these findings to improve your funnel and your conversions.

As an unrelated note, I cannot help smiling when I think of all the popular advice about leadership, psychology, and other disciplines that is placing so much emphasis on a leader's ability to empathize. Indeed, the more the leader develops his ability to empathize, the more effective he becomes, so they say. And yet, stop for a second and look around your workplace. Who has made it through the ranks in your firm? And ask yourself...have they got there for their ability to feel for others, or is it something else?

3.6 Copy and feelings

I often meet copywriters who produce beautiful copy while paying little or no thought to the feelings or behavior that the copy is intended to trigger. However, in the right hands the copy of your website is a powerful tool, and can make all the difference between great success and mediocrity. Take a classic experiment by psychologist John Bargh and his team at New York University, who asked two groups to put together a set of four-word sentences from five available words. The first group was allocated words associated with the idea of "old": Florida, forgetful, bald, gray, and wrinkle. The students left the classroom with no realization that the important part of the experiment was only just beginning. Bargh and his team measured the amount of time it took students to walk from the beginning to the end of the corridor, and found that students who were exposed to the concept of "old" walked down the corridor significantly more slowly than the second group did. (Kahneman, 2011) Similarly, in an experiment that primed people with negative feelings such as sorrow, grief, and heartbreak, the people stated that they would pay less money for a box of chocolates than a control group were prepared to pay (Dolan, 2015). And in yet another example, a wine described as expensive ($90 per bottle) was perceived to be a better wine than it was when it was presented as a $10 per bottle wine. (Bloom. 2011) As psychologist Richard Wiseman concludes: "The ways in which we think and feel are frequently influenced by factors outside our awareness...Just reading a sentence can influence how old we feel and our recall of general knowledge. A simple smile or subtle touch can influence how much we tip in restaurants and bars. The music played in shops...influences the amount of money we spend." (Wiseman, , 2007, p. 148) Another common mistake made by many content writers is using complex vocabulary that looks good on paper. However, studies by Oppenheimer found that "couching familiar ideas in pretentious language is taken as a sign of poor intelligence and low credibility" (Kahneman, 2011, p. 63). The moral of the story is that if you are a Poundland-like business, a pawnbroker that deals in luxury goods, or a fork-lift truck company, simple does it. This is also true for the fonts you use for the copy, and every SEO audit must include a check of readability of your copy. For example, Oppenheimer also found that passages written in a font which was difficult to read impacted negatively on the perceived intelligence of the author. (Wiseman, 2010) The conclusion: if your goal is to improve the perception of your website, easy to read copy really does make a difference. Readability, Grammar, and Yoast's SEOs are just a few examples of tools that have inbuilt readability modules. At the risk of repeating myself let me say that these ideas seem obvious, but in my experience content writers and web designers are often delivering something that shows off their skills but makes their site more complicated than it needs to be; it is your role as business owner to rein them in and provide appropriate feedback.

The name of your website and names of your products are another factor that can have a strong impact on the performance of your website or product. For example, in one experiment participants were asked to evaluate reports from two companies named Artan and Taahhut. Subjects gave more credit to the company they could think of more easily (Artan), presumably because they unconsciously avoided the cognitive effort of thinking about the more complicated name. (Kahneman, 2011) Another study found that companies with names that are more easily pronounceable (Emmi, Swissfirst or Comet) did better than companies with more-difficult names (Geberit, Ypsomed) in the first week after their stock was issued. (Kahneman, 2011) I experienced this first hand when, as a training project, I was building my first website for a translation agency I was looking to launch. After much deliberation I decided to go with "Bestranslations.co.uk". At first glance this seems sensible; however, at a closer look you will notice that the letter "t" is missing after "Best". Every time I was trying to type the name of my company into Google I had to make a conscious effort to stop and think about the name, adding further cognitive pressure on myself to the point that I simply started to type "best translations" into Google. Of course, being newly built, my website was nowhere close to being on the first page in Google, which meant that any of my clients who typed "best translations" into Google were being served competitors' websites.

Let's conclude our discussion on copy with a review of the approach usually employed by content writers, SEO teams, or PPC consultants when writing copy. In a simplistic way the process goes something like this: a keyword research is carried out, groups of keywords are allocated to specific pages based on keyword themes, and content is created in line with the theme. Of course, very little thought is being paid to the finer conversion optimization actions as exhibited in the brilliant New York University experiment, where the words associated with being old affected the actions of the subjects. I only hope that you will now put plenty of thought into writing your copy.

3.7 Images and feelings

SEOs generally encourage website owners to include a variety of content on a page, with text, images, videos, and infographics often being mentioned. The idea behind this is that website visitors will find the page more interesting and relevant; thus time-on-site metrics will improve, which in turn will send signals to search engines regarding the relevance of your page. Again, too often designers, SEOs, or business owners pick up generic or cool Shutterstock images without much thought about the feelings these images might trigger subconsciously in their website's visitors. As long as it looks cool, clean and is somehow in line with the perceived brand identity, the designer is happy, and the client is happy as well. Furthermore, most business owners will very rarely, if ever, change images on their website. Of course, as you have probably already guessed, this is both a mistake and the loss of a significant lead generation opportunity. Take for example an experiment during which researchers served the participants with images of classrooms and school lockers, significantly increasing support rates for a school initiative; (Kahneman, 2011) or consider another experiment carried out in an office kitchen at a British University. For many years, staff members helped themselves to tea and coffee and paid by contributions to an honesty box, based on a list of suggested prices. Over a period of 10 weeks, researchers tested the changes in contributions when an image of a pair of watching eyes accompanied the honesty box vs. an image of flowers. Researchers found that during the "eyes" weeks contributions to the honesty box was three times as high as in the "flowers" weeks. In simple terms, researchers successfully triggered in the unsuspecting participants a feeling of being watched, which resulted in three times as many "conversions." (Kahneman, 2011) However, nowhere was the impact of images made clearer than in an experiment carried out by Gibson and Zillman. The researchers presented 135 people with two articles, a genuine one about wetlands and a fictitious one about Blowing Rock Disease, a non-existent disease supposedly spread by ticks, particularly to children. The articles were compiled in three variations: one with no image, a second one with a general image of ticks, and a third one had images of both ticks and of children that were believed to be infected. When presented with the child images, the article triggered a significantly higher emotional response, and the risk was considered higher than in the other two conditions. (Gardner, 2009) In essence, the perception of the article and the emotional response it triggered were down to the images used, rather than the text. And all it took was an understanding of the feelings to be triggered in the audience and employing the correct image to trigger them. This is the real power of imagery on your website. In the online world, as a web designer, SEO, remarketing specialist, or business owner, you must remember that arousing feelings is always more important than being cool. Always start with the end goal in mind: what feelings will trigger the conversion, and what images, copy, or videos will trigger the feelings? Now, you can start designing your website; choose your images, copy, and other assets that will trigger the appropriate feelings.

3.8 Videos and feelings

Given the huge leaps in machine learning technology, including Google's newly developed ability to "read" videos, SEOs have been increasingly encouraging webmasters and businesses to include videos in pages, and to repeat keywords and variations of them throughout the video. However, the power of videos impacts digital businesses well beyond the obvious SEO benefit. For a start, videos can get your message across and show off your products far better than any still image could ever do. I often come across websites where webmasters are posting generic, bland, and uninspiring videos with no other goal in mind than presenting a brand, service, or product. At times, webmasters go a step beyond that and mold the video around the optimizing guidelines provided by the SEO guy or his digital marketing agency. What a wasted opportunity to engage people with the product, service, or brand. I cannot re-emphasize enough the idea that it is not about being cool, but about the feelings you intend to trigger in the audience visiting your website. My suggestion is: incorporate SEO within your video if possible, but mold your video around the feelings that will trigger conversions. Start with the audience in mind, understand the emotions you have to trigger with your video, and only then create the video. And remember that people do not make logical decisions, they buy what they want not what they need, what they feel, not what is right. In the words of psychologist Bruce Hood: "Feelings are the reasons humans do anything. Feelings motivate us to go to work, fall in love...enjoy life or not." (Hood, 2009, p. 85) Similarly, what we feel about a website, product, or piece of content often determines what we do next within the funnel.

3.9 Sound and feelings

We have seen how images and videos impact the number of conversions on your website. There is one conversion ingredient whose role in converting audiences is even more often overlooked than images and video, and that is sound. Just as with images and videos, far too many websites display videos with no consideration to the feelings that the soundtrack needs to trigger. We all know that the right video and soundtrack on your website make us feel rapport with the seller, but don't seem to fully appreciate the impact they have on our decisions. Take an experiment where a bland, peaceful soundtrack was played with the goal of calming people down in claustrophobic situations, such as when taking an elevator. The soundtrack generated a 14 percent increase in the production of an important immune chemical, whereas jazz music generated seven percent, and no increase occurred when no music was played. In another experiment, people who were undertaking bronchial therapy recovered faster when listening to music by Bach. (Trivers, 2011) Yet another experiment found that in a supermarket, people purchased more French wine when the background music was French, but purchased more German wine when the music played was German. (Dolan, 2015) Trivers concluded that "the right kind of music can induce positive feelings," (Trivers, 2011, p. 133) while Nolan concluded that "listening to music...most strongly affects the brain region associated with positive emotions and memory in a way that no other input to our happiness production process can." (Dolan, 2015, p. 146) Of course, by now we know that when we experience positive feelings our perceptions change, we are more altruistic, rely more on the automatic and biased System 1, which in turn leaves us prey to external influences.

3.10 Familiarity and feelings

It seems that the more exposed we are to a product, the more we get to like the product; an idea which is referred to as the familiarity principle. The main reason for this positive predisposition to familiar products is the fact that "repetition induces cognitive ease and a comforting feeling." (Kahneman, 2011, p. 66) This being so, familiarity pays, which is why marketers go to great lengths to induce in us comforting feelings of familiarity. Byron Sharp explains in his book *How Brands Grow* that "familiarity breeds liking. Usage also breeds familiarity and brand knowledge. This in turn breeds liking." (Sharp, 2010, p. 91) Indeed, research shows that prior usage of a brand, website, or product leads to a person being more favorable toward it. (Sharp, 2010) Familiarity is one reason why remarketing campaigns are so effective. For example a 2015 article published by Wordstream concludes: "We've found that conversion rates actually increase the more users see an ad within remarketing campaigns." (Kim, 2018) In simple terms, the more people were exposed to ads, the better the conversion rates. Moreover, studies by psychologists such as Gary Klein have found that we are more likely to compare various options with our current choice when the option available to us is unfamiliar. (Klein, 1999) Thus, we scrutinize more an unfamiliar product, and compare it against competing products. By contrast, when familiar with the product, System 1 takes over, decisions are then made on autopilot, and habit provides an excellent shortcut by instigating repeat behavior. Charles Duhigg defines habits as "choices that we make at some point deliberately and then stop thinking about but continue doing, often every day." (Duhigg, 2012, p. xvii) As long as you continue to deliver what I expect, I will, from habit look forward to opening your emails. Two psychologists at the University of Southern California summed that up nicely: "Consumers sometimes act like creatures of habit, automatically repeating past behavior with little regard to current goals." (Duhigg, 2012) Moreover, a study by Duke University has found that 40 percent of the actions people take daily are not decisions but habits. (Duhigg, p. 2012) Of course, always remember not to disappoint my expectations: less but with great quality is better than more with mediocre quality.

3.11 And remember...not everyone sees red

Most marketers and webmasters will be familiar with the recommendations to make call-to-action buttons visible, to split test colors, positions, and other elements on webpages. For example, Amazon displays prices in red, a color that is often recommended as being more "action oriented". Browse around the web and have a look at some of your favorite websites. How many of these websites make use of colors to drive action and conversions? And yet research carried out at Oxford University indicates that red works more on men than on women. In fact, the study found that a red button made no difference to the purchasing behavior of women. (Jones, 2014) Now consider a website whose target audience is mainly women. The conversion optimization or SEO person may have learned from many tests that red converts best, so they go for it. Of course, they may not be aware that red has little or no impact on women, and end up diminishing, or losing altogether, their chances of improving the conversion rate of their website. Many DIY webmasters are influenced by this conversion-optimization-by-color convention. It is beyond the scope of this book to review the effects of every single color, but you now know that you should do your research on colors to find those best aligned to your target audience.

3.12 So, what did we learn?

To begin with, refrain from offering content or products that will not arouse some feeling in people. Informative but emotionless text, and video or audio created for SEO alone are just two examples of what we have been discussing. A/B split testing is another example. Webmasters test colors or sizes of CTAs, such as Buy Now buttons, images, and headings, with no consideration for the feelings these CTAs might trigger. For example, two different countries, one blessed with wonderful weather, the other not so lucky, may need different images and perhaps different colors. Most multinational companies translate and localize national versions of their website based on keyword research at local level. Keywords with higher search volumes and which enhance the theme of the website then dictate the content strategy for the page. The "right" user intent is often mentioned; after all, if I type, "buy sweater" into Google, I will mindlessly take the opportunity of clicking your large red "BUY NOW" button. You see this every day, even though research has shown that 90 percent of the time we will continue our search and your big red button will do nothing to convert it. Similarly, research tells us that if I am a woman the red color of your big button will have no influence on the likelihood of my buying your product. Nevertheless, we know that people's decision-making is prone to influence by many external factors, feelings, and emotions. Looking to increase conversions in a bad weather country? You may want to put extra effort into ensuring that your copy spreads some happiness first. Of course, if depression is what you're targeting, then suggestive images and videos and bad weather will be just the right mix; but, you will need to work much harder to change the contagious and annoying positive mood in the warmer and sunnier country. Looking to trigger a feeling of fear, maybe to sell a new security system? Just talk about the number of houses that *could* have been affected by a potential security breach recently.

Make people feel happy and safe; they will reward you with more trust and be more inclined to help, i.e., share, like, buy, subscribe. Provide people with distinct experiences; they will remember you more, as the Von Restorff effect—people remember the unusual—has proved. Expose them to and build their familiarity with your products in a non-intrusive way (e.g. Remarketing, Native advertising, Organic and Paid social, encourage initial usage, free samples); they will feel more positive toward it.

Remember that when feelings of reciprocity occur, people may not be able to explain why they have those feelings or the reason for their actions. And sometimes simply asking for a favor rather than offering one works better at triggering benevolence—the Franklin effect. Above all, a "purple cow" mindset is paramount at all times. Obsess about user experience, whether it be in the name of your website, speed, or on-page funnels; people's patience decreases as the pace of life increases.

To sum up, researching and understanding the feelings that will trigger conversions should always precede content creation and optimization, and that is of equal importance to, if not more important than, keyword research.

After all, there is little value in bringing people to your website if 90 percent will continue their search in pastures new. In truth, it is likely that, regardless of your efforts, people will continue their search on other websites. Thus, it is also important that your website, page, or product be remembered when the actual purchase decision is made. First impressions matter, last impressions matter, and the choices and experiences you offer matter as well, but the feelings that those things trigger are what matters most.

CHAPTER 4.
MORE...

4.1 Beware the large incentive trap...

One misconception marketers seem to have is that both large incentives and lead magnets will grow email lists and induce commitment. This misconception is mainly due to an assumption of reciprocity: the more I give you, the more you will give me. However, by offering high-value lead magnets or gifts you present your audience with the perfect way to explain away your gift: "It was the high value gift, rather than my appreciation of the website, that prompted me to download the gift and provide my email details." The negative impact of large rewards on people's perception of a task is well documented. Specifically, when larger rewards are being provided, people engage less in the activity they have been incentivized to perform. (Sutherland, 2007) This is because those people now associate their behavior with the large incentive rather than with enjoyment in performing the activity. Hence, your offer, gift, or lead magnet must be of a low monetary value but high intrinsic value to your audience. In my experience, website owners or digital marketers pay very little attention to creating lead magnets that will engage audiences with their brand, product, or website beyond the transactional level. In this context, business owners and marketers offer lead magnets with an "I give you this, you give me that in return" mindset. For example, some marketers provide discounts via sticky headers or various pop-ups as a mean of attracting new leads. You see pop-ups promoting discounts or special offers for new customers, brands running discount campaigns in supermarkets, and 50–70 percent reduction offers are being made by retailers throughout the year. The trouble is that, more often than not, discounts do not attract new customers, but rather reduce revenue. Indeed, research by Ehrenberg, Hammond, and Goodhardt revealed that most purchases during discounting campaigns came from people who had purchased the brand previously, hence from existing rather than new customers. (Sharp, 2010) And even when discounts attract new buyers, a large proportion of those buyers are driven purely by price and revert back to their previous buying behavior when the promotion ends.

Psychologists refer to this pattern as the "purchase reinforcement effect." (Sharp, 2010, p. 157) The motivation for this behavior is easy to see: the large discount allows website visitors to explain away the reason for their purchases in terms of "I bought this product because of the large savings rather because I am committed to the website, brand, or product." Of course, when promotional campaigns are aimed at increasing short-term sales vs. long-term loyalty acquisition, then price discounts will often meet your goals. In fact, research has shown that on average you can expect increases of around 25 percent from a 10 percent price cut. (Sharp, 2010) One classic example revealing how strong the impact of discounts is on people's behavior is a phenomenon accidentally discovered by an automobile tire company. The company had printed in error some batches of discount coupons that in reality offered no discounts at all. The surprise came when the response rate to theses coupons was as high as the response rate to coupons that were actually offering discounts. Hence, simply packaging the deal as a special offer was worthwhile. Another thing to keep in mind, though, is that before deciding on a discounting strategy you must consider yet another effect of price discounts, which is the decline in sales after the promotion. This could happen because people have purchased more than they would normally buy, or as mentioned above, because people revert to their earlier purchasing behavior. (Sharp, 2010) In the end, if commitment is what you are looking for, then large discounts will merely provide your audience with a way of explaining their purchasing behavior and the reasons for reading your article or for allowing you to add their details to your email list.

4.2 ...but don't be afraid of using Free

For all its popularity, it is surprising to see that many marketers dismiss "Free" as an outdated concept living its last days. The argument is that as people have gotten smarter they now see beyond "Free". In reality, the belief is caused by the misuse of "Free," with many businesses lacking understanding of why and how "Free" is supposed to work. Indeed, most businesses use "Free" more as a word than as a psychological principle. They offer "free this" and "free that," and when it's not working out as they wanted it to, they come to the conclusion that "Free" doesn't work. It was set up to fail. So when does "Free" work? Firstly, the idea of a free gift employs the reciprocity rule. We have already discussed reciprocity earlier in the book. A reminder: on receiving an unexpected favor we feel a significant urge to offer a favor in return. Very often, in order to reduce the cognitive strain we return favors much larger than the favors we receive. However, as previously stated, the free gift you offer on your website must be perceived by your audience as a purple cow, there simply is no way around it. Too often, people are being met with pop-ups, emails, or other online growth hacking techniques, demanding that they provide their contact details and loyalty in exchange for a product, report, or some other lead magnet that is of little or no value to the them. Even when it works and people do sign up, you are simply allowing your hard-earned visitors to explain away your gift: "I have downloaded simply out of curiosity." This, not surprisingly, results in an unsuccessful "Free" strategy. "Free" also employs the reciprocity rule in a more unexpected way. As a digital marketer you often come across various tools offering free trials. Leadfeeder is one such tool that comes to mind. Most people think of free trials as a low risk opportunity offered by companies to showcase their product. Given that digital products are very cheap, if not free, to replicate, free-gift customers most often don't cost you a thing. From the customer's point of view, as well, if they like the product they can of course sign up, and if they don't then no harm has been done. This perception is sound and makes sense at first glance. However, many experiments have shown that, in a cause-and-effect way, once you take the trial you feel an urge to reciprocate. (Cialdini, 2007) Remember the name of Steve Krug's book? It was *Don't make me think.* "Free" works in that sort of way, as revealed by another experiment by Dan Ariely. Ariely found that, when offered a choice between a 1¢ candy and a 26¢ candy, most people took the 26¢ candy. But when offered a choice between a free candy and the 26¢ candy, most people went for the free option. (Caldwell, 2012) I think we can agree that the difference between 1¢ and free is insignificant, and yet it made such a difference.

4.3 The power of (wrong) associations

We have discussed briefly people's tendency to presume associations between what may well be unrelated traits and characteristics. For example, confident or loud marketers are often associated with expert status; expensive products or great-looking websites are associated with great quality. This tendency is a powerful tool in the hands of marketers who leverage it for the purpose of triggering specific feelings in their audiences. Take one study of men who were presented with an advertisement for a new car. In one version an attractive woman was included in the ad. The result? Men rated the car faster, more appealing, more expensive-looking, and better designed than did the control group, which was served the ad without the attractive woman. (Cialdini, 2007) But why did they rate the car faster? The answer is provided by a very similar experiment carried out by psychologist James Roney. Roney first presented groups of young boys with two pictures, one of an attractive young woman and one of an older woman. When asked to fill in surveys which measured their different attitudes, Roney found that the group that was presented with the image of an attractive woman valued ambition, material wealth, and status more than the control group did . (Laham, 2012) And, when in a lustful mood men are more likely to cooperate if we go by the finding of an experiment where male skateboarders were asked to perform 10 tricks in a University of Queensland study. When the researcher was an attractive woman, the participants took more chances in performing more-difficult skateboarding tricks than they did when the researcher was a man. (Laham, 2012) It appears that when the attractive researcher conducted the study, men felt more adventurous and courageous, and adapted their behavior in line with their feelings. This is similar to why conversion optimization consultants encourage webmasters to add or increase the visibility of signs associating or linking their businesses with professional bodies, professional institutions and such like. By implication, these associations transfer credibility to the business and the website, acting in the same way that social proof acts. After all, if a company is a member of this well know professional body, then the company must have the same high values. Of course, if we look closer, there is nothing really indicating that that is true. Which takes me to the next interesting aspect of associations, which is the tendency people have to look for associations and patterns, even where none exist. The famous award winning "Linda" experiment carried out by Daniel Kahneman and Amos Tverski provides a brilliant example of wrong associations at work. The two researchers provided a description of a person they called Linda, and asked the participants whether Linda was more likely to be a bank teller or a feminist bank teller. Based on the information provided, the logic was clearly pointing out that Linda was more likely to be a bank teller, and yet surprisingly 85 to 90 percent of the subjects thought that her concerns about discrimination and feminism made her more likely to be a feminist bank teller. (Kahneman, 2011)

Online, tools like Sniply use the principle of wrong associations brilliantly: the high authority source of a Sniped shared article or product lends its authority to your snip. With Sniply marketers overlay a message bar on a popular article and share it under the assumption that people will extend the authority of the article or website to the Snip. After all, an overlay message would not appear on a high-quality website unless the content were valuable, right? Similarly, Birdsong enables you to share popular articles and display your own subscription pop-up, prompting people to subscribe to what they perceive to be the email list of the host website, the authority figure. Of course, both Sniply and Birdsong serve up a copy of the webpage rather than the original, but most people will not notice the difference. Do keep in mind though that, particularly in Birdsong, you are in fact tricking people into signing up to your list. This may work well in specific niches, though it most often would be inefficient in building engagement. On the other hand, a foot in the door may be better than nothing, and if the content or products you offer are consistently purple cows you may have a better chance than if you did nothing at all. You can leverage this principle in many other creative ways to improve conversion rates and the perceived authority of your page, product, or website. For example, sharing articles of influencers in your niche improves your being perceived as a knowledgeable person. Writing articles and quoting influencers and so forth can also transfer authority to your website.

4.4 Everything is relative

The relativity principle points to another strange behavior that we humans display, which is deriving enjoyment from comparing our achievements with the achievements of our friends and colleagues. (Sharot, 2012) One classic experiment by Kahneman found that people preferred to work for less money if their wages were higher than those of their colleagues. So, if you ask me to work for you for $30k, I will most often say yes if I know that other people working for you are being paid around $25k. But if you asked me to work for you for $35k and told me that those other people are on $45k, I would most likely see this as a loss. This is funny in a way, as research has also shown that after reaching a certain income level, we do not become happier with more money but become rather more stressed. To continue the financial example, we continue to push ourselves and sacrifice our time to earn more money than our colleagues, in spite of many studies showing that, beyond a threshold of $75,000, increases in earnings do not correlate with improvements in happiness and wellbeing. (Kahneman & Deaton, 2010)

Leaderboard tools leverage relativity by displaying real time updates on the progress and scores of game-players. This keeps people engaged; after all we don't want to be beaten by the Joneses—a cliché, I know, but ever so true. The great flexibility the tools offer in terms of the purpose of the contest means that marketers can again tailor the contest to the audience, and induce particular feelings. I must say that I do find it mesmerizing to observe how people share more, like more, or take specified actions more, simply to come out on top with no other reward than the feeling associated with winning. A truly great growth-hacking category of tools that leverage the power of relativity in a brilliant way.

4.5 Probabilities suck...

Study after study confirms that intuitive System 1 deals better with numbers than with probabilities, an idea labeled as the denominator neglect principle. Consider an experiment that was carried out on two groups of people. The first group was told that a certain disease kills 1,286 out of every 10,000 people. The second group was informed that the disease kills 24.14 percent of people. The results? People in the first group judged the disease to be far more dangerous than the people in percentage group. (Kahneman, 2010) You may therefore find that "7 out of 10 people recommended us" works far better than "70 percent of customers recommended our product." Another aspect of framing is people's tendency to pay attention to copy that evokes negative feelings. In one experiment a number of physicians were presented with two descriptions of risks associated with the treatment of lung cancer by surgery or radiation. When the stats for surgery were presented as, "The one month survival rate is 90 percent," 84 percent of the physicians opted for surgery vs. radiation. But when the same stats were presented as "There is a 10 percent mortality rate in the first month," 50 percent of the physicians proposed radiation. The simple act of framing surgery as something bad was sufficient to decrease "conversion" by 34 percent of the sample group. (Kahneman 2011) In yet another experiment, beef that was described as "75 percent lean" was rated much higher than when presented as "25 percent fat." (Gardner, 2009,p. 94) Similarly, a 75-percent-fat-free burger is perceived as different from the same burger framed as a 25-percent-fat burger. (Taleb, 2007)

4.6 Give people a reason...any reason

One surprising concept I have come across while reading Robert Cialdini's *Influence: The science of persuasion*, is that of providing people with a reason to take the action you require. We seem to be wired to always seek an explanation for anything that happens; as the old saying goes, "Everything happens for a reason." And, when no reason exists we find one, weird though it they may be. Take an experiment carried out by Ellen Langer of Harvard, when 94 percent of the people queuing to use a Xerox machine allowed her to skip the queue when she provided a reason for having to do so. Must have been a very compelling reason, right? In fact, no. Langer simply added to her request, "because I am in a rush." Her request became, "May I use the Xerox machine because I'm in a rush?" By contrast only 60 percent of the people allowed her to use the machine when she provided no reason for it: "May I use the Xerox machine?" Things got even more interesting when Langer provided another reason: "May I use the Xerox machine, because I have to make some copies?" Of course, everyone was queuing to make some copies, and yet simply providing people with a reason delivered a "conversion" of 93 percent. (Cialdini, 2007) So, next time you write and promote your offer via a pop-up, email, social locker, or similar growth hacking tool, you may want to split test, giving people a reason for performing the action you require, e.g., "I have worked n days to write this article"; "Buy this product because…"

4.7 The tick that makes the difference…

After all that I've been saying about getting people committed to your brand, content, or product, you may be puzzled by this assertion: sometimes, getting people to subscribe is simply a matter of the way you frame your request. Consider a 2003 study of organ donor rates, which found that people's decisions to sign up were down to the manner in which the question was being asked. In countries with high donor rates the question was being framed in an opt-out form, which meant that if you did not want to sign up you had to untick the box. Ok, you may think, but surely the difference for opt-in conversion rates cannot be that high; after all, if you don't want to sign up it only takes a second to opt out. Well, organ donor rates in Austria were close to 100 percent vs. only 12 percent in Germany, while Sweden had a rate of 86 percent vs. 4 percent in Denmark due to that simple difference. (Kahneman, 2011) In fact, I now pay more attention to how the "subscribe to our newsletter" forms are presented to me on websites. Try it yourself; you will be surprised how often you will have to untick the subscribe box. One word of caution, though: this opt in or opt out approach may work for organ donor recruitment and similar goals. However, if engagement is what you are looking for, then this approach will be very inefficient. After all, why would I feel engaged with something I never signed up to in the first place?

4.8 And...ask them a question

People love questions, which seem to be far more effective than simple statements. For example, an experiment carried out by Robert Burnkrant and Daniel Howard found that people were more likely to support a policy when the arguments were presented as questions than when they were presented as statements. (Pink, 2013) But how do we apply this online? It is actually quite simple, and pop-up tools such as Hello Bar offer the option of preceding the core pop-up offer with a question. Neil Patel is one digital marketer who comes to mind for having used a Hello Bar with the preceding, "Do You Want More Traffic?" encouraging people to click on YES before continuing to its core lead magnet.

4.9 Money counts...just not in the way you may think

People expect online prices to be on average eight percent lower than High Street prices, under the assumption that online businesses incur lower costs. (Jones, 2014) Similarly, I don't know about you, but for me, special offers somehow seem more "special" online. Thus, as a general rule of thumb, promoting the idea that people get better deals online is beneficial. And, creating the illusion of lower prices as opposed to actually offering lower prices can go a very long way. You can observe this principle at work both on the High Street and online. For example, slogans like "Sale now on" do not say much about the size of discounts, and yet we rush in, full of expectations of massive discounts that we will benefit from.

Let us turn our attention to some of the principles and concepts that marketers leverage, or should leverage, to further improve their conversions and margins.

One of the marketing tools most often used is the contrast principle, which plays to the tendency people have to perceive different products and assess them based on contrasts between the products. For example, if a second product is very different from a first, we perceive the second product as being more different than it actually is. (Cialdini, 2007) Online retailers leverage this principle by selling expensive products first, and follow up the sale with cheaper upselling products that will complement the purchase. Given the contrast to the high cost of the first purchase, the lower-cost product is now perceived as a bargain. By contrast, if your first purchase is of low cost, a higher-cost product will then seem excessively expensive. Psychologist Robert Cialdini tells the story of a real estate salesperson who started his routine by taking potential customers to see rundown properties at inflated prices. Only after this process did the real estate seller present the house he actually intended to sell. This house was now perceived as a bargain when compared with the houses presented earlier. (Cialdini, 2007) So, when constructing your sales funnel, you may want to promote your most expensive product first, and follow up with less-expensive add-ons. You might also consider presenting two products side by side, offering one product with simple functionality at an inflated price, and the second full functionality product for only a slightly higher price. The goal is to reduce the appeal of the cheaper version, prompting the audience to purchase the product you really wanted to sell in the first place. Many of the tools I present in this book leverage this principle by showing side by side a product with limited features and a second full functionality product for a small increase in price. Psychologist Dan Ariely also provides several examples of the contrast principle in practice. Take the restaurant owner introducing the highest-priced item so he can sell the second highest-priced item. Or the TV salesman who intends to sell his $850 Toshiba TV by displaying it on the same shelf with a $690 Panasonic and a $1480 Philips. (Ariely, 2009) A derivation of this principle is the practice of surrounding your object with dissimilar objects, in order to make your product stand out, or surrounding your product with similar products when you need your product to blend in and be associated with more-popular products. (Gilbert, 2007) Another way to influence your audience is by displaying three products side by side. In this case you are trying to persuade website visitors to choose the middle option. This is a very common practice in the digital world. You reach the pricing page, which displays a basic low-priced package, a middle-priced pro package, and an expensive enterprise package. Most often the middle-priced package is clearly underlined and a "Most Popular" badge is visible as well. For example, you can observe this principle on the pricing page of the Moz Local tool. Also note how packages are being lined up, starting with the lowest value, followed by the middle package, and, on the right hand side, the enterprise package. Many other websites add an extra package, having Free, Basic, Pro, and Agency packages. You may not consciously pay attention to the order of packages on the page; however, many studies have shown people to have a preference toward items on the right hand side of the display. In one experiment psychologists Richard Nisbett and Timothy Wilson set up a display table outside a bargain store and presented passers-by with four pairs of nylon pantyhose, displayed on a table. They labeled the items A to D from left to right. As they passed by, people were being asked to assess the quality of the items and, overall, pair A was preferred by 12 percent of people, pair B by 17 percent, pair C by 31 percent, and pair D by 40 percent. The catch is that all pairs were in fact identical and the only variation was in their position. (Wilson, 2002) This experiment and many other similar studies suggest that improving sales and conversion rates may at times have less to do with the product and more to do with positioning your core package as far to the right side as possible. An example would include displaying your packages from left to right as Free, Basic, Enterprise (most expensive) and Pro (advertised as most popular).

Let us now revisit a sales technique that we discussed a bit earlier in the book: the "door in the face" technique. Online marketers often employ this method when looking to sell lower-priced products by offering a more expensive product first. However, at times, "door in the face" may not be the most appropriate approach. This could be for a variety of reasons, including a price sensitive audience, new untested products, and first-time customers who are unwilling to splash out without testing a product. In these cases, Cialdini proposes the "foot in the door" technique and suggests that offering a lower-priced product will gain people's commitment to a product or brand, making it easier to subsequently upsell other products. As always your lower cost product must be a purple cow, though it should not represent your core business. This is important, as offering a core product at a lower price first will only devalue it by setting up the wrong anchor price and associations of quality; i.e., cheap equals bad/OK quality. But how does "foot in the door" actually look in practice? To better understand the workings of this technique consider the following scenario: like many people, you agree to display on your car/house window a small sign promoting safe driving. This simple action makes you feel good about yourself, and reinforces your ideal self. Two weeks later you are approached again. This time you are being asked to place a large, ugly-looking sign in your garden displaying the message, "Drive Carefully." This would change the look and feel of your garden, and there are problems of space limitations and flexibility. Having already accepted to place a small sign in your window, would you agree to it? Many of us are certain that we would resist and refuse. However, if we consider an experiment by Jonathan Freedman and Scott Fraser, 76 percent of us would in fact agree to displaying the large, ugly banner. (Ross & Nisbett, 2011) Of course, you may argue that given the nature of the good cause people would have accepted anyway, therefore no psychology mumbo-jumbo here. However, further findings of the study will contradict you: only 17 percent of people agreed to display the large, ugly sign when the "foot in the door" technique was not employed. Hence, getting people to commit to taking a small step initially resulted in a large majority of people subsequently agreeing to a larger concession. Digital marketers often employ this principle for building momentum in selling their higher-priced products. Some examples include digital marketing tools offering free trials or lower-cost packages with limited functionality. Retailers also push lower-cost or discounted products followed by more-expensive products via recommendations such as, "People who bought this also bought this," or by recommending discounted products which have higher prices or margins. To complement the "foot in the door" technique you can use what is labeled as the "diminishing sensitivity" principle, which refers to the subjective difference between the way people evaluate products or offers. Specifically, the higher the prices of the products, the lower is perceived the price difference and the easier to upsell the more expensive product. As a practical example, the subjective difference between $900 and $1000 is much lower than the subjective difference between $100 and $200. (Kahneman, 2011) As a customer you experience this principle regularly. Take something as simple as buying a suit. You enter a shop having a set budget in mind; you look around, and find a suit within your budget. But then you notice another suit. You really love this suit and it only costs $50 more. You decide to buy the slightly more expensive suit even though the $50 gap took you over your maximum budget. I am guilty as charged for falling prey over and over again to this simple trick.

From another perspective, though, price levels may at times have little to do with intrinsic worth, and quite a bit to do with manipulating the expectations people hold. Many experiments have shown that people use prices as cues for assessing the quality of products. Take an experiment where a bottle of wine was presented with a $40 label and subsequently with a $7 label. People perceived the higher priced wine as being of better quality. Funnily enough, the fMRI studies carried out throughout the experiment found that the part of the brain associated with sensing pleasure experienced more intense activation when people believed the wine was more expensive. (Caldwell, 2012) OK, so marketers do make more money out of the $40 bottle. But sometimes, price sensitivity can be an issue. How to get around it, you may ask. Marketers use another brilliant trick in encouraging the purchase of more-expensive products. And the winner is...monthly rates. Monthly rates represent in my opinion one of the smartest and finest inventions marketing has ever seen. First, as a marketer, by deferring payment over a period of time, you reduce the perceived risk and cost. Second, you are increasing the overall price of the product. In one telling experiment people were willing to pay up to 50 percent more for a product when allowed to defer the payment, a principle labeled the "hyperbolic effect." (Caldwell, 2012, p.106) Third, you can more easily offer upsells—available at a low monthly rate, of course. And fourth, the customer is primed to buy again or upgrade at the end of the agreement.

One mistake many online stores are prone to making is pursuing incremental price discounted strategies. Many online stores introduce discounts at a lower rate, let's say 30 percent, and incrementally raise the discount rate because the product is not selling. For example, if I visited the clearance section of your website and purchased a product discounted by 30 percent, I might see the same product at a later stage with a 70-percent discount tag. You really don't need to be a psychologist to deduce that I will feel cheated and experience a feeling of loss. In one study people found in a catalogue that a discounted product they had already purchased from that source was being offered at a greater discount. Those people promptly reduced their purchases from the company concerned by 15 percent, an average of $90 per customer. (Kahneman, 2011) I am hoping you have recognized loss aversion at work there, with the loss being perceived as real, in spite of the savings associated with the initial discount.

I have been employed in commercial environments for most of my working life, whether managing hotels as a General Manager, running digital marketing campaigns for both SMEs and iconic brands, or managing various language projects as part of the conference interpreting agency I have been running. I have liaised with a variety of teams in marketing, revenue management, sales, brand management, and digital. It always goes the same way: we talk about the company, its identity, its clients, the segmentation of the clients, and so forth. But at no point do any of these experienced professionals ever ask a very important question: who's paying? Allow me to explain. You and I both know that while purchasing for ourselves we conduct more research; we compare more and we scrutinize a greater variety of product features and price options.

In contrast, when we purchase on behalf of someone else, be it a company, boss, or client, the "other people's money'" effect applies; that is, we scrutinize less and are willing to pay more. The funny part is that we do not consciously act in this manner, we just do it. The "other people's money" effect works by removing the emotional barrier of parting with our own money. (Caldwell, 2012) In simple terms, as we are not using our own money, we experience less emotion; i.e., we experience no feeling of loss when missing out on a better deal. In fact, we are happy to "satisfice" our decision-making when spending other people's money, yet we are significantly more exacting when spending our own cash. A result of this is that by segmenting your audience into own money and company money can achieve some great benefits in terms of both sales and margins. Decision makers, such as purchase managers, marketing directors, and department managers are much quicker to part with the cash, and they scrutinize less.

Finally, let us briefly touch on the moral aspect of the so-called social values so proudly displayed by many brands and companies. The past couple of years marked the rise of a new type of charity work: companies donating a portion of their profits to charity with every purchase people make. And it works, for many studies show that simply by framing the product in this way leads to people's purchasing more of it. For example, one company's sales went up by 15 percent when the product was framed as giving away 5 pence with every purchase. In fact, when introducing a 5 pence donation you might as well raise your price by 10 pence! (Caldwell, 2012) Putting aside the moral aspect, in terms of influencing people the reason behind the success of the "5¢ to charity with every purchase" advert boils down once again to feelings: feelings about who we are, how we perceive ourselves, or how we want to be perceived by others. As always, marketers are quick to take advantage of our feelings, and the biases that come with them. And as a marketer charity is a great tool too.

4.10 Don't invite them to get into the bed on your first date

In his book *Entrepreneur Revolution*, Daniel Priestley introduces the idea of an Ascending Transaction Model. The model points to the fact that at an initial stage customers are looking to try something out without too much risk, to spend a little money for a quick gain. (Priestley , 2014) If your product is a purple cow they will "ascend" toward buying complementary products that may well end up earning you more profit than your core product. In this situation, offering a guarantee will further reduce the perception of risk. (Caldwell, 78) As another example consider one of the many tools presented in this book, SEM Rush, which offers free versions and incrementally priced packages. It may seem a simple idea, but many underlying principles are at work in your attempt to lower the perceived risk in trying your product. For example, by offering a free or lower-risk product you employ the "foot in the door" technique, described earlier. The "low risk" initial purchase works because humans are typically risk averse, as Daniel Kahneman's experiments have shown.

4.11 But when you get them in your bed... don't go and spoil it all

One common mistake a lot of marketers make after winning commitment from the audience is to fully automate their follow-up strategy. Email marketing or push notifications are being used to deliver a myriad of products or content meant to cash in on the newly acquired asset. The truth is that people simply don't have the time to read all your emails. Take me; I've signed up for several industry-specific publications, only to find myself inundated with emails, sometimes three in one day from the same publication. Of course, I simply do not have time to read them, and a very interesting thing has happened: I stopped reading their emails altogether. Furthermore, my decision not to read some of that email made it easier for me to devalue it, and ultimately give up reading it altogether. By contrast, I look forward to SEOBook's newsletter, which gets delivered to my inbox throughout the year, and which never disappoints in terms of quality of content. Less is more. In fact, there is something very interesting about how I feel on receiving SEOBook's newsletter, as I know I will receive great quality content. I began to reflect on that feeling, and I came across the famous experiments of Russian psychologist Pavlov, who was first to discover the principle of classical conditioning. Classical conditioning describes the process of manipulating a stimulus in order to create an association with a new condition. In his experiments on dogs, Pavlov managed to condition the salivary glands of the animals to leak at the sound of a bell. He achieved this goal by training the dogs to associate the bell with food. (Slater, 2005) In effect, Pavlov managed to change the behavior of the dogs by introducing a stimulus they looked forward to—food. In a weird way I feel the same excitement when receiving the SEOBook's newsletter; in my case the stimulus being the great content, hacks, and interesting opinions I have gotten accustomed to. Of course, a stimulus can be a regular newsletter with great discounts, the newest products coming to market, the hottest trends, and so forth. As a user, I am conditioned to "salivate" at the receipt of your email. As long as you don't disappoint my expectations, you can rest assured I will rush to read your email as soon as possible. Why? Because, like most people, I am curious, and if I do not satisfy my curiosity, deep down inside a pain emerges, a situation that economist George Loewenstein refers to as situational interest. (Heath & Heath, 2008) This being said, nowadays most content delivered automatically after my initial experience of your purple cow is of far lower quality, and is simply promotional, affiliated marketing offers, or is otherwise commercially focused. For me, it is far too easy to explain away the reason I subscribed in the first place, and also to explain my decision to unsubscribe from many of these blogs—what a wasted opportunity for webmasters or marketers. Bottom line, provide consistent value to your audience, and never forget why they signed up and committed themselves to giving you some of their scarce attention in the first place. Many websites are going a step further with these crazy methods and automatically signing you up to their databases and newsletters without asking; they scour the internet for email addresses, download emails lists from LinkedIn, buy email lists, and use many other devious approaches. Many tools I present in this book are available to perform these actions; however, using these strategies exclusively will most often deliver mixed results, for reasons we have been discussing already.

Another example of marketers making a move on their audiences too quickly is provided by the misuse of various email or social share tools meant to capture contact details of the audience. We lure someone to a page, they start reading a great piece of content, and halfway through a social locker pop-up interrupts their flow by hiding the remaining content. They are given the choice of continuing to read by performing an action, such as sharing the article, liking it, following it, or emailing it. What should they do? Firstly, note that at this point we have already gained our audience's commitment to reading the article. We now offer the reader the choice of taking an action, e.g., "Continue without sharing," while giving them a reason to share the article, which might be, "I have worked two days, five hours and twenty-three minutes on this article." Thus we eliminate their ability to falsely rationalize their reading of our article or for taking an action, e.g., sharing the article. One observation, though: many marketers position the locker after the first couple of paragraphs. This is a mistake, as readers have not been given enough time to get into and commit to the content. In such cases, we will often observe increases in our bounce rates. To prevent this from happening, we should allow visitors to read at least 50 percent of our content before locking it. By this time, readers will have committed their time, and if they liked our article and we have followed the rules, they will most likely "freely" decide to take our targeted action, i.e., share, like, email, or follow. The loss aversion principle is at work here, as well, since most readers explain the time spent on reading the first part of the article in terms of "I must have liked the content; after all, why else would I read the article?" And, as we will see a little later, they now adapt their preference in line with their behavior: they love our content more, they share it more, and recommend it more.

4.12 Make them work for it...and time it well

Throughout this book I emphasize the importance of your offer, gift, or product, and the idea of allowing your audience to decide whether or not to provide their contact details. Providing this option, though, is not to be confused with making it easy for them. Offer your purple cow too easily and you may be devaluing your great product in your visitors' eyes; after all, as you offer it so easily it must be because your product is not all that good, right? In fact, many experiments have demonstrated that the more effort we put into achieving a task, the more we value it once we have completed it. Take a classic experiment where participants were subjected to different levels of pain or embarrassment prior to being accepted into a group. The more difficult the process was, the more interesting and exciting they judged a recorded discussion to be, and the greater the number of people within their new group they perceived as being attractive and sharp. These perceptions were interesting, given that researchers construed the discussion particularly boring and dull. By contrast, people who were easily accepted into the group more accurately rated the discussion as boring and uninteresting. (Trivers, 2011) The moral of the story is that if your purple cow is to be taken at its real value, you should think hard about ways to make your audience work for it. In his book *Predictably Irrational*, Dan Ariely captured this idea brilliantly with a passage from Mark Twain's *Tom Sawyer*: "He had discovered a great law of human action...namely, that in order to make a man or a boy covet a thing, it is only necessary to make the thing difficult to attain." (Ariely, 2009) Of course, you must also ensure that the quest of obtaining the gift is engaging and of interest to your audience; simply making it hard will most often increase your bounce rates. The principle works in a reciprocal manner, as well: the more effort we are perceived to put into our product or content, the more people will appreciate it. For example, in an experiment by psychologist Justin Kruger participants were asked to rate a piece of abstract art. One group was led to believe that the painting took four hours to create while the other group was told it took 26 hours to create. As you have probably guessed, people in the 26 hours group rated the piece of art significantly higher on attributes such as quality, value, and likeability. (Bloom, 2011) Hence, framing your pop-up offer, Social Locker share message, or similar growth-hacking tools, with something like "It took me three days, six hours and fifty-two minutes to create this content for you," is likely to positively impact on the perception of quality attributed to your offer, product or content. Getting people to perform some sort of mental activity such as doing a quiz or entering a competition, results in yet another benefit for online marketers, in addition to achieving more-committed audiences. Most people are confident of their ability to resist "noise," and in their ability to "freely" decide to perform an action, whether purchasing, sharing, liking, tweeting or subscribing. Indeed, we believe we are quite good at evaluating choices and making conscious, unbiased decisions. Of course, our confidence is nothing but an illusion. As we will see throughout this book, subconsciously we are all prone to many biases that influence any decisions we take. Moreover, psychologists like Roy Baumeister have demonstrated over and over again that willpower is not a fixed trait, but rather works like another muscle. Baumeister noticed that the more effort we put into performing mental tasks, the more tired we become, and the more control we delegate to the automatic but highly biased System 1. Labeled as ego depletion, this effect has two ramifications: first, our willpower is being diminished, and second, our cravings increase. Stress, in particular, depletes willpower, and with it our ability to control our emotions, behaviors, and cravings.

(Baumeister & Tierney, 2012) Indeed, when we have low reserves of willpower we become "cognition misers," often making decisions without much deliberation; we compare less, "satisfice" more, and focus on one feature of products, e.g., the cheapest, the best, the most available, and so forth. (Baumeister & Tierney, 2012) Jonathan Levav beautifully demonstrated this effect in several experiments. In one instance he asked MBA students to choose a bespoke suit. In another experiment he studied the behavior of real customers purchasing accessories for their new cars. As expected, in the beginning people would carefully weigh up the choices and study a multitude of features. As they got tired, ego depletion set in, System 1 took over, and people settled for the default option. An even more interesting finding was that by manipulating the order in which various accessories were presented, customers purchased accessories that were on average $1.5K more than a control group did. So, when defining your sales funnel, simply by presenting your target products earlier or later makes a big difference to your sales. (Baumeister & Tierney, 2012) As Baumeister concludes, "decision fatigue leaves us vulnerable to marketers who know how to time their sales." (Baumeister & Tierney, 2012, p. 103) Maybe we should take some time to reflect on this, if only for one minute during our daily routine. We start our morning full of energy and willpower. We go to work, work on a variety of tasks and goals, and deal with a variety of people, whether bosses, colleagues, supplier or clients. Our willpower is already being depleted. As we go through the day, the mental tiredness settles in, we have less and less willpower and we "automate" our behavior toward the evening when we have little or no willpower left. The "brain dead" feeling kicks in. What now? We enter a shop and purchase stuff we did not intend purchasing; we stop making price comparisons and go with whatever is easier, and may as well purchase the strategically placed bars of chocolate, gums, and other sugary stuff by the checkout counter. Incidentally, supermarkets also leverage the contrast principle in this case, as after gathering goods worth much more, 60¢ for a chocolate bar will seem a bargain. Supermarkets also know that with decreasing levels of willpower, people crave glucose and sugar. It is why your local supermarket welcomes you with products that are most likely already on your shopping list, such as fruits, vegetables, and salads. After a long day at work, and what seems like an even longer trip around the supermarket aisles, you reach the checkouts and find yourself in Candyland. And your brain shouts, "Sugar! Sugar! Sugar!" Lots of us do this, whether we have the Snickers bar, the Krispy Kreme doughnut, the sweet popcorn, jelly beans, or a sugary drink. Now ask yourself: was this purchase on my list? There is nothing innocent in the decisions of supermarkets in placing their products; in fact, just like digital marketers, supermarkets continually split test the position of the products throughout the shop, the sweets provided at the checkout, and the shelves they place the different products on.

The supermarket example shows that marketers are quick to take advantage of our "cognition shortfall". But how far can it go? One of the most celebrated experiments ever on willpower was carried out on eight parole judges in Israel. The judges were reviewing parole requests throughout the day, a very-high-stakes situation that required a high degree of integrity, lack of bias, and clear heads. The study found that 65 percent of the requests were granted after the judges had had a meal, and decreased during the two hours prior to the next meal. Researchers concluded that as judges were getting tired and hungry, they reverted back to their System 1 default position of denying requests. These findings are disturbing, as they imply that the release or otherwise of convicts was determined in large measure not by potential good deeds performed over the years, but rather by their appointment times and the state of the judges' bellies. Judges were not at fault, either. After all, their intentions were good, and the intense mental effort allocated to the reviews reflected integrity, as well. They just haven't considered that depletion in glucose levels and intense mental effort depleted willpower.

But what does this have to do with online marketing? Quite a lot actually. Take the quiz or contest tools I have mentioned, and the effort spent by an audience in the process of completing the quizzes or contests. While engaged with the quiz or contest, the metal effort can be taxing. And, when a person completes the quiz or contest, they are provided with a score, and product recommendations for improving their skills. Assume you are a client; you achieve a quiz score of 68 percent, download your gift, and find yourself redirected to a Thank You page. The Thank You page displays a cleverly marketed purple cow product that could help you improve your competency score to 80 percent. The sugary products strategically placed at the supermarket checkouts have taught us that you are now more likely to take up the offer. Or, consider the findings that most people engage more on social media in the evening. Most marketers attribute this behavior to work patterns. The popular view is that as people are at work during the day, they are less likely to interact on social media. However, marketers miss out on a much finer piece of information, which is that the evening is also the time when willpower levels are at their lowest, after a hard day at work. The result is that as people get closer to the evening they become more tired, cede more control of mental activity to System 1, scrutinize less, compare less, and are more prone to being influenced and to "satisficing." Of course, you may now think, the later in the evening, the more vulnerable my audience is. You may decide to move your outreach efforts from your current schedule to later in the evening. However, this view would be inaccurate. As the parole judges experiment suggests, people are more susceptible to influence as they get tired, and between meals when glucose levels are lower. This knowledge alone should help online marketers to better tailor sales funnels, email targeting, notifications, pop-ups, and paid advertising. In effect, your audience is more vulnerable when returning home after a long day at work and before having a glucose-rich evening meal. You may dismiss using quizzes or contests as an influencing tool, and you would be right up to a point. However, when timed well, quizzes or contests may be just what is needed to nudge people into the triggering of the action you want. Remember that players use more effortful System 2 when doing quizzes or contests. And many studies have found that people often put less effort into a subsequent task, cede more control to System 1, and are more prone to being influenced. I am sure you can think of many other creative ways to engage your audience in some sort of mental effort at the right time of the day, and of other tools to use, before creating your strategy. Some other ideas that come to mind include: long articles are less likely to be read in the evenings; shorter posts do better. Instagram posts do better than LinkedIn articles in the evening; the latter will do better at the beginning of the day.

4.13...but keep it scarce

Calls to action come in many shapes and forms. For example, many of the growth hacking tools I present in the section on tools display countdowns emphasizing the limited time of the offer. This kind of offer leverages the principle of scarcity, that is, people value goods and services that are less available more than goods that are available in abundance. (Jones, 2014) Wording such as, "last 24 hours," "Only 10 items left," "limited to three per person," or "Sale must offer on Sunday" often make people feel they will miss out on the offer unless they act promptly. The principle is powerful even in situations when price discounts are not necessarily significant, as the action bias is triggered by scarcity rather than price. For example, a supermarket ran a 10 percent-off promotion for Campbell's Soup by running two different messages: "No limit per person" and "Limit of 12 per person." The supermarket found that customers purchased twice as many cans of soup in the "scarcity" condition. (Kahneman, 2011) But why do we buy more than we need? People erroneously attribute their decision to the opportunity of saving money; they feel that by saving money they are in fact gaining money. But saving money cannot explain why people buy less when the scarcity advert is removed; after all, the price remains the same. It is the mindset we adopt while purchasing the product that makes the difference. We assume that our decision is based on a perception of gaining/saving money and we rush into purchasing before the offer ends. In reality though, exposure to the offer raises a fear of losing something, of missing out on a saving. The "Limit of 12 per person" generates the mental image of hordes of people fighting for Campbell's soup, taking up the entire stock available. And nothing will be left for us; we would have lost something, maybe the opportunity of saving money. Of course, this sounds like a perfect task for System 1, which, on detecting the imminent danger of missing out on the very last discounted cans of Campbell's Soup in the universe, jumps into action and impulsively purchases the product. In brief, the opportunity of saving money ranks lower than the fear of losing out on the offer. Psychologists refer to this finding as "loss aversion"; the alternative of possibly losing out is cognitively more painful than is the laying out of money to make the purchase. A simpler example of this principle is an experiment described by Daniel Kahneman in his exceptional book *Thinking Fast, Thinking Slow*. Participants were presented with the scenario of tossing a coin, with an opportunity of winning $150 if the coin showed heads but losing $100 if the coin showed tails. Surprisingly, in spite of the larger potential win, for most people the fear of losing $100 loomed larger than the opportunity of winning $150 and they would not accept the gamble. In fact, the average "loss aversion ratio," calculated in several experiments, was between 1.5 and 2.5. (Kahneman, 2011) Back to our Campbell's Soup example: people purchased twice as many cans when fearing they would miss out on the promotion. The loss aversion ratio in this case was two to one. Furthermore, scarcity has an unexpected impact on perceptions of quality. The scarcer the product is, the more positive our attitudes toward the product, as one classic experiment by psychologist Stephen Worchel has confirmed. Worchel asked two groups of subjects to rate the quality of a cookie. One group received a jar of two cookies (scarcity condition), while the other group received a jar of 10 cookies (abundance condition). As you might have guessed, people in the scarcity condition rated the cookies far more positively than did the comparison group. (Cialdini, 2007) As Cialdini concludes, "not only do we want the same item more when it is scarce, we want it most when we are in competition for it." (Cialdini, 2007, p.

262) Finally, marketers leverage scarcity to induce a feeling of regret in their audiences. One example that comes to mind is the "When it's gone, it's gone" slogan, which implies that you will regret it if you don't take the offer now. And it does work; many studies found that when people are reminded of the possibility of feeling regret for not taking an action, their behavior reflects an increased preference for conventional options, and a preference for leading brands over generic products. (Kahneman, 2011)

4.14 The myth of "less is more..."

In his book *Don't make me think*, Steve Krug advises website developers to "get rid of half of the words on each page, then get rid of half of what's left...it makes the useful content more prominent, it makes pages shorter." (Krug, 2014, p. 49) This idea has become a widely accepted "law" of conversion and seems to be supported by findings in traditional psychology, as well. For example, in one famous experiment, when presented with more choice —24 types of jam—people were less likely to buy than when only 6 types of jam were being offered for sale. (Laham, 2012) So it makes sense that "less is more" was widely adopted by SEOs, PPC consultants, digital marketers and website designers. To understand the extent of this idea you only need look at any conversion optimization tool like Unbounce where all templates inspire simplicity and very little text or distractions from the main calls to action. I personally find the obsession with simplicity *too* simple, even naïve. The "less is more" idea assumes that people reach your page—either via organic or paid search—and are already in a buying mindset, which implies that more text or information would act as a distraction from the main call to action. Indeed, the assumption is that people reach your splash page and happily take action with no more information than a couple of paragraphs on the main product features that you have provided. Moreover, in addition to the "noise free" approach, let us not forget the prominent "Buy now" button, so clearly displayed on many of these landing pages. However, there is plenty of research indicating that most people are in anything but a buying mindset when reaching your website. For example, a report by Interbrand shows that customers spend increasing amounts of time on researching various websites before making a decision. (Jones, 2014) And, despite all the talk about mobile overtaking desktop, you may be surprised to learn that about 97 percent of shopping carts are abandoned when accessed via mobile. Similarly, research carried out at Pennsylvania State University found that as much as 90 percent of user searches on Google are informational or navigational, with only 10 percent of searchers being in a transactional mindset. (Jones, 2014) Basically, these reports underline the fact that people are spending more time than ever in the research phase, seeking information, and comparing alternatives, features, prices, and so forth. With this in mind, you should not really take the traditional "Buy now" button advice too seriously; after all, most people are visiting your website for research purposes, rather than to buy something. Think twice before accepting traditional advice from digital marketing agencies or web designers regarding the design of your website; they may in fact affect your business negatively. There is, however, a catch. We cannot simply generalize and assume that a whole 90 percent of the visitors who are in a research mindset will necessarily need or want to read more text. An important distinction must be made when considering the amount of text targeting the 90 percent "research phase" visitors to your website. Research by Gary Klein, reported in his book *Sources of Power*, suggests that experts make decisions in a different manner to less-experienced people. Specifically, Klein observes that experts generally make intuitive decisions that are grounded in their extensive practice and experience in their work. By contrast, less-experienced people scrutinize more, compare more, and pay more attention. Applying this idea to online shoppers, we can see how experienced buyers know instinctively what to look for in a product or offer. In their case, simplicity is key; not much info is required, and less really is more. By contrast, less-experienced shoppers tend to seek more information, more text, and more resources on the page. Thus, in their case less is definitely not more.

The fact is that we scrutinize unfamiliar websites, products, or brands more, an operation that initially is in the remit of System 2. However, as we become more experienced in performing a task, our cognitive input reduces, performing the task becomes easier and more intuitive, and ultimately System 1 smoothly takes over from System 2, performing what has now become a familiar task. The level of expertise or familiarity your audience has with your product is important, as it will dictate your content and conversion optimization strategy. For example, if your audience has plenty of experience of your product or category of products, then "less is more" may apply, as your audience already knows what to look for, and more text or resources will prove of little interest to them. By contrast, when your audience is less experienced, then more information is often needed. We are simply talking about user intent: experienced users will generally seek no information and prefer action-oriented pages. In contrast, less-experienced users, who are not familiar with your product, will want more information and will carry out more research as well. In this case, providing less information will prove detrimental, as you searchers will move on to another website that provides the information they need.

If you think about it, this is why Google varies the amount of text it ranks in various industries. Google simply acknowledges that different industries have different audiences, different user intent and different needs of volume and depth of information. It is also why you should not get overly stressed about the green color of your Yoast SEO plugin or similar tools that are using static benchmarks such keyword density, minimum of 300 words of copy per page, and so forth. For example, a report by Searchmetrics found that in 2017 desktop content was one third longer than mobile content, and that the number of words per page of the top-ranked websites varied by industry. (Searchmetrics, 2017)

4.15 Monkey do, Monkey believe...

Hundreds of experiments have shown that after taking a decision we are more committed to it, and even change our behavior in line with our decision. (Sharot, 2012) This principle has been branded, "the endowment effect." (Ariely, 2009) For example, in one classic experiment race bettors were more optimistic and self-assured about their choice after having purchased the tickets. (Cialdini, 2007) Hence, if you convince me to download your gift, to share, like, or follow your article, or simply to purchase a product, I will become more confident that I have made the right choice, and I will love your stuff more as well. And, as I cannot explain away my reason for subscribing to your email list, sharing your article, or buying your product, it must be that I really liked it. I now adjust my preference in line with my behavior, becoming more committed to your stuff. This inference has been studied at length, and is the core idea of the self-perception theory: people infer their preferences by observing their choices. (Sharot, 2012) The principle was beautifully demonstrated in an experiment in which doctors were tricked into giving a short lecture about the benefits of a drug. Soon after the lecture, the doctors began believing their own words and started to prescribe the medicine more. (Ariely, 2012) In another experiment, when people committed themselves to losing weight by tweeting about their efforts they lost an average of one pound for every 10 Tweets. (Dolan, 2015) Another interesting experiment found that students who nodded their head up and down, which is the equivalent of saying "yes" from a body language point of view, were far more impressed by an editorial arguing a policy that would increase tuition fees. (Gladwell, 2001) This suggests that incorporating some sort of vertical and repetitive movement of the visitor's head would make ads, website copy, and conversion attempts more effective; the assumption here being that my behavior—nodding "Yes"— primes me into bringing my preferences in line with the behavior, thus becoming more favorable toward a product. OK, so I adapt my preferences in line with my behavior, thus becoming more committed to your stuff. What next? Well, as I like your content, I am now happy with your sending me emails and high quality "gifts" via tools such as MailChimp or SendinBlue. Of course, please send me some push notifications via PushEngage, ensuring I do not miss out the content I have grown so fond of. Next time I receive your newsletter, I will be more inclined to open it; after all I chose to receive it. And, since I shared your great article, promotion, or product, I will most likely continue to do so without having to be prompted again.

4.16 The white bear challenge...

Another mistake often made by many marketers is being too "in your face" with customers, talking too much about their own business and the advantages it offers; and doing too much prompting of people to keep the business's products in mind next time they're buying. Of course, reminding people about your product is one of the main goals of remarketing. People are being hit with product promotions and advertising messages all day long, and it is quite easy for them to forget about your product. In fact, Sharp concludes that the main purpose of advertising is to maintain market share by cancelling out the advertisements of competitors. Sharp: "If a brand's advertising reaches them, if they notice it, if it refreshes, reinforces or builds the memory structures that make the brand more likely to be noticed or come to mind in a buying situation...then it nudges their propensity to buy the brand." (Sharp, 2010, p. 141)

Thus, remarketing works by keeping your product fresh in the memory of your cognitively busy audience—if you didn't do it, people would easily forget about their earlier interaction with you. This would present a problem, as we have seen that 90 percent of people browse the Internet in research mode, reviewing a myriad of options on every single feature of the product they are looking for. If you have ever completed a research online you will be familiar with the feeling that you simply can't remember all the options, websites, or products you have seen during your research. So why keep trying to get people to remember our product? It may be time to think of alternative ways of getting people to remember us; after all, it is clear that the share of attention for each product is being reduced day by day; there is simply too much choice and too many products and services vying for our attention. I would like to invite a bit of controversy and encourage you to consider ways of asking your audience to forget the benefits of your products, forget the reasons why they should or shouldn't choose your products, forget about your products altogether. This may sound counterintuitive; after all, why would I ask my audience to forget about my products? However, plenty of research indicates that trying to suppress thoughts has the exact opposite effect: thoughts keep reappearing in our minds. The classic illustration of this concept is the "White bear" challenge. If I specifically ask you to NOT think about a white bear, and re-emphasize that you must not think about the white bear, what do you suppose you will be thinking of? Of course, a white bear will come into your mind. Stephen Hayes and his colleagues once again demonstrated the concept in several experiments. The researchers asked participants to not think about a yellow jeep for couple of minutes. What happened? Well, participants reported that the thought of yellow jeeps came into their minds for days and even weeks after the experiment. (Cabane, 2012) Of course, your approach as a marketer will need to be more subtle, though I am confident that you can think of many creative ways of incorporating this concept into the copy of your website and any other digital marketing devices you may have on the go. Actually, no....FORGET about it!

4.17 Launch to the Moon: the power of expectations

Up to this point we have discussed products that have already been launched and their promotion. But what happens with a purple cow you are just about to launch? There is no better example of the preparation for launching a product than the launching of Hollywood movies. All the world tours, previews, trailers, advertisements, and interviews are intended to build both familiarity with the product (hence better attitudes toward the movie) and a sense of increased expectation: you look forward to the movie, and the closer the launch the more you look forward to it. So, what happens? Let's start by explaining what dopamine is. In simple terms, dopamine is a chemical that fuels the reward network in the brain. The pleasure we feel after viewing a movie we have been expecting, at a new iPhone being launched, or a new online tool or product becoming available, is all down to dopamine being released inside our brain. (Robertson, 2012) Understanding the process that delivers pleasure is essential when launching your new product online. Unfortunately, many marketers launch purple cows with no prior preparation for building feelings of expectation and familiarity, and rely entirely on paid advertising or other types of publicity. All that potential flow of dopamine surging through their audience's brains...wasted. If you are looking for a vivid image of the impact of anticipation, simply visit any Apple store on the morning of the launch of a new iPhone and be amazed at the hordes of people waiting outside the shop for a product they could get their hands on with much less hassle the very next day. One great experiment carried out by economist George Lowenstein points out the impact of anticipation on the perception of the actual product or service. After learning who their favorite celebrities were, Lowenstein asked undergraduate students at the Carnegie Mellon University to state the price they would pay in return for a kiss from their favorite star. The price points were different, depending on the timing of when the kiss would be offered: in one hour, three hours, 24 hours, three days, a year or ten years. The study found that people would overall pay more for a kiss in one year than for receiving it immediately. (Sharot, 2012) The moral of the story is clear: anticipating a new product is as enjoyable, if not more enjoyable, than the actual experience of the product. I experienced this first hand when studying for my MBA. On the one hand, working very hard for it made me value the degree more. On the other hand, I significantly overestimated the level of happiness I would feel on receiving the degree.

4.18 There is hope for OK products too...

OK, so our decision to "freely" commit to an action such as downloading, sharing, buying, or liking will impact our perceptions of the product. Specifically, by performing an action we infer a perception and bring that perception into line with the action. For example, I signed up to your newsletter, and as I cannot explain it away it must be that I like your stuff. I am now more likely to become committed and like your stuff more. Of course, this was possible because I was not given an opportunity to explain away my downloading, sharing, or liking of your product. Thus, it pays off to stay true to your purple cow strategy and the principles we have been discussing throughout this book. However, for all the talk about purple cow products, you may find yourself pleasantly surprised to learn that there is hope for building loyalty to "OK" products as well. This is achieved by leveraging the concept of cognitive dissonance, which refers to our difficulty in acknowledging that we have made a mistake or done something wrong, particularly when we have invested time, emotions, effort, or money. In fact, the more we've invested the harder we find it to acknowledge that we were wrong. Now, as we try to fix this state of dissonance, a state of mental discomfort arises, ranging from minor unpleasant feelings to more advanced anguish, relative of course on the resources we have invested. (Tavris and Aronson, 2008) Subconsciously, we are now looking for a way to remove our mental discomfort, this unpleasant feeling. But how do we go about it? The answer is simple: we justify our decision and become more committed to it. (Tavris and Aronson, 2008) An interesting insight into how the brain resolves this conflict has been provided by several fMRI studies, which have found that upon receiving information that disagree with our opinions, the reasoning areas of the brain simply shut off. In brief, people rejected immediately any evidence that increased their mental discomfort. (Tavris and Aronson,2008) Remember the students who rated a boring lecture as interesting when they had to work hard to be accepted into the group? This is a prime example of how people become more committed to an OK product, or even bad one, when they have worked harder to obtain it.

Yet another principle that marketers can leverage from time to time for promoting OK pieces of content or products is the sunk-cost fallacy. The sunk-cost fallacy concerns people's tendency to invest resources in products that are not as good as they would like, instead of investing fresh resources in something better. This occurs simply because people have already invested time in the less good product and are reluctant to experience and acknowledge the feeling of loss that would come with abandoning it. (Kahneman, 2011) So, when reading your article I expend some of my scarce time and attention. When the Social Locker comes up halfway through the article, I am presented with a choice: admit I was wrong or explain my actions in terms of, "I enjoyed your piece of content, product or offer." Then, since I have convinced myself that I enjoyed your article, I become more committed to it: I am now more willing to share, like, follow, or email. Of course, I also ignore the niggling little voice in my head; otherwise I would be forced to consider the possibility that all my effort up to that point has been a waste of time. This is cognitive dissonance and sunk cost at their best. I have experienced this principle many times myself, bad movies being one example; I have continued to watch a boring movie because I have already invested 30 minutes of my time in it. Of course, I could have spent the remaining hour of the movie in a more productive way, and yet I would go along with it and waste more of my time.

There is also another principle at work here, which psychologists have labeled the "Zeigarnik effect," after the Russian psychologist Bluma Zeigarnik. Zeigarnik found that uncompleted tasks or goals often pop up in our minds, and once completed they simply stop doing that. (Baumeister & Tierney, 2012) So, when I read your article and get interrupted by your Social Locker, I feel an unconscious urge to finish the task.

In the end, psychologists Tavris and Aronson concluded that "the more costly a decision in terms of time, money, effort or inconvenience...the greater the dissonance and the greater the need to reduce it by overemphasizing the good things about the choice made." (Tavris & Aronson, 2008) One word of advice though: sunk-cost works when used occasionally, and when you have been building a large amount of goodwill with your audience. However, the principle can act as a double-edged sword: my time is scarce, so I have strong feelings about spending it on reading your bad or OK article. As a result, I may not visit you website again, or I may end up being guilty of confirmation bias by concluding that all your content, products, and offers are poor. Again, I experience this with many of the publications I sign up to when great articles are followed by average or overly commercial pieces of content, which leads me to unsubscribe from those email lists.

4.19 Further thoughts....

So what have we learned? To begin with, we learned that our end goal is a website visitor signing up to an email list or taking up our offer because he likes our stuff. And as he likes our stuff he is more likely to genuinely engage with us at later stages, e.g., in email campaigns, receiving push notifications, and when making subsequent purchases. It all starts with a purple cow lead magnet, which is being promoted via pop-up tools, email marketing, social sharing lockers, push notifications, and other growth hacking tools. We then engineer our sales funnels to eliminate any possibility of our audience explaining away their action, whether that be signing up, sharing, liking, following, or buying. Specifically, we must ensure that people cannot rationalize their action by saying, "I had no choice but to provide my details," or to devalue your lead magnet by telling themselves that It's free/cheap, thus it cannot be any good. Furthermore, to increase the likelihood of gaining genuine commitment and engagement from our audiences, we must provide them with some sort of control, or an illusion of control, over deciding whether or not to offer contact details, to share, like, follow, or email our content or product. This is important, as in the words of psychologist Timothy Wilson, "The more people feel like they are forced into something, the less likely they are to enjoy it and want to keep at it." (Wilson, 2011, p. 132) Trivers has also confirmed that people need to feel that they have control over their behavior, that they act out of choice, even if the feeling is an illusion. (Trivers, 2011) A simple scenario could be a pop-up that allows website visitors to download a lead magnet free of charge if they choose to, while also incorporating an optional sign-up feature. You can be creative with your copy, e.g., I have worked x days, y hours to provide you with this article and would love to send you any fresh information. I am no copywriter; however, in this simple scenario people have control over providing their details, they imagine or "feel" your efforts, which triggers feelings of empathy and ultimately increases your chances of gaining commitment and leads. Some people will sign up to your updates and some will not, which is perfectly fine. After all, the ones who don't sign up would not have opened your emails anyway. By contrast, people who do sign up have done so freely, of their own accord, and cannot explain away your gift. And once they take an action, people adapt their perceptions to their behavior: after all, "If I took this option freely, I must like your stuff." In fact, if I think about it, I now like your stuff even more than before, in the way that the study of race bettors revealed. Entrepreneur Daniel Priestley takes the idea further, encouraging businesses to offer gifts and expect nothing in return. His line of thought is that free gifts are a token of your business's greatness and should prompt people to want to learn more about it. (Priestley, 2014) Priestley provides examples of free events organized regularly by Rolex, Qantas, Kia, and Red Bull. I almost bought into the idea until he gave a last example, which was the free browsers, calendars, maps, and apps that Google provides. In the chapter on Future I will explain that there is no such thing as a free lunch with Google. In fact, as I will discuss in the section on the future, Google is far from disinterested and has at heart its own self-interest, which involves gaining access to ever more data. That being said, products offered by Google are a great example of purple cows that we use every day, and we happily reciprocate by conceding access to some of our data. In the end, the fact is that our lead magnet must generate some sort of action, whether giving personal details, sharing, following, liking, or purchasing. At the same time, the path to achieving these goals is important, particularly when our goal is to engage followers who are optimistically anticipating our offers, emails, products and content. Any offer, product, piece of content, or sales funnel we create must be preceded by meticulous research on the feelings and emotions that will trigger our desired action. For example, if fear or reciprocity is likely to increase conversion rates, then copy, images, videos, and audio must all work together in a funnel that both generates and provides solutions to alleviate those feelings, reducing cognitive pressure. Take time to nurture your target feelings and do not ask the audience to get into bed with you on the first date. Why would they? Remember Daniel Priestley's Ascending Transaction Model? Priestley points out that people are looking for low risk and guarantees when first trying your product. You need to work hard to get a committed audience, but when you do achieve your goal do not revert to default content, products or experiences; remember why people signed up with you in the first place and do not fail their expectations.

We have also been discussing several other psychological tricks you can use to further improve both conversion rates and commitment. For example, simply providing people with a reason can be powerful, as Ellen Langer's Xerox experiment revealed. Framing your request will boost conversion rates when automatically ticking the subscription box, as we have seen in the organ donors example. Leveraging the denominator neglect principle can greatly help to increase your conversion rates. We have also learned that by building anticipation we can improve the actual experience of our product, as suggested by the Carnegie Mellon study of students postponing the pleasure of getting a kiss from their favorite celebrity. Don't sell yourself too easily though. Make people work for your purple cow lead magnet, and point out to its scarcity; they will value it more. And, as we have seen in studies on willpower, timing your offer well can make the whole difference with regards to the level of receptivity of your offer. Finally, remember that less is not always more, and the level of experience with a category of products will dictate the amount of information and website copy people need.

That's it.

CHAPTER 5.
GROWING A SOCIAL MEDIA FOLLOWER BASE

L et's consider for a moment why brands, influencers and businesses are so keen on increasing their social media base of followers. One obvious reason is social proof. The reality is that without a large enough follower base acting as a cue to the greatness of your product, content, brand, or website, most people will not even give you a try. For a practical manifestation of the importance of social proof, you only need to think of Stanley Milgram's pedestrian experiments. In these experiments people did not look up when one person alone looked up; they looked up when several people looked up. Or consider the discussion we had in the reviews section: you will not purchase a book with no reviews. The book could be a great work, but given the lack of social proof, nobody will read it—sad but so true. It is why many top-end restaurants pay people to queue up, providing social proof that the restaurant or club is busy and popular. (Ariely, 2009) By doing that, restaurant and club owners leverage the principle of "herding behavior," which describes our propensity to assume that something is good or bad based on other people's behavior. (Ariely, 2009) Indeed, how many times have you entered an empty restaurant? The restaurant must be empty for a reason, right? As in the case of restaurant owners, marketers and webmasters acknowledge that great products will not sell without some help from the herd. And, in an attempt to grow their social following, marketers sometimes take advantage of social media automation tools, which work on principles such as follow/no-follow, like, share, or by spinning comments. Moreover, many companies go as far as buying fake followers, a simple action if you consider that all you need do is enter "buy fake followers" in Google Search. I have experienced this first hand with clients who initially purchased fake followers and likes, and subsequently increased their follower base by a combination of great content, natural and machine-generated comments and likes, and by using follow/no-follow tools.

Many white hat SEOs, social media consultants, and the like dismiss the practice, and will strongly advise you against it. I believe this is more down to ego and self-perception than to common sense. The truth is that the rich get richer, and more reviews attract more purchases, more people willing to connect with you and more business. "OK," the white-hat professional will say, "but people check your social profile and identify your connections as fake." Let me just ask that person a question: how often do you go on LinkedIn, filter people by keywords, and then start an investigation into the type of contacts they have? In reality, the process you will follow is more likely to include a search based on your targeted keywords, an assessment of the legitimacy of the profile information—i.e., the image information—and sometimes the number of connections. You then send or accept the invite. So, it is the actual number of connections that provide the cue, and trigger your action.

One major benefit of growing our social media followers base is that the followers become part of a group of people with some sort of similar traits or backgrounds. The membership to various groups represents a perfect opportunity to exploit and leverage principles of similarity. Psychology professor Richard Wiseman points out that, "Regardless of whether the similarity is in dress, speech, background, age, religion, politics, drinking and smoking habits, food preferences, opinions, personality, or body language, we like people who are like us, and find them far more persuasive than others." (Wiseman , 2010, p. 62) And countless psychology studies document the tendency of people to conform and to internalize a group's beliefs, often at the expense of personal beliefs. A classic example is provided by an experiment carried by Solomon Ash, a psychologist who asked participants to identify a line, out of several lines of different lengths, that matched a standard line. At the start, participants were told that they were taking part in an exercise in visual perception. Within the group all the members were accomplices of the experimenters, apart from the unaware subject. The subject was scheduled to answer the question on the correct line last, after all the other members of the group had provided their answers. Throughout the experiment, the stooges were often pointing to the wrong line, in spite of the correct answer being obvious. Of course, as a rational person you would predict that subjects contradicted the group and pointed to the correct line. After all it was so obvious, right? As you have probably guessed, the body language of the participants showed disbelief to the group's choice, and yet 50 to 80 percent of the people went along with the group. (Ross & Nisbett, 2011) What this experiment also demonstrated was the principle of polarization, which is the tendency of a group of people to become more extreme in their beliefs. Let's look more closely at how this works in practice by looking at recommendations as an example. In our section on the future, we will discuss the important role of recommendations in filtering information and helping us choose. Tools like Amazon's "People who bought this also bought this" help us avoid the decision paralysis triggered by almost unlimited choice. But why do we trust recommendations? Why do we actually trust Amazon's algorithms and other people's preferences? Consider books. Every time I buy a book on growth hacking, psychology, or the future, I associate myself with the type of person that reads book like these: innovative, open-minded, a bit on the cool side, and so forth. Of course, the group of people purchasing the same book must also be innovative, open-minded and cool too. Thus, I infer the traits of the group from their purchasing behavior. Also, given the research on similarity, I know that I trust people who are like me more than I trust others; hence I trust their recommendations more too. Unintentionally, I am now a member of a group of people with similar reading interests and purchases. Now, when the group purchases a new book, I have to purchase that book, as well; after all, it is what innovative, open-minded, and cool people do. And when I buy a new book, another member of the group will be influenced by my purchasing behavior, too. This process is captured well by psychologist Robert Trivers , who concludes "Within each group, individuals are misoriented in the same direction, easily reinforcing each other." (Trivers, 2011, p. 252) This is polarization. One interesting point to make is that people in general do not actually influence my purchasing behavior. It is rather the stereotype associated with the reading behavior of the group that makes the whole difference. But how powerful is the impact of the stereotype I associate myself with? Several studies testing this effect have found that, when reminded about their membership or perceived membership of a group (e.g., race, gender or—why not?—book preferences), people are three times as likely to be influenced by the stereotype associated with that group. (Sharot, 2012) Thus, I am three times as likely to purchase a book when people similar to me "bought this" and "also bought this." Social media networks are prone to conformity and polarization, too. Of course, as we will see later, the type of social group you are part of makes all the difference.

What other reasons may we have for growing our social media follower base? Increasing the reach of our content or products, of course; no surprise there. Indeed, we think about the number of people who follow us on social media as the potential number of people we can reach. I have 1,000 followers, hence I can market to 1,000 people, right? This is an oversimplification, as we will see in the section on the future that with social media giants the reach of your organic posts is significantly reduced. For example, we will see that Facebook posts only reach around 16 percent of your friends organically. However, for simplicity purposes, let us assume the equation expected be reach equals the number of followers/friends. The interesting thing, though, is that plenty of research indicates that in reality your product reaches far more people than your 1,000 social media friends. Let's have a closer look at how social connections work. The power of connections was initially popularized by psychologist Stanley Milgram who conducted his famous "Six degrees of separation" experiment in the 1960s. Several hundred people from Nebraska received a letter for a businessman in Boston. The people did not know and had never heard of the businessman before. Also, note that Nebraska is more than a thousand miles from Boston (Thank you, Google). The subjects were asked to send the letter to a person they knew personally, a "connection," who they thought would be more likely to know the businessman. The result was amazing, even by the standards of today: the letters changed hands only six times before they reached the businessman. (Christakis & Fowler, 2011) Nowadays, given the advancement in technology, digital progress, and the presence of social media, the six steps of separation have reduced considerably. In fact, psychologists Nicholas Christakis and James Fowler carried out numerous experiments, laying down their findings in their brilliant book suggestively named *Connected*. What they found was that "if your friend's friend's friend gained weight, you gained weight...if your friend's friend's friend stopped smoking, you stopped smoking....if your friend's friend's friend became happy, you became happy." They "packaged" their findings into a principle called the three degrees of Influence, to conclude that everything we do influences people at our first, second and even third connection level. In terms of social media, LinkedIn for example considers that we influence people at up to two degrees of separation (first degree and second degree connections). Consider one of the main services offered by LinkedIn: job advertising. We all receive LinkedIn messages from recruiters who promote various job vacancies. If you think a bit about it, you have not actually met or known these people, and yet it is often these second-degree connections that will get us our next job. This is exactly what Stanford psychologist Mark Granovetter found when studying people who changed jobs. Granovetter wanted to understand how often people have seen the person that helped them in obtaining their job. The assumption was that the more times you saw the person, the closer you are connected. Granovetter was surprised to find that only 17 percent had met their connection "often," 55 percent "occasionally," and 28 percent had "rarely" met the person. (Christakis & Fowler, 2011) This study clearly points out the real power of second and third degrees connections. Christakis and Fowler carried out another great study, which further exemplified the influence of second and third degree connections. They looked at three piano teachers and how they were acquiring clients in Tempe, Arizona, and found that the teachers mostly acquired customers by word of mouth. But most importantly, 38 percent of the recommendations came from people who were three connections away from the teachers. That is 38 percent of the business leads coming from the teacher's friend's friend's friend! Returning to our conversation on social media, you should now understand the extent of your influence on your 1,000 connections, their friends and the friends of their friends. This is powerful indeed. Another great observation Christakis & Fowler make is that as your family and friends become better connected, you also become better connected. (Christakis & Fowler, 2011) What this means is that the type of followers you have really does matter. Earlier in this chapter I discussed buying fake followers for social proof purposes. While I encourage this strategy as an initial growth hacking step, I have to admit that at times I have had to rein in some clients from purchasing further fake followers. Once they got the taste for easy gains, some of my clients wanted more and more. Back to the Milgram's pedestrian experiment: another brilliant find was that when the accomplice group consisted of five people, almost as many people looked up as when the group consisted of 15 people. Thus, 500 social media followers could provide the same social proof as one million fake followers. It makes no sense to further purchase fake followers and the like after reaching your goal of social proof, as more fake followers will add no further value to your business.

Another great piece of research found a probability of 52 percent that you will be lonely if a person you are directly connected to at one degree of separation is lonely, and a 25 percent chance if a person at two degrees of separation is lonely. (Christakis & Fowler, 2011) Which leads me to the point that 100 well-connected influencers will reach more people than 10,000 poorly connected people, and will definitely reach more people than one million fake followers. Christakis and Fowler explain this point best when discussing their studies on obesity, smoking, drinking, or even the impact of being widowed. (Christakis & Fowler, 2011) They found that if one of our friends becomes obese it nearly triples the likelihood of our becoming obese as well. Similarly, when people quit smoking, their friends, their friends' friends and their friends' friends' friends are influenced to mimic that action. (Christakis & Fowler, 2011) And, a Harvard study found that when 10 percent of their friends got a flu shot, subjects were 8.3 percent more likely to get a flu shot themselves. (Christakis & Fowler, 2011) This makes sense, as friends cluster together and perform the same activities together. So, if James is friends with Nicholas, Nicholas will most likely have an influence on James. The study also found that if James does not consider Nicholas to be a friend, then Nicholas will have no influence on James. In other words, you may increase your social network artificially using various tools such as follow/no follow, likes and mentions, shares, or comments, but this will have very little influence in a large social network where people do not consider you a friend. Furthermore, the more relevant, qualified, or influential your LinkedIn or Facebook friends are, the more people will associate you with their traits, in line with the "principle of association" we discussed earlier. (Cialdini, 2007) To sum up, having quality connections matters. You may use automation and fake followers to build an initial base of followers for social proof purposes. Then the really hard work begins, as you must now grow your connections—the right type of connections. Seth Godin has made this point eloquently when stating that marketers cannot afford to reach the masses anymore. Instead, Godin advises marketers to reach out to sneezers, the people who both share and have influence online. (Godin, 2005) Of course, we don't want just any sneezers; the more like you they are, the greater the chance of reaching the influencer. As a simple example, a digital marketing consultant is more likely to share a great digital marketing article or tool than an accountant is. Or consider the more practical example of the well-known blogger Matthew Woodward. Matthew has launched his Private Blogs Network course mainly targeted at beginner to mid-level SEO professionals. The launch was preceded by four free introductory videos in which Woodward recalled several occasions early in his career in SEO when he had little information and had often learned what to do by trying things out and making mistakes. This is a prime example of how the blogger was using the principle of similarity to instill into his audience the idea that "I am like you; I've been there as well; we have the same background; I understand you and I am here to support you." Triggering a feeling of empathy with his audience was an important goal of the videos. After all, as Chabris and Simons rightly point out the more we empathize with someone the less critical we become of their message. (Chabris and Simons, 2010) Every experienced SEO knows that Private Blog networks are a "no go" SEO strategy, and yet in Woodward's case the empathy we feel toward the blogger and his being associated with expertise lead us to hold a more positive perception of private blog networks. By pointing to his earlier mistakes, Woodward was also leveraging the pratfall effect, meaning that occasional slip-ups can enhance your likability, and make you seem more human. (Wiseman, 2010) And, by emphasizing the common goal of beating Google, the blogger was leveraging the shared adversity principle, which refers to the fact that sharing adversity brings people together. In fact, the more adverse the experience the more intense the bond. (Brafman & Brafman, 2011) Thus, the more intense that SEOs perceived the battle with Google, the bigger the bond between the blogger and his prospective students. Now, assume for a moment that the course was proposed by an unknown John Doe digital marketing guy, rather than a respected influencer like Matthew Woodward. Would your perception of the proposition change? I suspect, you would laugh off the idea of private blog networks, while also seriously questioning the level of expertise of the John Doe marketer.

Every marketer knows that people perceive more positively and trust more a message or product when respected influencers have endorsed it. Which is why tools like BuzzSumo offer Influencer outreach modules, and digital marketing agencies allocate large resources to reaching influencers. But why are influencers so important? Why do we still let ourselves be influenced by people whom we perceive as authorities in their field? How much influence do these influencers actually have on the followers we long to getting access to? And is paying influencers to sneeze about our brand or product worth it?

We consider ourselves to be the masters of our own minds, and we are sure of our ability to decide the quality of a product solely on its merits. Indeed, we tell ourselves that we are too smart to let ourselves be unduly influenced by biased people's recommendation of a product. Unfortunately, this perception is yet another lie we tell ourselves. Of course, we are influenced by celebrities endorsing products, and by online influencers sharing or liking articles or products or promoting products on social media sites. In fact, psychologists and marketers have been aware for a very long time that "arguments produce more attitude change in the people who read them when they are attributed to well regarded (that is, attractive, trustworthy, or expert) communication sources than when they are attributed to poorly regarded sources." (Ross & Nisbett, 2011, p. 71) But how much effect do influencers actually have on our decisions? How far can the influencer go before we decide that enough is enough? And can we prevent ourselves from being influenced? Stanley Milgram to the rescue again, with his most famous experiment on "obedience to authority". Milgram was looking to understand the extent to which authority figures impacted the behavior of people. Via newspaper ads and direct mail he recruited hundreds of people from diverse backgrounds. The cover story was that people would be taking part in some fictitious studies regarding the impact of punishment in the learning process. The first experiments were carried out at Yale University. Milgram devised a scenario where unsuspecting subjects were being asked to gradually increase the electric shocks they were applying to a "learner". Unknown to the participant the learner/victim was an accomplice of the experimenters. Several conditions were tested, including a remote condition with the accomplice placed in a separate room, but allowing the participant to hear his kicks on the wall, presumably caused by the pain inflicted on the victim. In another condition—voice feedback—the victim was still located in another room but this time vocal protests were introduced, that is, the subject could hear the protests of the victim. Other conditions tested were proximity and touch-proximity, where the victim was in the same room, close to the subject and even touching the participant. The subject was acting at the commands of a laboratory technician who was wearing a grey technician coat. The technician's clothing, attitude and association with the University conferred on the technician a perceived status of authority. Of course, both the victim and the technician were accomplices of the experimenters, and they both played their roles in a very realistic manner. The victim in particular was well trained, and managed to mimic brilliantly the pain and anguish associated with the different levels of shock received. Participants were being told that the researchers were looking to understand the impact of punishment on the learning process. The participant was supposed to teach the victim a paired-associate learning task. Every time the victim gave a wrong answer, the technician would ask the subject to increase the level of the shock applied to the victim. The aim of the game was to assess how far the subject would go in obeying the technician, despite the screams, apparent pain, and the requests the victim made that the experiment be stopped. Many factors were tested. It is beyond the purpose of this book to detail the experiment, though you can of course read all about it in Milgram's book *Obedience to Authority*. So how far did the participants actually go with the shocks? For how long did they obey the technician's commands to increase the level of shock? Well, in the remote condition 65 percent of the people obeyed the authority and went up to the highest available level of shock. In the voice-feedback condition 62.5 percent went along with the experimenter. In the proximity and touch-proximity conditions 40 percent and 30 percent respectively went along with the experimenter. (Milgram, 2010) It is easy to see that the greater the distance between the victim and the subject, the more the subject obeyed the technician. Of course, keep in mind that it was not authority per se that drove the subject in his obedience but rather the perception of authority provided by cues such as the University of Yale setting, the technician's coat, the technician's control of the experiment, and the confidence displayed by the technician. How does this transfer to the online world? Well, online marketers encourage business owners and marketers to build presence online on LinkedIn, Facebook, and Reddit, to answer questions on Quora, and to contribute on Blog4U or on similar platforms. The premise for this action is that it both drives traffic to the website and builds the website's authority profile. During my career I have met many mediocre self-made "experts" in various industries, and I know of many more. These "experts" are perceived as authorities based on their significant online presence, even when the content presented is well below the quality I would expect at their particular level. In the section on future I will introduce you to the case of a mediocre SEO expert that has provided my team with an expensive but subpar lecture on SEO. Throughout his lecture he showed little to no understanding of current principles, SEO issues and tools, advancements in machine learning, or the impact of Rankbrain on SEO. Only after the lecture did I understand the reason behind his insistence on being paid in advance. I can only assume he had received lots of similar negative feedback in the past. And what do you know? Yes, you guessed it—he's a LinkedIn influencer. He talks at conferences and he is very active on Facebook and Twitter, as well. He certainly generates quite a bit of noise. In a nutshell, as shown in the Milgram experiments, the appearance of authority or expertise is sufficient for confident behavior to be wrongly associated with actual expertise. Take another experiment described by Chabris & Simons. Groups of four people who had never met before were asked to solve several math problems. Every participant was first asked to take a personality test measuring how dominant they tended to be. Researchers then recorded and closely analyzed the solving sessions. They found that people whose personality was more dominant had most often taken leadership of the group, even though they proved no more expert or competent than the other group members. So, how did they end up being leaders or influencers? In the words of Chabris & Simons, " the answer is almost absurdly simple...They [the dominant influencers] spoke first...people with dominant personalities just tend to speak first and most forcefully...If you offer your opinion early and often, people will take your confidence as an indicator of ability, even though you are actually no better than your peers. (Chabris & Simons, 2010, p. 98) You experience this contradiction throughout life: incompetent bosses who talk their way into a job, group brainstorming sessions hijacked by mediocre "leaders," confident influencers and professionals who are forever "everywhere" online with nothing much to say. Of course, this is one powerful lesson you can leverage as a marketer looking to leapfrog more experienced influencers in your market: the mere appearance of being an influencer can be as strong as actual expertise. Like that seasoned but mediocre SEO consultant, you can talk your way into it. Fortunately, confidence is often associated with expertise, a helpful bit of knowledge to leverage when competing against more-established influencers.

Milgram's studies, while shocking, give us a glimpse into why we go along with what influencers or perceived authorities say or do. We trust and believe recommendations provided by influencers. And when a John Doe provides the same recommendations we most often dismiss them. In the words of psychologist Paul Bloom: "Other people's actions are driven not by how the world really is, but by how they think the world is." (Bloom, 2011 p. 161) Thus, focusing on growing your network with quality connections, rather than quantity, is paramount for leveraging social media as a growth strategy. Using automated follow/no-follow tools exclusively is therefore not indicated. Many people fall prey to the promises of fast growth, particularly given the granularity of filtering offered by these tools: you can follow or invite only people who have profile images, who posted a given number of posts within a given amount of time, who posted comments, or have a certain number of followers or friends; or you can choose them based on a keyword, and so forth. This level of granularity is one reason why I often encourage a balanced approach in using both automation and organic growth. However, automation alone will never deliver the engagement you are looking for. While people may accept your automated invitation or follow you in return, they will do so not because they love your product or content, but rather as a polite gesture, returning the favor, getting access to your first- or second-degree connections or for other such reasons. In conclusion, more is not always better. This is particularly important on social media platforms like LinkedIn, which is limiting the number of invitations you can send. So, use you invitations wisely, go for quality and well-connected people, gain access to their first- and second-level networks and see the reach of your product or content skyrocket.

Christakis and Fowler also explain that if influencers are to be successful, one more ingredient is needed: influenceable people. (Christakis and Fowler, 2011) While it may seem obvious, many marketers forget this aspect when choosing audiences, whether organic or paid for on Facebook, LinkedIn or other social media networks. If you are looking for proof, take a look at your email inbox or monitor your search experience; how many automated emails or remarketing ads do you receive from websites you've visited without engaging with them? And how many times have you reached a website and been welcomed by a pop-up offering basic information or lead magnets you don't really need? One way of keeping people engaged, though, is the traditional old school special offer. Yes, it does work, as a study by Nielsen has shown. The study found that special offers were the main reason why people followed brands on social media, a finding backed up by another study by the *Marketing* magazine. (Jones, 2014)

To sum up our conversation on growing social media networks: remember that people have the tendency to associate themselves with people who share some degree of similarity with them, such as background, history, experiences, or education; before devising your social media growth strategy, you must ask yourself several questions:

- Who is your target audience? Is your audience relevant? If it isn't, the size of your network will be irrelevant as well. Do you exclusively automate your social media growth? You should be aware that influencers most often will not follow you back and do not interact with automated comments or likes, either. Moreover, by growing your network solely on automation you will find yourself at the periphery of the network, perceived as a follower rather than an authority, and your pitches, whether articles, posts or promotions, will go largely unnoticed. Conversely, choosing a relevant audience and building a perception of authority will improve the reach of your message throughout the network, up as high as your third degree of separation connections.

- How many connections do your friends or followers have? How about the friends their friends have? What type of connections are they? We have seen how 100 well-connected people reach more people than do thousands of poorly connected "friends." A hundred influencers will connect you to thousands, hundreds of thousands and even millions of second- and third-degree connections. By contrast 1,000 poorly connected people will connect you to a far smaller number of people.

PART 2.
CONCEPTS & TOOLS OF THE TRADE

CHAPTER 1.
INTRODUCTION

When I first started in digital marketing, I used to consume an unhealthy amount of digital marketing content, watch every tutorial I could get my hands on, test every tool I read about, and sign up to dozens of industry publications that quickly started to clutter up my inbox. I was particularly interested in tools that professional digital marketers and agencies used, but also tools that those consultants were not aware of but which could have improved their workflows. At the same time, I was not, and still am not, a very technical SEO, and I could not write a piece of code even if my life depended on it. Thus, I had to find a way to close those skill gaps by using technology and tools. In the beginning, it seemed that digital marketers made use of such a lot of tools, and it all looked so complicated...understandably, as a non-technical person I felt anxious. The aura of magic surrounding the SEO and digital marketing professions did not help, either; after all, if all those people took years to learn these skills, how could I do it in just a couple of months? Pompous-sounding terms such as growth hacking and digital growth marketing strategies further increased my anxiety, raising images in my mind of Einstein-like geniuses breaking into the FBI's or NASA's computer systems...how would I ever match them? However, as I started my research into tools and digital marketing concepts, I quickly realized that behind the veil of jargon there was nothing magical or difficult about these tools and concepts. The more I learned about how digital marketers performed their stuff, the more aware I became that behind the jargon lay very simple and uncomplicated concepts. Moreover, I quickly realized that for whatever task I needed to perform, there was a tool out there to enable me to do it. That is when I also realized that these tools could benefit a wider audience, beyond digital marketers. In fact, non-technical marketers, sales teams, small business owners and entrepreneurs would all benefit from running their own digital marketing campaigns, and save themselves money in the process. This chapter came to life from a desire to help people and businesses that find themselves at a great disadvantage when competing against mammoth companies with mammoth budgets. I also wanted to help marketers that, just like me, do not have the technical knowledge associated with many SEO and digital marketing tools. Yet another goal of this book was to demystify the unnecessarily complicated jargon used by digital marketing specialists to give apparent weight to tasks that are really very simple to perform. As a client who may be sacrificing some of your already limited budget in the hope of growing your business, you deserve respect, rather than a smooth-talking marketer who dazzles you with their spiel. If you decide that you simply do not have the time for DIY, my hope is that after reading this part of the book, you will find yourself in a far better position to challenge your digital marketing consultant or agency to do better. I am fortunate in that I work in an agency that empowers my passion for customer service, although from my experience with other agencies and colleagues, I know that this is not always the case. Another point I want to make is that some of the tools presented in this chapter include various types of practices that may go against the arguments put forward in the chapter on psychology. Do keep in mind that the purpose of this chapter is make the reader aware of what is possible and of the various tasks that currently can be performed. In the end, every business is unique, and only you can decide the tools, psychological principles, and practices to best match your goals. I also encourage you to perform further research and online training before deciding which tools to use, as this will both maximize the results and minimize costly mistakes, such as in the use of tools like the ones described in the social media automation section. I have always found YouTube and Udemy my main go-to channels for learning more about various tools and their functionality. Finally, when it comes to social advertising, the scope of this chapter is not to provide in-depth training in that field, but rather to make you aware of how easy it can be to employ a DIY approach, and give you the confidence to do so. The truth is that new settings and features are being introduced all the time, and by the time you read this book, any specific information it contains could be on features that have already been updated; always check. Again, I have always found platforms like Udemy and YouTube very helpful in learning about various features and which strategies to apply when running social advertising campaigns on a variety of platforms.

CHAPTER 2.
SEARCH ENGINE OPTIMISATION

In my previous book *HACKING DIGITAL GROWTH 2025: Exploiting Human Biases, Tools of the Trade & The Disturbing Future of Digital Marketing* I discussed at length the future of SEO. Back to the present time: let us shift the discussion to the more practical and current part of SEO. As an entrepreneur or business owner, you will often perceive SEO professionals as wizards using the magic power of knowledge for the purpose of ranking your website on the first page in Google. My intention in the next section is to demystify SEO, provide you with a good and easy-to-understand interpretation of the jargon, the key areas you should focus your efforts on, and the tools used by experienced SEOs when working on a website. After reading this section you should feel fairly comfortable about auditing your own website, from a technical point of view, performing various optimizations to your site and learning new ways of benchmarking your competitors. Finally, you will notice that many of the tools presented are WordPress plugins. WordPress is a content management system that I recommend to every small business owner, marketer, or entrepreneur who requires great flexibility, user friendly design, and a DIY capability; it enables them to make quick changes, add features, and integrate with any third-party tool you can think of.

2.1. SEO Technical Audits

SEO technical audits are essential to ensuring that your website is visible to and indexed by search engines, such as Google or Bing. After all, if they can't see it, they can't rank it. A typical technical SEO audit investigates issues such as indexing of your website content, Google cache for key pages, title tags, duplicate content, site architecture and internal linking, broken links, correct use of 301 and 302 redirects, 404 page errors, 500 server errors, JavaScript, iframes, flash errors, Google Search Console and Bing Webmaster tool errors, xml sitemaps, canonical versions, correct implementation of rel canonical link tags on the site, page speed issues, compression, caching, minify CSS/JS/HTML issues, mobile experience, hrefllang/rel alternate implementation, analytics tracking code, filters for internal searches, local SEO, structured data, funnels, setting up goals and events, and more. If you are new to SEO, do not worry …by the end of this Chapter it will all make sense.

Unfortunately, far too many nice-looking websites are being built with no consideration being given to search engine optimization. Most often, this situation occurs due to a disconnect between the Web development team and the online marketing team. It is imperative that the two teams work together in planning the project, as opposed to designing and building the website, and only at a later stage considering the website's goals and its SEO strategy. Needless to say, these nice-looking websites most often come at a cost with no ROI, and are nowhere to be found on search engines like Google or Bing. They deliver no leads, no enquiries, no business.

What is an SEO technical audit?

An SEO technical audit should be included as a default in any SEO package offered by your SEO agency or consultant. A technical audit focuses on the fundamental mechanics of your website; it is the very first step you will take when optimizing your site. In simple terms, all your efforts will be in vain if your website cannot be seen or found by search engines like Google and Bing. In the end, neither Google nor Bing can rank your website for content that they cannot see or find. There are many errors that can appear on your website from a technical SEO point of view, but the main issues occur around response codes 200, 4XX and 5XX, indexation, canonical issues, hreflangs, errors found in Google Search Console and Bing Webmaster tools, XML sitemaps, 301 and 302 redirects, redirect chains, meta descriptions, page titles, title tags, and demographics, to name just some of the areas.

What is a 200, 404, or 500 response code, and how do you fix errors?

You can think of response codes as diagnostics. Whenever you run your website through a technical SEO tool, the tool crawls every page of your website, following every URL link it finds. If the crawler finds a page through the link, a response code 200 is generated, which means that no action is required. However, if the crawler follows a URL link and finds no page associated with it, then, most often, a 404 or 500 message is returned. A 404 error message indicates that no page was found at the URL address the crawler followed from your or an external website. This can occur for various reasons, though most often it indicates that the page has been deleted or moved to another URL. For example, you might have a Web shop and add or remove products regularly. When you remove a product from your website, search engines will continue to crawl the URL, get to a dead end, and return a 404 error. In another example, you optimize (that is you change your URL address to incorporate keywords and the correct user intent in a natural way) but forget to redirect the old URL to the new URL. Now, when Google crawls the old URL it reaches a dead end, as the page isn't there anymore. The solution is simple; every time you remove a page, a product, a team member, a case study, or other element, you must redirect the URL associated with that element to the most relevant page on your website. Now, when crawling your old URL, the search engine crawler is directed to the new page via the redirect command.

A 5XX, most often a 500, error is generally related to a server issue on your Web hosting server. It occurs for various reasons, and appears as a crash of your website, restricting access to parts of the site or to the whole site altogether. Sometimes, 500 errors are only temporary; often, waiting for a short while and retrying will work—most Web hosting teams are very good at identifying faults and working out fixes. If a 500 error persists and your SEO technical skills are limited, contact your Web hosting technical team. Your SEO specialist or Web developer should, in most cases, also be able to quickly diagnose the problem and take the right course of action.

What are page titles and how do you optimize them for SEO?

When creating a new page, product, case study, or other element, you give it a name, hence the name *page title*. There are still SEO consultants who insist on including as many keywords as possible, and, if possible, putting them at the beginning of the title. While this practice was valuable a couple of years ago, it is of little worth nowadays. As a matter of fact, Google's machine learning algorithms have improved at such a high pace, they are now able to assess the value of the title in relation to the content and too many other factors. In brief, over-optimize your pages and you risk losing in rankings. Of course, you can include keywords or variations of them at the beginning of the title, if possible; however, always ask yourself: is my title relevant to the content on the page, and am I offering the visitor what I have to sell in the page title? A page with a title that is not reflective of the page content leads to visitors bouncing back from your page, and lowers your time-on-site metrics. Lower time-on-site metrics send signals to search engines such as Google...your page is not relevant to the title you are presenting, and you will lose rankings.

What are meta descriptions and how do you optimize them for SEO?

A meta description is a small paragraph—up to 320 characters—used by search engines like Google to decide when and where to display your page within search results. In simple terms, when searching for, say, "Romanian translator" in Google, you are served results that Google believes to be best matched to your user intent. Let's take the first page in Google as an example. You see several websites, and their descriptions include a title on the first line, the URL on the second, and the meta description on the third line. A few years ago, meta descriptions were optimized with keywords, and the practice was abused by webmasters and SEOs. Nowadays, though, Google puts very little to no value on the content and optimization of meta descriptions and title tags. You will however notice that most websites ranked on the first page in Google still have keywords in their title tag and meta description. Some SEO consultants still talk of the benefits of optimizing meta descriptions and meta titles, and continue to promote this myth, giving weight to the supposed need for their services. The truth is that meta descriptions and title tags are important because they drive user action, rather than influence search rankings. Specifically, an enticing description encourages visitors to click through to your page, and if your content accords with the meta description, the query term, and the user intent, the visitor now spends more time on your webpage. Hence, the term *time-on-site metrics*. In a very simplistic way, higher time-on-site metrics will lead search engines to conclude that your website is relevant to the query, and will reward your website with higher rankings. In brief, forget the myth, and focus on optimizing your meta titles and meta descriptions for better click-through rates, rather than stuffing keywords.

What are meta keywords?

A long time ago, in ancient SEO times, search engines used to encourage webmasters to include, within their code, keywords that described their business, category, or service. Search engines used meta keywords for understanding what websites were about, and ranked them accordingly. It is hardly necessary to point out that webmasters abused this feature, adding keywords that were irrelevant to the website content and user intent, and the results returned to searchers were consequently of low quality.

Nowadays, search engines have made it very clear—and this is confirmed by numerous tests—that meta keywords have no value for SEO. Hence, if your SEO consultant talks about optimizing your meta keywords, this will be a strong signal that they have little understanding of SEO, or place little value on integrity and transparency.

What is a canonical?

A canonical is a way of telling Google which page to consider relevant, from two or more pages with the same content. Let's assume that you have two pages with the same content. Google crawls these pages but will not be able to tell which page should get the authority and the ranking rewards. You can fix this by implementing a canonical tag on secondary pages, pointing to the page you want Google to consider the authority page. You may ask: but why would I have two pages with the same content? Or you may argue that you do not have two pages with the same content. This is where things can get a bit complicated. Canonical issues appear for various reasons, too many to describe here. I will, however, focus on the need to establish canonical versions of your site via 301 redirects, and within the Google Search Console. While you may perceive your website as one entity, Google sees your website as several different properties. Specifically, Google considers the www, non-www, https, and non-https versions of your site as four separate properties with the same content. This creates a duplicate content issue which can be resolved by telling Google in Search Console that you would prefer that it consider your main website the www version, say, or the non-www version. This step is also called setting up a canonical version in Google Search Console. Finally, you need to ensure that all subdomains of your site are re-directed via a 301 redirect to your preferred canonical version of the website.

Getting canonical issues wrong can have a negative impact on your website, though not in the way that many inexperienced webmasters explain it. Specifically, less-experienced webmasters may support the idea that Google penalizes your website for having a lot of duplicate content. In reality, this explanation is born out of ignorance, and Google will not penalize your website. However, as Google doesn't know which is the canonical version of your website, it will distribute your rankings between the different copies of your site. This, of course, will lower your ranking. Moreover, when canonical versions are not being set via redirects, you may also experience potential loss of ranking-benefit from your authority page, with some links pointing to your https version, others to the http version, and others to the non-www version, for example.

What does the Index/Noindex command do?

You will use the index command to inform search engines that you are happy for them to index your page and its content, hence allowing users to find and access your content online. By contrast, you will use the noindex command to inform search engines that they should not make that particular page available and visible on the Internet. Suppose you are building a new website, and are in the process of refining your content. Throughout this process, you do not want to make the content available in its current form. You would apply a noindex command initially, and remove it before your website launch. In this way, Google will only index your website in its final form. Other examples include pages with information that you may not want made visible to your users. Many errors occur when webmasters accidentally noindex content on their website, or even the whole of the site, resulting in lost traffic and lost visibility.

What is NoODP?

NoODP (No Open Directory Project) tags are meta robot tags providing search engines with a description of your business in directories such as Yahoo or the now defunct Dmoz. You generally use it to control the display of your meta description within these directories, hence preventing Google from generating the meta description for your listings automatically. Think about it as a meta description of a page; if you don't specify a meta description, Google picks up automatically up to 320 characters from the page. This is undesirable; it affects negatively your click-through rate, and indirectly affects your SEO efforts.

What is hreflang?

Think about hreflang as an interface between two languages. When your website is available in two or more language versions, the hreflang interface ensures that the correct version is delivered to the user. An hrefllang error could, for example, have the effect of delivering the English version of a website when the user has chosen the German version, or some content might be delivered in English and some in German on the same page.

What are redirect chains?

To understand redirect chains you need to have an understanding of what "link juice" is. In a very simplistic way, link juice represents the authority that Google is believed to confer to a particular backlink based on the authority of the page, website, or blog that the link appears on. The higher the authority of the page or website where the link is, the more link juice and authority this link passes to your page and website from a ranking perspective. Let's assume that, for whatever reason (e.g., the product is not available, the news release is out of date), you remove a page from your website. We have learned that in such a case we must redirect the old page to the most relevant page on the website, or Google will return a *404 not found* error. When this happens the link juice authority of the old page is lost. By contrast, redirect the old page to a new active relevant page and the new page will receive an estimated 90+ percent of the authority from the old, say, product page. Now, let's assume that the initial product page is being redirected to another product page, which in turn becomes redundant and is further re-directed to yet another page. You now have a redirect chain. Think about it this way: old URL passes 90 percent authority to new URL; new URL redirected to another URL, passes on 90 percent out of the 90 percent received from the old URL. To sum up, the more redirect steps you add, the more link juice you lose. To fix a redirect chain, the solution is to go back to basics; redirect the initial old product page to the last page in the chain directly, with no intermediate links, thus passing 90 percent of the original authority to the final page.

What is an XML sitemap?

The XML site map is a map of all the URLS of your website. The XML map is submitted to Google and Bing search consoles, for example. The rbt.txt file allows search engines to better understand and index your website. Once it is submitted to the Google and Bing search consoles and referenced in the rbt.txt file, both search engines are regularly updated on the current content of your website, indexing the content better and faster, and more often.

What are 301 and 302 redirects and why do they matter?

Earlier, we discussed 404 response codes, which are returned when search engines cannot follow a URL location that they have searched for. We also discussed redirecting redundant pages to relevant pages on your website. Redirections can be performed via either a 301 redirect or a 302 redirect. A 301 redirect is a permanent redirect, communicating to search engines something along the lines of "please pass all the authority of the old page to the new page I am redirecting you to." By contrast, a 302 redirect communicates to search engines, "I am only temporarily redirecting you to the new page, while I refurbish my existing page; hence, please keep my page authority as it is and do not pass authority to the new page." If you intend to redirect old pages, products or other URLs, then 301 redirects should usually be performed. Always investigate 302 redirects to ensure you understand the reasons behind them, and replace 302 redirects with 301 redirects if the intent was to permanently redirect the old page to the new page.

2.2 Building your website

WordPress, Avada and Visual Composer

If you do not own but are planning to build a website, then WordPress is the best content management system (CMS) you can use, particularly if you are a non-technical person. The WordPress platform has too much functionality for me to even attempt to explain it all here, and it distinguishes itself through flexibility and customer friendliness. Its most powerful feature is that it enables you to quickly add plugins for virtually any task you may need to perform. Do you need a testimonials section? Or maybe a team area, a shopping cart, a carousel, a contact form, or integration with any third-party platform you can think of? There are plugins to do all of those things and many more. And, if you have chosen your theme well, you may have very little need for plugins, as great themes provide inbuilt functionality to add any element you can think of to your website, in an easy-to-use drag-and-drop manner. Avada is one such theme I would strongly suggest you check out. If you already have a WordPress website but are fed up with the continuous charges imposed by your developer, just add the Visual Composer plugin to your website and gain instant access to all the elements you need in an easy-to-add drag-and-drop manner. You can find many courses on Udemy and YouTube that will show you how to build or upgrade your own website; I have personally built dozens of websites following various online training courses. Put the time in to take these courses; it will be worth it.

GoDaddy

When researching online, you will often find that various bloggers recommend mostly the same hosting platforms. Most often, though, they have never actually used the products named, and their recommendations are based on the highest-paying affiliations. Make no mistake: choosing the right hosting provider is essential for your website. You simply cannot make this decision well without thorough research.

One trustworthy Web hosting provider is GoDaddy. GoDaddy is cost effective, high performing, and has one of the best customer service teams around. I know of a hotel that made the wrong choice of a Web hosting package and the management have had to upgrade their server. They have been quoted almost $4,000 a year by their current provider. GoDaddy has provided a quote for half that sum, with the same server specification. Of course, GoDaddy is just one example. However, the point is that you need to put the time in to research and choose a good Web hosting provider.

To sum up: don't let yourself taken in by exotic hosting proposals; most bloggers are monetizing their posts with very little concern for your business.

2.3 Technical audit tools

Google Search Console

If there is one tool you must use in carrying out your SEO technical audits, it is Google's Search Console. Within its search console Google makes available information about your website, relevant technical issues, recommendations to improve its visibility, tools, and much more.

There is too much functionality within the search console to list everything here. However, some of the tasks you will perform or review often include html improvements, concerning such as: title tags; duplicates; meta descriptions; the structure data highlighter tool; the analytics tab; setting up international targeting; indexing status and crawl errors, such as 404s; robots.txt visualization and testing; XML sitemap submissions and errors; and links to various Google consoles.

Within the Search Console you will create http, https, www and non-www versions of your property, and set up the canonical tags we discussed earlier. A common technical issue with many websites is that only one version is created in the Google Search Console. This means that Google does not know which version is the canonical property. The solution is to create all four versions of your website in the search console and identify the canonical version with canonical tags. Of course, this is an oversimplification of one of the many functions of the search console, but it is an essential tool you cannot overlook in your SEO technical efforts.

Bing Webmaster Tools

Bing Webmaster Tools is Microsoft's equivalent of the Google Search Console, and overall it provides similar functionality. One of the primary reasons for using Bing Webmaster Tools is creating and verifying your website—proving that you own it—and submitting your XML sitemap. You can use either Bing or the Google Search Console for the remainder of the tasks.

Screaming Frog

Screaming Frog is an industry-leading SEO technical audit tool. Indeed, this is the preferred tool of most of the SEO consultants I know. A free version is available and it should suffice for crawling small websites. However if you are crawling larger websites you will need to purchase a yearly license. At £149 per year this is the very first investment you should make when starting your SEO career, or when auditing your website as a business owner.

What does it do?

It would take a whole book to cover the various functionalities offered by Screaming Frog. Examples of just a few of the tasks it undertakes are: pages or elements blocked by rbt.txt files; response codes; URL analysis; detailed analysis of H1s and H2s; page titles; meta descriptions and meta titles; image optimization; canonical issues; and index/noindex issues. A must-have tool.

SEO PowerSuite

If you are a cost-conscious marketer and your limited budget may not be sufficient for online marketing tools such as SEMrush, Moz, or Raven Tools, then SEO PowerSuite is a great alternative. This tool has various pricing plans and is far less expensive than the more established tools. SEO PowerSuite has been developed a bit differently than all-in-one tools; it comprises four different modules, which can be purchased separately: WebSite Auditor, SEO SpyGlass, LinkAssistant, and Rank Tracker. As you have probably guessed, the WebSite Auditor module will provide you with specific technical SEO capability. SEO SpyGlass is concerned with any tasks you may need to perform related to backlink profiles, and a large variety of metrics is included. LinkAssistant is a complete link-building and outreach tool. Finally, Rank Tracker will monitor your ranking position, and a wide choice of metrics is on hand to provide an in-depth understanding of your keywords' performance.

Siteliner

Siteliner is a tool that should be part of every technical and on-page SEO audit that you carry out. One of the functionalities provided by the tool is benchmarking your website's performance against the median performance of other websites. Of course, do bear in mind that the median will only provide you with a broad-view topline benchmark; in reality the median differs, based on various factors, such as the industry or the type of website.

To get started, simply input in your URL and enjoy the wealth of information brought to your fingertips. Some of the main areas you will be looking at when running your website through Siteliner are:

Duplicate content (i.e. the percentage of duplicate content found at sub-domains). This will provide you with a quick overview of potential issues that could be caused by such as canonical or sub-domain-related errors;

XML sitemaps. You will be provided with information on whether a sitemap has been found on your website, and whether it is referenced in the rbt.txt file;

Statistical information on the number of words on each page, the text-to-html ratio, the number of outbound links, the number of inbound links, and the total number of links per page; "broken" links.

CachedView

A cached view of your website is the version held by Google on its servers; it is how Google "sees" your website. The version of the website seen by users must be the same as the cached version. You will need to investigate any discrepancy. To re-emphasize an earlier point, Google cannot rank what it cannot see. Hence, you will be reviewing your website's cached view, and you will do this page-by-page, focusing on your main landing pages first. To sum up, Google must hold as its cached version the correct version of your website.

When auditing a small-to-medium-size website, you may check the landing page using the traditional method: take the page URL, drop it into the Google Search bar, click the little arrow by the URL, get the cached view. When you work with larger websites, you will use various tools; one of them is CachedView. There are many tools available, of course, and CachedView is just one of them.

Responsinator

If you are a digital marketer, then for you the following words will state the obvious: mobile search is big, and it will soon overtake the more traditional desktop search. It is therefore essential that your website's mobile version is user focused; this is not a nice-to-have; it's a must-have.

But what do mobile users want?

It depends on many factors, such as the type of business, user intent, type of products, and services. But two needs and wants are universal: mobile users want speed, and they want to get what they're searching for. And, the look and feel of your website on various mobile devices is crucial in delivering great user experience on devices such as the iPhone and tablets, in vertical position or landscape, and so forth.

One tool you can use for this purpose is Responsinator. Simply input your URL, click Go, and several devices displaying your website will populate the screen.

Google Mobile-Friendly Test

We have discussed the importance of your website being mobile friendly. Google has already moved its focus from desktop search to mobile search by announcing that it is moving the desktop index to mobile. In brief, it is highly unlikely that you will have any chance of ranking prominently if your website is not perceived as mobile friendly by Google.

How do you know whether your landing page is mobile friendly?

Simply run it through the Google Mobile-Friendly Test tool. If the label returned says "mobile friendly," great! Otherwise, you will need to put things right. The tool will also provide you with information on any loading issues, links to resources, and even an overview of how your page looks on a mobile device.

However, I prefer Responsinator when reviewing the look and feel of my page on various devices, due to its having a greater number of devices available and its landscape-versus-portrait image feature.

SEObook keyword density tool

There is lot of debate regarding the impact of keyword density on SEO. The idea behind the debate is that, as Google's RankBrain algorithm gets smarter, it will be able to quickly learn, make associations, and understand what websites and pages are about, even without keywords being present on the page. We are not quite there yet, and many top SEOs acknowledge that keyword density is still important. For the time being it makes sense that the keywords must be on the page, and, of course, semantic analysis should dictate your on-page keywords strategy.

To discover the keyword density of a page or text you can use a tool called the SEOBook Keyword Density Tool. You can complement your analysis with another tool, TagCrowd, which generates a tag cloud, an image displaying the most-often-found keywords on the page, thus providing you with an overview of the page's keywords strategy and semantics.

You can use these two tools both for SEO technical audits and to spy on your competitors, unveiling their keyword strategy or identifying new keywords you may not have thought of.

BuiltWith

BuiltWith is one of my all-time favorite tools. Simply input the website URL and the tool will provide information about the technical components the website is built with. Some of the information you receive will be related to the site's Web server, its email services, hosting providers, content management system (CMS), widgets, and much more.

You will be able to use the information provided by BuiltWith in various ways. For example, every time you receive an enquiry from a potential client with a website, the first task you should undertake is to run the website via BuiltWith. You will in this way understand how the website was put together, i.e., the CMS, the hosting company, the plugins that are on the website. You can also use BuiltWith to spy on your competitors. And finally, you will use BuiltWith to continuously learn from what other successful bloggers do: what plugins are they are using on their websites, what hosting, and so on.

Who.is

Another tool that complements the information provided by BuiltWith is Who.is. There is a large number of tools available online providing the same functionality; Who.is is one of them. Input the targeted URL and a wealth of information will be instantly available at your fingertips: registrar info, date of website registration, expiry date, when it was last updated, server names, similar domains, detailed information on the registered owner, and domain history reports, to list just some of it.

Just as with BuiltWith, you will be able to use who.is both to evaluate what you are working with and for competitor benchmarking purposes.

WordPress Plugin Checker

You will sometimes need to gain a more in-depth understanding of the plugins available on particular WordPress-created websites. You may also be a curious person and sometimes like to learn about the plugins being used by your competitors or even bloggers you admire. You may then decide to research these plugins on YouTube, learn about them and assess their potential value for your own website.

One tool you can use is WordPress Plugin Checker. Input the URL of the website, click Check website and enjoy a wealth of information about the plugins installed on the target website.

What WordPress Theme is That?

As with WordPress Plugin Checker, you will sometimes need to better understand and learn about the WordPress theme used to build your own or a competitor's website. You can use What WordPress Theme is That? for this purpose; again simply input the URL of the website and click Search.

Web URL Opener's Sitemap.xml checker

You will generally use Siteliner or the Google Search Console to assess whether your website has an XML sitemap and whether the XML sitemap is referenced in the rbt.txt file. However, at times you will find yourself in situations where, for various reasons, you will not be able to use either of these two tools. When this happens, you can use a tool called Sitemap.xml checker from Web URL Opener. Input your URL and find out whether your website has an XML sitemap in an instant.

Web URL Opener's Robots.txt Checker

At times you will also want to check if a website has an rbt.txt file, and the content of the rbt.txt file. Most often, the Google Search Console should be sufficient for the task; however, you will sometimes have no access to that search console. You will still need to carry out an SEO audit, and one tool you can use is Web URL Opener's Robots.txt Checker.

WayBack Machine

WayBack Machine is a fantastic tool, providing information on the history of your website, changes that have been made, cross-checked against factors such as decreases or increases in traffic and rankings.

How does the tool work?

WayBack Machine acts as an Internet archive; it crawls the Internet and archives webpages at different times. This means that the tool archives multiple variations of your website, compares them, and presents the information to you at the touch of a button.

In addition to its obvious SEO benefits, the tool can also be used as a competitor benchmarking tool. You can spot changes on your competitors' websites, overlaid with increases in rankings or traffic—which you can analyze with tools such as SEMrush—understand changes in their strategies, and emulate successful practices, if appropriate. Many other creative ways can be devised for putting this great tool to good use.

YouGetSignal

Many times, websites are being hosted on shared Web servers, as dedicated servers are still quite expensive for a blogger or a cost-conscious entrepreneur. There are various reasons why you may want to learn who you share the server with. YouGetSignal can tell you. Simply input your domain name and press Check.

Isbanned

When your website shows significant loss in rankings and traffic you will want to investigate the reasons behind it. The Google Search Console, SEMrush, and WayBack Machine are some of the tools you can use as part of the process. Another tool you may want to consider is Isbanned. As its name suggests, Isbanned carries out a check to see whether your website has been banned by Google.

Barracuda's Panguin SEO Tool

You will also need to check if your website has been affected by Google's Panguin updates; Baracuda's Panguin tool will carry out that check. Again, it's simple to use; connect to your Google Analytics account and you are good to go.

OpenLinkProfiler and WebMeUp

In the Competitor Benchmarking chapter we will be discussing various ways in which you can use competitor backlink analysis as a sales tool, in benchmarking strategics, and for intelligence gathering. Indeed, the old-school approach of walking through a competitor's car park and writing down leads is highly ineffective, yet it is very much alive in the arsenal of many sales and revenue professionals. I have already named several tools you can use to conduct backlink analysis. Raven Tools and SEO PowerSuite are two of them. Other recognized leaders, but perhaps too expensive when you are on a low budget, are Majestic's Site Explorer, Ahrefs and Moz's Open Site Explorer.

What if you can't afford these tools?

Fortunately, two good, free alternatives are available: OpenLinkProfiler and WebMeUp. These tools will generally provide some good results to get you started!

Google's Structured Data Testing tool

Structured Data is important to Google to the extent that Google provides a Structured Data Testing tool within its Search Console. The tool makes it extremely easy for any non-technical webmaster to add appropriate markup to their website. Structured data provides Google with information about the specific parts of your website and the type of data the parts provide. This helps Google to improve its ability to match user intent to your website.

Make no mistake; structured data is important to your SEO efforts, and too many websites still have errors in this area, or no structured data at all. To check the status of a website, input its URL to the Google Structured Data tool and click Enter.

Google PageSpeed Insights and GTmetrix

One of the three tools you will use to check page speed scores is Google's own PageSpeed Insights. This tool provides you with a good understanding of any improvements that need to be made to your website. You will be provided with a score out of 100 (the maximum achievable), and three colors are used to indicate the page speed health of the website: red is bad, orange means you need to do some work, and green is good. The tool includes two tabs, one indicating mobile page speed performance; the other indicates performance on desktop. Details are provided with regard to any improvements needed, and links to Google's own resources make it easy for webmasters to learn more about the various issues.

You should double up Google's PageSpeed Insights check with GTmetrix, simply because this tool has more-comprehensive information, allowing you to pinpoint very quickly the main speed issues on your website.

There are many other tools out there; Pingdom is another that is very often used in conjunction with Google's PageSpeed Insights tool and GTmetrix.

2.4 WordPress Plugins for fixing main website technical errors

W3 Total Cache

One plugin you can use for WordPress page speed optimization is W3 Total Cache. This really is the ultimate caching plugin, and is one of the most downloaded plugins on the Internet, with over one million downloads. Its functionality includes various caching options, browser caching, minifying, content delivery network (CDN) support, and many other features.

WP Fastest Cache

Optimizing your WordPress website for speed can at times be a very frustrating process. You will find that W3 Total Cache works best in most cases; however, at times it has little impact on a website. When this happens, you will generally try various alternatives, testing speed, monitoring improvements, and continuously repeating the process until you achieve acceptable results.

So, if W3 Total cache isn't working, you can try WP Fastest Cache, another highly popular caching plugin. This plugin is easy to install and configure, more like a ticking exercise. However, please do your research first, as some options, for instance minifying, can break (damage) your website. The same advice applies to any plugins you install on your website, of course.

WP Super Cache

Tried W3 Total cache and WP Fastest Cache and still not working? Try WP Super Cache as well. Like W3 Total Cache, this plugin has had over one million downloads; hence, it is highly trusted and well tested by developers.

ShortPixel

One of your biggest problems when auditing a website is page speed. You will most often collaborate with a developer when working on a non-

WordPress website. However, when working on a WordPress website, things are a little different; you have far more flexibility in trying various plugins, settings, and tools. One regular page-speed challenge on most websites is optimizing images for the Web. You will generally work with one of three plugins for image optimization, but I've found ShortPixel to deliver the best results in terms of compression and quality of image. Other compression optimization plugins you might use are WP Smush and TinyPNG.

TinyPNG and JPEG Optimizer

We have seen that one common cause of poor page speed is image optimization; image size in particular can be a problem. Think about how often you download some high-quality royalty-free or paid-for image and upload it to your blog with little or no consideration to compressing the image. If your website has been built on a WordPress platform there are various plugins you can use to improve speed by compressing an image that is already on your website. ShortPixel, Tiny.PNG, and WP Smush are three examples we have discussed. Yet again, the more plugins you add to your website the higher the likelihood that your website will be slowed down. Moreover, various other technical issues can occur, such as various plugins not working well together; that is why you should really keep the number of plugins on your website to the very minimum.

The solution to the image optimization problem is to compress your images before you actually upload them to your website. You can use two tools for this purpose: Tiny.PNG and JPEG Optimizer. Having tested quite a few such tools, I know that these two will usually deliver good results in terms of both size reduction and quality preservation.

WP-Optimize

WP-Optimize is by far the best WordPress plugin for optimizing databases. You can use it in conjunction with ShortPixel, W3 Total Cache and Autoptimize.

It is easy to set up and its main features are selected in advance. This means that you can optimize your databases at the click of a button

Autoptimize

Autoptimize is another popular WordPress plugin. This plugin provides functionality to systematize scripts and styles, minify and compress scripts, add expires headers, and cache. Another prime feature in improving your Google page-speed score is moving styles to the page header and scripts to the footer. You can minify HTML code, and quite a few other advanced features are included as well. Overall, a great plugin that will most often speed up your WordPress website.

Redirection

One error you will often have to deal with when conducting website audits is 404 returns. These errors appear for a variety of reasons, such as pages having been removed but the link not having been redirected to a relevant page, products removed, and development issues; the list could be continued. The point is that these pages drain "link juice" authority. 404 pages should be redirected to relevant pages, enhancing the link profile and page authority of those pages, while also maintaining a tidy back end of the website.

One plugin you can use for redirection purposes in WordPress is called Redirection; it is very easy to use and free. All you need to do is install it, sign in as a new user, copy and paste the old 404 page URL into the "from" field, paste the new URL into the "redirect to" field, click enter, and that is it. For non-WordPress websites dropping your redirections in the htaccess file will do just fine, although you should not attempt this yourself if you are unfamiliar with the process.

UpdraftPlus

When working on a website, things can go wrong; websites can be "broken." This can happen for various reasons, such as development issues, various plugins not working well together, or problems with the themes. You may, for example, update some of your plugins and everything goes down. *I know, I know*, you will say, *if I'd followed best practice—set up test environment, update plugins—I wouldn't have had that issue.* But then, let's be neither naïve nor superficial, we know these tasks take time, and most of the time (999 out of 1,000 times) we will simply check the plugin configuration, confirm that the plugin is up to date, and go ahead. And sometimes, a website breaks. When it does, the first action you would take is to try to install a backup copy. Most of the time you will do this via your hosting panel, but you can also use a plugin, such as UpdraftPlus, one of the most downloaded backup plugins. You can set up regular backups to be emailed to you, to your Dropbox, or your Google Drive, and so on. As best practice you should create a backup of your website prior to performing any technical changes to the site. Back it up, email it to yourself, and if the worst thing happens, simply reinstate using the backup.

CHAPTER 3.
LOCAL SEO

When someone types a keyword such as "Hotel" in its search bar, Google aims to determine the context of the query: are they searching for services, publications, reviews, or something else? Once the user intent is determined, Google matches the query to the company best suited to it on the first page relevant to the term "Hotel." Once you have convinced Google that your website is relevant for the "Hotel" query, you must "convince" Google that yours is the most relevant hotel in the location of the user, or in the location of the user's search. In simple terms, if someone searches for hotel services in Berlin, Google delivers the most relevant local result; the same for the UK and for any other country. So, the aim of the game is to send Google as many signals as possible to "own' that location, that is, to make sure that Google will pick your hotel in preference to your competitor's across the street. The good news for you is that small local businesses in particular are really bad at local SEO, which makes it easier for you to leapfrog the competition at the local level.

If you want simplicity of implementation, as a business owner there are several actions you can take right now to significantly improve the local SEO of your website.

-        Submit your business to Google My Business and fill in all fields within your console;

-        Perform a local SEO search for your business on MOZ Local;

-        On-page SEO—optimize your page and website for keywords, including variations, such as dentist in London, London dental services, postcodes, areas etc. (We discussed at length on-page SEO in the SEO section of the book);

- Implement structured data on your website—this step will further inform Google about the content and purpose of your website. If your website is built on WordPress then you will find a lot of resources and local SEO plugins at www.rankya.com. Of course, many other plugins are available to provide similar functionality. If your website is not built on a WordPress platform, then look no further than the user-friendly Data Highlighter tool offered within the Google Search Console;

- Improve the number of reviews received by your business. It can be confusing to understand which review websites you should focus your efforts on. The easiest way to find out is simply to search for your targeted term in Google, pick up the websites included by Google in the local pack, and have a look at the review websites included in the results. You can now put in place a strategy for improving your local reviews score;

- Build as many backlinks as you can pointing to your website from websites within your local area. You will find that with regard to backlink profile, local SEO is quite different than global SEO. Specifically, for link-building purposes, you would usually search for websites with high authority and within your "ecosystem," your sphere of activity. And many SEOs still recommend the same approach at a local SEO level. However, at a local level your focus must change. You must gain as many local links as possible. To sum up: you should not concern yourself with the authority or the theme of a website, as long as the website is relevant to your local area. You will most likely already have quite a few opportunities to gain local backlinks to your website; some examples and ideas are: pay for sponsorships; volunteer; join a local club; attend local meetups; register with local directories and local review websites; sponsor local events; make use of local resource pages, local blogs and newspapers; support local charities; be listed in local calendar pages; join local business associations; support local schools, homeowners associations, and other community organizations.

Google My Business

If there is one platform you must register your local business on, it is Google My Business. You can think of Google My Business as a tool provided by Google to inform its algorithms about the location of your business, its website, and its images; in fact, anything that will enhance your website's relevance to a local search.

If you are running a business, particularly a bricks-and-mortar business, then you must submit and verify your business via Google My Business; there is no way around it. Why? As explained previously, Google is obsessing about great user experience and serving the most relevant results to its users' queries. Google considers local SEO a major factor when ranking your website.

How does it look in practice?

A person finds him- or herself in Wimbledon, and they're looking for an Asian restaurant. They type "Asian restaurant" in their Google Search bar. Google's algorithms present them with a restaurant that meets their query— Asian restaurant—matching the perceived user intent: they are in Wimbledon, looking for an Asian restaurant; hence, they are most likely looking for Asian restaurants close to their current location. Of course, this is an oversimplification, as other ranking signals are also taken into consideration. Overall, the aim of the game is to provide as many local signals as possible to convince Google that yours is the most relevant Asian restaurant in your location. And, submitting your business to Google My Business will be the very first step toward achieving this.

Google I Search From

Google aims to deliver the best Asian restaurant as conveniently as possible to the searcher. This includes matching the Asian restaurant to their current location. Hence, when they Google "Asian restaurant" from New York they are served a very different result than when searching from London.

Depending on your product, business, service, or other factors, you may find yourself having to monitor your Google rankings for targeted keywords in other countries. Moreover, as an SEO consultant, you will often work with businesses operating in various locations around the world. The truth is that many clients you will work with, particularly small and medium-size enterprises (SMEs), will simply type their target keyword in Google and expect to see their website on the first page of results. Google I Search From will save you from the embarrassment of situations such as praising your client's ranking position in Google, while the client cannot find themselves on the first page when searching from their country. Google's I Search From is easy to use; simply choose your target country from the dropdown, input your query, and search. You will now see the same results as your client sees. A great tool for a quick check of your rankings the old fashion way, even at local level.

MozLocal

Another signal that was found to improve local search rankings in Google is local citations. Many companies offer services such as submitting your business to thousands of directories, promising that they will rank your website on the first page in Google, and so forth. The problem is that very often these services may do more harm than good. The days of directories having strong impact on SEO are long gone, and Google places very low or no value on links from directories that are not relevant to your business, directories which exist only for link-building purposes, and so forth. Moreover, when employing these services you will often not know what directories your business is submitted to, their authority, quality, or location. And even when this information is provided, you may conclude that after all, these directories are not relevant to your business. To establish a consistent local presence, one of the best tools available is MozLocal. MozLocal helps you establish a consistent business listing in all five relevant aggregator databases: Factual, Central Index, Thompson Local, Foursquare, and other directories and popular websites. Moz used to have an option of £179 per year for a professional package in the UK.

You would get hundreds to thousands of business listings, Local SEO analytics, Google My Business Insights, Customer Action, and Listing Alerts. However, they temporarily withdrew the offer from the UK market, although it's still going strong on the US market. It is very likely that the tool will be brought back to the UK at a certain point in a much improved version. In the meantime, you can quickly audit your MozLocal score: simply input your company name and postcode, click Check Listing and review your Local Score report. Now, all you need to do is use the report to register your business with that websites manually.

Google and Yelp reviews

Several Harvard Business school studies by Michael Luca found that reviews on websites such as Yelp have improved the ability of smaller independent restaurants to compete with established brands (Brynjolfsson and McAfee, 2016). We have already discussed at length, in the chapter on psychology, how reviews work; hence, you should now be aware of how important managing your reviews really is. And I believe that you can easily guess the number one reason why people do not leave reviews of your business. Most of the time the answer is simple: they do not need the hassle. As a customer you may ask yourself: Where should I leave a review? How much time will I need to spare? Or, even worse: many small to medium businesses are not even asking or encouraging customer reviews. Let me ask you a couple of questions: do YOU know where to post a Google review of a business? Does your team or the business owner know? When was the last time you posted a review about a small business?

How do you go about it?

There are many tools available to support you in improving the number of reviews received by your business. Plugins I often use when working on WordPress websites are from Rich Plugins. These three plugins support Google, Yelp, and Facebook reviews respectively. Purchase a license, download a plugin, then upload it to your WordPress website; configure, personalize, and add your shortcode to reveal a great-looking box displaying reviews and inviting people to review your website. These plugins make it easy for your website visitors or clients to post reviews about your services: they click a link, choose the type of review they would like to leave, e.g., five stars, leave comments, and they're done. But for real power, the plugin Rich Snippets enables a great deal of customization that you can apply to the reviews section. For example, you can choose to display only reviews with higher ratings, only reviewers who have avatar images, change your business image, choose the number of characters to be displayed before the Read More button and much more. In this way, you can screen out negative reviews by choosing to display only four- and five-star reviews, reviewers with avatar images—hence real people—and allow 155–200 characters before the Read More button, priming your audience with more-positive perceptions. You can also add a Write a Review button, encouraging more people to write reviews and improving your overall rating score.

CHAPTER 4.
DATA INSIGHTS

4.1 Intro

L aunching a digital marketing campaign without having a strong strategy planned for monitoring and using the results of that monitoring to optimize the campaign is a mistake many marketers and business owners make. Most often, small business managers type in their keyword in Google, review whether their website is being ranked on the first page, and accept this result. Some are going further and, from time to time, having a quick peek within their Google Analytics account to assess the number of visits to the website, and maybe the channels that are driving the traffic. This will of course provide very little understanding of the actual performance of the website, let alone the behavior of its users, or whether the website could convert more users into leads. In fact, what you gain is an illusion of knowledge, which in turn gives you confidence that you are on top of your online campaign, and makes you less alert to signs that the campaign is not maximizing its potential. For example, I have shown in my previous book HACKING DIGITAL GROWTH 2025: Exploiting Human Biases, Tools of the Trade & The Disturbing Future of Digital Marketing for Growth that being ranked in the third organic position and lower will do very little for your website traffic, and even the first and second organic positions receive very little market share of visibility. Hence, being on the first page is a very skewed way of reviewing your organic search performance. To combat this illusion of knowledge it is important that you have the right data presented in the right format. Indeed, some business owners are moving to the other extreme, and dwell far too much on data. However, as the jam experiment suggested, too much data generally leads to decision-making paralysis.

In a nutshell, a comprehensive tracking system must be in place to measure results, split test, adjust, and improve, while also developing accountability regarding SEO agencies or consultants. By the way, you will sometimes be met with the following statement: But this is a brand awareness exercise; we do not care so much about leads at this moment. Huh!?

4.2 What kind of information should you track?

Keyword ranking performance

Monitoring the ranking performance of your keywords in search engines like Google or Bing is essential in measuring the performance of your SEO campaign. After all, one of the main digital key performance indicators (KPIs) you will be setting for yourself, in addition to increasing traffic to your website and leads, is improved keyword rankings. In the keyword research section we will be discussing notions such as keyword search volumes, keyword difficulty and user intent, competitor analysis, analysis of keywords' "ecosystem," search engine scraping of the suggest box or scraping of the top-ten-ranked websites. A keyword ranking analysis complements the data insights collected via Google Analytics and Heat Maps, and answers questions such as: what keywords is my website ranked for? What positions are these keywords ranking on? Have my rankings improved or deteriorated? What keywords have been gaining market share and which haven't? Why? How valuable are these keywords for my business, and where should I focus my efforts? Which landing pages are being ranked, and in what positions? Furthermore, when keyword ranking performance is used in conjunction with competitor analysis, you will also gain a better understanding of your performance vs. that of your competitors.

Paid Search reporting

Paid search advertising, whether pay per click, social media advertising, or content amplification, represents a great opportunity to companies looking to win by using paid-for strategies. While SEO provides longer-term benefits, paid search is instant, and most often necessary, in blending short-term commercial goals with longer-term and more-strategic SEO goals. Given the cost associated with paid search, leveraging the data insights gained from running your campaign is essential. You will assess the impact of paid search on your goals, and so more confidently explain its potential to other stakeholders. Overall, it is important that you understand the contribution of your paid advertising campaign to delivering metrics such as website traffic; engagement, e.g., likes, video views; numbers of impressions and click through rates; cost per action; cost per click; conversion rate and cost per conversion; goals and events completed; sales funnel completions; traffic sources; individual campaigns; group ads; actual ads and individual keywords performance; landing page conversion rates; heat maps and A/B split test results; to name just some of the items. And, of course, you will need to remember that more information is not necessarily better, as the jam experiment has shown.

Website Health reports

Technical improvement and maintenance of your website represents a core KPI that you need to set up as part of your campaign. After all, if search engines cannot find your website or content, any further SEO effort is pointless...neither Google nor Bing will rank content it cannot see. Many SEOs still consider technical SEO more of a means than an end, and you could argue that technical SEO is a given. Hence, of itself it cannot represent a KPI, the argument goes. In reality though, your website's technical health must be considered a KPI in its own right. A good website that performs well from a technical point of view is one factor that supports the sustainability of your long-term online marketing efforts. Too often, websites are optimized using various "grey hat" and "black hat" methods, ranked on the first page, just to go back into obscurity soon afterwards. SEO is a long, assiduous and continuous process of technical, on page and off page optimization; there really is no magic formula. Neglect in this work will affect your website, in both the short and the long term. You should review your overall website health report monthly, and you must track progress alongside technical improvements. A typical report is generated via one of the many tools available; your website is crawled and a report is generated. The report includes data such as indexation of your website by search engines, headings, meta descriptions and meta titles, image optimization, duplicate content issues, text-to-html analysis, 4xx and 5xx errors, and more. You can now compare your current report against previous reports and assess progress.

Backlink Audit reports

Backlinks to your website are still a top ranking factor within search engines. In fact, out of over 200 ranking SEO factors known nowadays, backlinks to your website consistently come out top. You should therefore consider this factor as a KPI in its own right, rather than just a means of delivering better rankings. As with general website health, your backlink profile health will be a good indicator of whether your website will continue to deliver great performance consistently. Your monthly report should include information on your backlink profile: how many backlinks to your site, how many toxic links, how many links have you gained or lost since the last report and why, disavowed (unwanted) and removed links, the linking websites, and the quality of the links pointing to your website, and so on.

Organic Social media and Brand monitoring

Monitoring of your social media and brand mentioning on the Web are other areas you will to need to pay attention to. Overall, you must assess the performance of your social campaign against your engagement KPIs. Some of the questions you may need to answer are: What is the size of your audience for each social media channel? What is the pattern of engagement of your audience on each channel? What is the top content-generating engagement, and what is the growth over a period of time? How many shares, likes, views or comments? How do your results compare with your competitors'? And, most important: Are you getting leads and achieving your KPI targets?

Competitor Performance analysis

Most of data analysis we have been discussing can also be applied to benchmarking your competition. What keywords are they ranked for within Google or Bing? How about the performance of their keywords over time, website health, social media channels, paid search campaigns, backlinks analysis? Most SEO tools work by crawling the URLs of the website you input to the tool. Hence, you can easily perform an analysis of a competitor's website by asking the tools to crawl the competitor's website URLs in the same way that you applied the tools to your own website.

4.3 Tracking results— tools of the trade

Often, you will need to install snippets of code on your website. This may sound complicated, but let us try to make it really easy.

Head, footer and post injections

When working on a website you will often need to add snippets of code for Google Analytics, Google AdSense, Google AdWords, Conversions, Heat Maps, Improvely, VigLink, Inspectlet, and other apps. One easy-to-use WordPress plugin to help you with this task is Head & Footer Code—user friendly, very intuitive, and no coding skills required. If you have a WordPress website, this option is a no brainer.

Google Tag Manager

You will work with websites built on a variety of CMS platforms. Some of these CMSs are flexible, and some will make it particularly difficult for non-technical people to add tracking code. However, developers are overprotective of their own interests with regard to providing access to these websites, acting as gatekeepers and charging clients ridiculous amounts of money for what is in effect a simple task.

Google Tag Manager is the most complete tool with the functionality to add code in any area of your website. For example, you can create events, conversions, or funnels, and add code to individual pages. The tool also includes a number of preset tags and templates integrating with most leading third party tools, such as Crazy Egg. Its functionality of previewing and testing the installation of the code on your page is also a very useful feature—overall, the easiest way to add code and events to your website. Moreover, Google Tag Manager is similar in look and feel to the Google Analytics admin area. Granted, it's a bit difficult to learn initially for the typical nontechnical person; however, once you get the hang of it, you will absolutely love it.

So, what tools do I use for tracking results?

Google Analytics

Google's analytics tool is the undisputed website data analytics leader. In fact, the large amount of analytics information provided by Google can seem overwhelming to many entrepreneurs. This generally happens due to the "cool' aspect and the depth of information; most inexperienced users of Google Analytics are easily drawn into analyzing more and more data, leading them to information paralysis. Hence, more information is not necessarily more valuable. Examples of information you can retrieve using Google Analytics are: the number of visitors to your website; number of sessions, number of page views, page views per session, average session duration, bounce rate, funnels, main landing pages metrics.

Heat maps and live visitor recording

While Google Analytics is highly valuable from a numerical analysis perspective, it does have its weaknesses. As mentioned, it can at times be overwhelming. It is also difficult, though not impossible, to understand the behavior of your website's visitors on the page: Where did they click? How far down the page did they scroll? What are the low and the high click areas of the page? When did they enter your website? This information is useful both as an analytics tool and in supporting informed conversion optimization decisions. This is where heat maps come in handy, providing information such as the areas of the page clicked on by your website's visitors, and how far down the pages they scrolled. Needless to say, heat maps meet the needs of both digital marketers and entrepreneurs by delivering comprehensive, visual and, most important, user-friendly complex analytics information. Heat maps complement Google Analytics, and I recommend that you use heat mapping on all your main landing pages. In addition, leading heat map tools incorporate another fantastic feature, which is live monitoring of the behavior of your website's visitors. Thus, you can actually watch the movement of a visitor's mouse on your page and the menu pages clicked on. You can monitor behavior vs. targeted funnels. Indeed, this is invaluable information for conversion optimization purposes. I have found Crazy Egg to be the only tool I ever need for both heat maps and live behavior analysis.

Improvely

As a marketer you are being measured, and you must deliver results. Improvely is a third-party tool enabling better tracking of the impact of paid search and social advertising campaigns. One example of Improvely becoming very useful is in monitoring the results of your AdWords Campaigns. You will, of course, use AdWords and Analytics reporting, and heat maps will measure the behavior of visitors on targeted landing pages. However, you will most often find AdWords and Google Analytics to be far from user friendly, and they lack the ability to enhance collaboration with your non-technical client. Your clients must, at all times, be able to judge the performance of their campaigns, and you can use Improvely both as an extra layer of reporting and for sharing details of projects with the client. The client can log in to his project dashboard and instantly have visibility of the performance of the campaign.

Improvely will really provide you with that extra level of granularity and insight, and enable better visualization of results on its very user-friendly dashboard. You can easily set up tracking links and A/B split tests of various ads, funnels and conversions. The tool is also popular with affiliate marketers.

To sum up, if you have been working hard to deliver results through your PPC campaign, if you aim to build trust and transparency with your client, gain further insights into your campaign's performance, and A/B split test the results and improve them, then Improvely is the tool for you.

SEMrush

SEMrush is one of the top tools used in the digital marketing agency environment. You would be forgiven for believing that you could not do without it.

What can SEMrush do?

One of the top features provided by SEMrush is the ability to track your organic keyword rankings for many key metrics: keywords indexed by Google; keywords Google ranks for and their positions; trends and changes in keywords' performance; comparison with competitors; backlinks analysis, and many more. Pay per click campaigns are also monitored, and a wealth of information on your campaign's performance is offered. You can apply the same process to your competitors, gain in-depth insights into their digital strategies, use data insights for decision making, build SWOT analyses of their businesses, and win.

How does this look in practice?

You have a competitor named Hotel X. Input their URL address in SEMrush and click Start. You may see that your competitor is being ranked for keywords such as Hotels in London, but also for Hotels in Wimbledon: you have just uncovered a potential niche, or keyword, you could focus your efforts on. You could ask questions such as: Why is Hotel X ranking for this keyword? Any potential clients or leads in the area? You may perform a keyword search and find that Hotels in Wimbledon has a very high search rate; a great opportunity to refine your strategy and gain some market share. In truth, there are just too many questions that could be asked, and too many insights that could be gained for them all to be listed here.

In addition to organic search, SEMrush will provide you with information on the performance of your or your competitors' paid search campaigns.

How does that look in practice?

You can see the keywords your competitors are bidding on, and the performance metrics associated with those keywords. You can gain an understanding of the markets they target, their budgets and digital strategies, uncover sales opportunities you may have missed, keywords you may want to target organically as well, get visibility of their ads, and more. And the depth of information can be as detailed as you want it to be.

Another great feature offered by SEMrush is its technical audit tool. SEMrush crawls your website, providing detailed information on required improvements and an overall Health Audit score. In addition to your own performance you can also monitor your competitors' website health, understand their challenges and opportunities and the budgets they allocate to digital.

Two of the great sections I love in SEMrush are the social media and brand monitoring sections. Both sections perform the same actions but in different channels.

The Social Media monitoring tool will enable you to monitor your and your competitors' social media mentions, your competitors' profiles, what they post, when they post, the engagement with their posts, and most other information you might need.

The Brand Monitoring tool extends the functionality of the social media tool to all Web mentions of your brand, based on the keywords you have specified. The value of these tools is enhanced by the fact that 99.99 percent of traditional sales and revenue teams make very little use of this functionality.

What answers should you expect from using SEMrush?

First, you will be able to paint a picture of your competitors' strategies: what social media channels they are leveraging, what strategies they are using on individual social media platforms, what PR campaigns are they promoting (i.e., new offers, new products), what publications they appear in and why. The list could go on.

SEMrush also provides a backlink analysis section. You can assume that 99 percent of the traditional sales, revenue, leadership and management teams continue to approach business development traditionally, with little progress in adapting to and leveraging the advancements of competitive digital benchmarking. A backlink analysis of your competitors will provide information such as who their suppliers are or where they are featured on the Web and why. And most important, a backlink analysis can generate leads, eliminating the traditional and inefficient practice of walking the car park of your competitors in order to get leads. Let's assume a client of your competitor recommends the competitor's hotel on their website; maybe a university is holding courses in the area and recommending your competitor. A backlink analysis will discover the link; you now follow the link and get to work to move that business from your competitor. Or assume that a new company moved to the area, and recommends your competitor's website to their international staff. Of course, you will now know about it, and initiate Operation Steal.

A more recent option offered by SEMrush is the Lead Generation Tool. I find this idea ingenious and commercially minded. As a digital marketer you are always trying to attract your website visitors into a sales funnel and what better way than to offer a free technical audit? SEMrush has made it very easy for digital marketers; simply copy and paste a piece of code and you can now provide free SEO audits and receive resultant emails. Now, every time a visitor inputs their website information, you receive the lead and they receive a partial report on their website. A win–win situation. SEMrush continues to evolve and has recently introduced these tools: Social media Poster, allowing automation of social media posts; Link Building Tool; PPC Keyword Tool; Ad Builder; and Content Analyzer.

Raven Tools

Raven Tools is another set of tools popular with digital marketing agencies. The tools provide some of the functionality provided by SEMrush, such as SEO Audits, and backlink research. However, you may find both the backlink research and SEO audits more comprehensive in Raven Tools than in SEMrush. Where Raven Tools complements SEMrush and where it excels is in its reporting function. There is no other tool I know of that can provide better, more tailored reporting than Raven Tools. As a marketer you are being measured by KPIs, and the truth is that having flexibility in tailoring your reports is paramount to how you will present your data.

What type of reports can you tailor in Raven?

You can either choose preset blocks of reports or choose individual metrics. The latter is the most powerful feature provided by Raven Tools. You can present your metrics as individual KPIs, pie charts, standard charts, tables, and more. The granularity provided in reporting your KPIs is unmatched by any similar tools. The tool also supports a large number of integrations, including Google Analytics, AdWords, AdSense, organic traffic, LinkedIn campaigns, Email campaigns, and other social media business. Many more integrations are available to support you in reaching your goals.

Social Mention

Social Mention is a great free tool enabling marketers to search social media mentions based on your choices. Of course, you can use the tool both to review mentions of your business and services, and to benchmark the content marketing strategy, results, and metrics of your competitors.

You can also discover current trends, and mentions of your targeted keyword. In fact, you will get access to most social mentions available online related to or including your targeted keyword. Simply input your keyword; Social Mention now searches for it in blogs, microblogs, bookmarks, images, videos and questions. You can actually choose which of these categories the tool should crawl, or let it to look into everything. Finally, a comprehensive report is provided, including information on how your keyword, competitor, or product fares from a social media point of view. The report includes data on metrics such as strength, sentiment, passion, reach, average seconds per mention, last mention, retweets, top keywords and mentions, top users, and top hashtags.

Overall, Social Mention provides a great variety of social media insights. You can put it to good use in developing your strategy and in staying up to date with news about your industry or about competitors. Of course, many tools provide this information; SEMrush is one of them; however, Social Mention is a great social monitoring tool and it's free. BrandMentions is an alternative tool that provides similar functionality to Social Mention.

Free Review Monitoring

Free Review Monitoring is another tool you can use to monitor your reviews in real time. You can opt to receive notifications when new reviews are posted online. It's free and offers great reporting, and great insights regarding your brand reputation online; you will really like it.

Talkwalker and Google Alerts

Another option allowing you to stay on top of what's happening in your industry, or simply to monitor new mentions of particular keywords and brands, or mentions of your competitors, is receiving notifications via tools such as Talkwalker and Google Alerts. These tools will notify you every time new content related to your specified keywords is posted online.

CHAPTER 5.
CONVERSION OPTIMIZATION

I include the section on conversion optimization in the analytics chapter as from personal experience I know that many marketers and business owners do not fully grasp the meaning of what conversions really are. As a result, the wrong data is being reviewed and wrong decisions are often made, or no decision is made at all. But what can constitute a conversion? First, conversions must be aligned to your business goals. For example, a hotel with a strong sales focus will consider booked rooms as conversions. By contrast, reaching the contact page may not be considered a conversion if it does not result in a sale. Ash, Ginty and Page provide a very good explanation of what a conversion is:

"A conversion happens when a visitor to your landing page takes a desired conversion action that has a measurable value to your business. The conversion action must be defined ahead of time, it must be trackable, and its business value must be clear." (Ash, Ginty and Page, p. 15) Depending on your business goals, a conversion could be a purchase, the completing of a contact form, a membership registration, moving the user through a sales funnel, and so forth. Hence, conversion optimization is the art of "converting" your website into what you consider to be a lead. The one book you will never need to read is Steve Kruger's Don't Make Me Think. Its idea is simple—make it as easy as possible for visitors to convert to a lead. A website that is not well designed will be associated with lack of professionalism. Similarly, a website with no visible contact details, or that in some other way seems untrustworthy, may deter people from interacting with your business. A page with too many calls to action will distract the user from your main goal. Colors have also been shown to impact conversion rates.

In converting your visitors into leads you will also need to deal with another matter, which is modifying your website and having the necessary skill set. For example, you may need to create new landing pages, shift various elements around the page, split-test variations of calls to action, colors, text, and other items. This takes both time and skill to carry out. In this context, achieving "Don't make me think" standards for your website is more difficult than you may have initially thought, particularly when you are an entrepreneur or marketer with little digital marketing or programing skills. Let us now discuss some of the tools that will improve your workflow and make it easier for you to implement a conversion optimization strategy without being a qualified programmer.

Landing pages

One mistake you will always be at risk of making is over-reliance on your Web designers. You may want to set up a PPC campaign and find yourself in need of high-converting, professional landing pages. You may need to build a sales funnel, or simply add a few pages to your website. Of course, as you are not a Web designer you will most often call the developer. My experience of developers, though, is that they are slow. It is hard to find good developers, and when you do find them they are expensive. And quite often they use page templates, make a couple of changes, and charge an astronomical price. As an alternative, one of the tools you can subscribe to is Unbounce. However, you may find it too expensive if you are a price-conscious marketer or entrepreneur. Another great tool is OptimizePress, which is cheaper and charges a one-off fee. If you find OptimizePress still too expensive, other, cheaper alternatives are available. ProfitMozo is one; ridiculously low-priced, it has a professional look and feel, a large variety of templates, and free hosting for the page if required. Two other available tools are ProfitBuilder and Landing Page Monkey.

Everfunnels

We have been discussing several pieces of software that can be used for building high-converting pages. However, if you're looking for an even quicker solution, you should consider the software Everfunnels. This software provides prebuilt and highly customizable sales funnels, in a quick and easy way. You can choose the sales template you prefer, turn on or off various sections of the sales page, e.g., the Testimonials, Ratings, Countdown, FAQ, and About the Instructor sections. You have areas where you can input your privacy policy, features, links, and much more. This software is ideal for building courses, sales pages, membership registration pages, and webinar funnels. Another really fantastic feature for non-content-writers is a variety of pre-written email funnels, including banners, images, text, and more. The funnels include pre-registration emails, post-registration welcome emails, induction emails, and post-registration email series. In addition, you can set up post-course survey links, resources, webinar bonuses, gift offers, questionnaires, and testimonials. Of course, you can adjust, personalize and add new assets to the email series. The point is, everything is done for you. And if you are a complete newbie to creating a webinar course, then you can use http://everlesson.com/saas1/, which is created by the same company as Everfunnels. With EverLesson you can build and customize highly-professional-looking webinar courses, with no programing experience required at all. This is really easy to set up, with lots of customization, and it integrates with the majority of complementary providers, such as PayPal, MailChimp, and Slack.

Simple Page Tester

You have used Crazy Egg to understand the behavior of your website visitors on page. Based on the data collected, you are now ready to perform changes to your pages and improve conversion rates. Surely, all the hard work you have put into creating and amplifying your content must deliver your goals, which most often are leads. Indeed, bringing traffic to your page is of little value if you cannot convert the traffic into customers.

Many marketers, armed with the powerful information provided by tools such as Crazy Egg will make changes to their pages, driven by a sharp entrepreneurial spirit. They will then wait a while, most often until a month has passed, review results, and make more changes as required. In these cases, conversion optimization decisions are based on the intuition of the entrepreneur, with no measurements or KPIs used to assess the impact of the changes. Improvements following the changes further complicate the problem, as success may be unjustly attributed to the changes, with little consideration given to the growth rate of competitors—the marketer may be growing but may also be losing market share.

If you are to maximize the results of your campaigns you must become an A/B split-test addict. You must be able to assess the impact of your various on-page conversion strategies, and continue to improve your pages regularly. There are two tools that you can use to conduct A/B split testing; which one depends on the complexity of data required and the CMS platform you are working with.

Simple Page Tester is an easy-to-use and quick-to-deploy A/B split test plugin for WordPress. The plugin is intuitive, and once installed it becomes available in the editor section of each page. Start by clicking the "Set up New Split Test" button and choose between the three options: Duplicate page, Create new page, or Add to existing page. Next, choose the delivery percentage for each page; this would normally be 50%, thus delivering each page to an equal number of visitors. Now, simply create conversions and you are all set. Finally, click the Choose Winner button when you decide to bring the test to an end. How do you know which page is the winner? The analytics module includes a quick overview with regard to the performance of each page: total views, unique views, total conversions, and conversion percentage.

When your website is built on a different platform than WordPress you will most likely have to choose a more premium offering such as Optimizely which is one of the best A/B split test tools available, though it does come at a price.

LivechatInc

You will feel excited about being ranked on page one in Google for your chosen keywords. However, always keep in mind that ranking keywords represents the means, not the goal. LivechatInc is a tool that impacts directly on the conversion rate of your page. When reaching your website, 90% of your visitors are in a research mindset, comparing the offers of various providers. In fact, very rarely will people reaching your website buy without any further research. Visitors reach your website, navigate around it, then visit other websites and may subsequently return to make a purchase. One opportunity to interrupt this research process and drive people into your funnel is live chat. Interacting with website visitors while they are on your page provides a great opportunity to present the benefits of your product, promote special offers, and build rapport. And, if you do your job well, by conducting the conversation you will, at the very least, have contact details, requirements, and an undertaking to follow up. Many other live chat tools are available of course: ClickDesk Live Support, Zendesk, Quick Chat, Olark, and Casengo are just some of them.

Hello Bar

If you are looking for a market leader in creating pop-ups, Hello Bar is one of the most popular tools available. The high degree of customization possible and its ease of use make it an ideal choice for most marketers who can afford the $149 yearly subscription for the PRO version. A free version is also available; hence, if you do not mind their logo on the bar this should be sufficient for most needs. Some of Hello Bar's great features are: it provides comprehensive analytics data; it is very user friendly; it enables A/B split variations of your pop-ups; it offers integration with a variety of email marketing providers; and it provides a contact capture list.

Convertful

If you are on a low budget, then Convertful is the pop-up tool for you. It does pretty much what Hello Bar does, and it provides some great templates. At $29 a year it's a far more economical choice than Hello Bar.

Acme Feedback

Imagine yourself browsing a blog with a large amount of interesting content. You have read couple of articles and you are preparing to exit the website. On leaving the website, a pop-up appears. A video is included in the pop-up window, and you are being thanked for visiting the website. In the same window you are also being asked to complete a survey. Several links to the best articles and a feedback box are also made available. As a marketer you have gotten so used to exit pop-ups that you may not really notice them anymore. Most often, you will simply click the close button and move on. This plugin may just be the one to alter this behavior. Almost on autopilot, you might play the video, check the most popular links, and even read another article.

Video Lead Box

Video Lead Box is another clever plugin; it provides the functionality of building pop-up sales funnels, in addition to your standard pop-ups. You might create a pop-up as step one, lead people to complete a second pop-up—step two—and so on. In fact, this feature may remove the need for a sequence of landing pages altogether. The plugin is highly customizable; you can add text, subscripts, and even videos. It also includes 30 pre-set templates. Finally, the plugin offers the option of locking the content, encouraging people to subscribe before they access your content. Thus, it offers great support in building your email list, as well.

Leadfeeder

A tool you must consider for lead-generation purposes is Leadfeeder. One of the biggest challenges you have as a webmaster is that of driving all the best traffic to your website, but you have little information on who has actually visited your site. You will, of course, try to capture as many leads as possible, using conversion optimization, remarketing, and other practices we have or will be discussing in this book. However, the conversion rate generated will be a relatively low proportion of the total number of visitors to your website. Leadfeeder can help you to significantly improve the number of leads by telling you exactly who has visited your site. Some of the information provided is: the name of the company, frequency of visits, market segment, company website and phone number, social media accounts, and LinkedIn profiles of the company and its employees. This is a powerful tool, particularly at local level, providing a large amount of hot leads. The only disadvantage I can see is the fact that the tool will not provide you with the name of the person or department generating the visit. This will prove a challenge when your website is being visited by an employee of a large or complex business, as you will find it difficult to track down the individual. By contrast, with many smaller or flatter businesses it will be far easier to reach the person in the business who is responsible for the area associated with your products. After all, in a small business everyone knows everyone else. Connect the tool to your Analytics account and that's it...you are ready to learn more about your website's visitors. This is a particularly powerful tool when running PPC campaigns, given the commercial intent of your audience.

Virtual offices

Most likely, when you start an online business you will at first need to keep your monthly fixed costs low. Renting an office is one cost you may want to avoid. However, not having an office, or even having it in the wrong location, may have a strong impact on the success of your business. People wrongly associate un-related factors, as we have seen in the section on psychology. For example, if you work from home, you must be bad at your job. However, if you operate from a central London office you must be successful; and people also tend to associate success with competence. As you are competent and produce results, surely you can charge higher prices as well? Thus, the contact details on your website have a strong impact on converting traffic to profitable leads. A way around the problem of not having a high-profile address is to set up an office in central London for a fraction of the cost you might expect to thus incur. I am talking, of course, about virtual offices. Simply type into Google "Virtual Office" and browse through the large variety of companies and packages available. You can pay as little as £90 a year for the right to use an address for your business, have your post forwarded to you regularly, and your telephone answered. You can even book a meeting room at the address, should you find yourself needing to do so. Various packages are available, catering to your requirements, and all without spending a single day in the office. You work from home, develop a strong brand image, and instill confidence that you are a legitimate business. Another option you might consider is shared offices, though this will generally turn out to be a more expensive alternative.

Virtual Numbers

Simply type "Virtual numbers" into Google Search and you will be presented with a variety of companies offering business phone numbers, with various price packages and various features. You are provided with a business phone number, enhancing your company image and inspiring confidence. The advantage of a virtual number is the high degree of customization. For example, you could set up individual virtual numbers for London, Norwich, and Brighton. You can set up 0800, 0333 or 01/02 numbers. You can also redirect the virtual number to your own number, have an answer menu or use voicemail. Many companies provide features such as text to speech, voice to email, email forwarding, analytics, extensions, and call recording. Finally, you may use virtual numbers to track the number of calls generated by your PPC campaigns via dedicated landing pages. I use a provider called Telecoms World; however, many other providers offer the same services.

Reverse Phone Check

For most businesses operating in a competitive environment, a missed call often mean a missed lead or a missed sale. When reaching your website searchers are most often looking for information, as opposed to taking some immediate action. As part of the search process, several companies will probably be considered. Now think about how many times you have called a company and no one has answered the phone. How many times have you subsequently dealt with their competitors? Have you called the first company again and got no reply, or have they called you back? Reverse Phone Check is relevant to both these types of situation. It provides you with information on the owner or owners of the phone number; their name, email, criminal records, address, social accounts, court records, and more. You can also use this tool for other purposes, such as researching your competitors or for sales research.

Geotargeting Pro

The idea behind Geotargeting Pro is simple yet very powerful. The tool provides the functionality of redirecting your website visitors to a page of your choice, depending on your visitor's location. Imagine that two visitors, one in the UK and one in France, reach your website and are looking for the prices of your services. They click on the Prices tab and this is where the magic happens. The tool/script tracks the location of the UK visitor and serves the page you have been developing for your UK visitors. When the visitor in France clicks on the same Prices tab, they will be served the page you designed for the French market.

How would it look in practice?

You can, for example, develop a pricing page written in French for your French market, and a German page for the German market. You may decide to set different services and prices for each market. You may even want to localize the content delivered to different regions within a country, e.g., Texas vs. New York. From another perspective, you might link Geotargeting Pro with Google AdWords. In AdWords you can then compile various ad groups to match the intentions of your visitors, their characteristics, locations, and so forth.

ClickKosh

One tool I really like is ClickKosh, a tool that is being marketed as "new technology that converts any simple image into attention grabbing shoppable hotspots in 52 seconds." But what does this mean? When I came across this tool, the first thing that came to mind was a room in virtual reality. You click or hoover on different items within the room and a dropdown provides you with information on the item, calls to action, the relevant email address or phone number, link to the website, price, and more. This is essentially how ClickKosh works: you upload your image, click on any element of your image, add a hotspot, chose the style of the icon from an unlimited library, and customize your call-to-action dropdown. In addition, an image editor is available that allows editing and customization of any image, whether your own or from several image partners. This really is a cool bit of software; large online retailers would benefit greatly from this idea, as well.

CHAPTER 6.
KEYWORD RESEARCH

6.1 Concepts

You have now audited your website from a technical point of view and fixed all errors. The time has come to work on your on-page SEO. Your first task in optimizing your website on page is to search for keywords that have the highest potential to meet both your micro and macro goals. Many consultants suggest keywords that are easy to rank but have low search volume or are connected with the wrong intent or location, or simply have the wrong meaning. No step is more important in optimizing your website than keyword research. Pick the wrong keywords and you may be ranked by search engines but get no leads or sales. Pick keywords with the wrong user intent, and the wrong people will find your website; again no leads or sales. Choose keywords too broad or not broad enough… no leads, no sales.

Your SEO consultant must accept responsibility for the impact of his actions, and for his contribution, or lack of it, in delivering on the KPIs they have agreed with you, the client. He or she must put the effort into researching, targeting and achieving ranking of relevant keywords. They must deliver on your KPIs, they must rank you for the most relevant keywords. Too often, SEOs explain away their failures by placing the fault on the client, who has been providing keyword suggestions. However, this is a delusion; experience must be right; and that often results in overconfidence and making decisions partly or wholly based on gut instinct. Cognitive dissonance also plays its part, driving professionals to commit to the idea that failure of a campaign cannot be their fault. As an SEO professional you may find yourself in a similar situation. Confirmation biases kick in, you start telling yourself that it was the client who asked to be ranked for the wrong keywords, or that in your experience the choice of keywords was right ninety percent of the time, hence you could not have predicted it would not work. You may continue your line of thinking and polarize you views. In fact, you have done your job and ranked the keywords provided by the client on the first page in Google; the problem must be the lack of demand for the services. Of course, you will most often not consider facts that contradict your point of view. Maybe you should have carried out more research and ranked keywords with a better volume, more attuned with user intent, and with more commercial potential. Maybe you should have challenged and educated the client on their suggested keywords strategy, and so on. Keyword research is important and a variety of tools, competitor research techniques, semantic analysis, and search engine scraping practices are available to help you discover the best possible keywords for your client.

What is a Keyword?

A keyword is a word you intend to rank on the first page in Google when people search for your service. Suppose you offer German translation services and would like to appear on the first page in Google when people type, "German translation services." "German translation services" would be your keyword. Of course, simply because you have chosen a keyword, and people are searching for it, it does not mean that your website will be automatically ranked on the first page in Google. In reality, you compete against thousands of other websites that will also want to appear on the first page in Google when people type "German translation services." A comprehensive keyword research must be carried out to identify the best keywords matching your goals, having the right search volumes, likelihood to rank, and the right user intent.

What is Keyword Research and why do you conduct it?

You decide that you would like to rank for a keyword phrase, say, "German translation services." You employ an SEO consultant, and you brief them on this particular keyword. At this point, your SEO consultant should use your keyword or keywords as a basis for performing comprehensive keyword research. This will allow them to discover the most profitable keywords for your website, and for your business goals. For example, he or she may carry out keyword research and discover that the term "German translation services" has a very low search volume with only 50 people using this query each month. The keyword may also have a high-difficulty rank score due to competition from other websites that are also trying to rank for it. However, your consultant may notice that keywords such as "German Translator," "German Interpreter," and "German translations to English" have higher search volumes and lower competition. You may now re-focus your efforts on these other keywords, while also optimizing on-page for the low-search-volume keyword. The main point is that you will focus your limited resources on high-potential keywords, while not turning your back on the less-promising keyword. You would be surprised how often websites need re-optimizing because SEO agencies or inexperienced consultants simply asked the client what keywords they wanted to rank for. There is no analysis, no understanding of keyword potential, no research into the competition or into search volume and keyword intent, and no consideration paid to the theme of the page. It seems needless to point out that these websites may end up being ranked for the wrong keyword, and deliver no leads, no enquiries, no business.

How do you conduct keyword research?

A typical keyword analysis starts with an analysis of your website's keyword density and the keywords your website is ranking for and already indexed for. This provides an initial idea about the services you sell via your website. You continue with a search using Google's Keyword Planner tool, which will reveal data insights on your targeted keywords, e.g., search volume and the competition. Google also provides suggestions and information regarding other keywords that are being searched for online and which may be relevant to your keywords. At this point, it is not unusual to discover keyword opportunities you have not previously considered. At times, you may also conclude that the keywords you've had in mind may not be as profitable as you had believed. The point to remember is that when trying to rank a page for a keyword you must consider its "ecosystem": synonyms, similar words, and meanings. You should always incorporate these keywords in the copy of your page as well. Why? Because Google is getting smarter. In practice, Google associates the concept of "German Translator" with the concepts "German Interpreter" and "German translation services." Hence, if I type "German Translation services" or "German Interpreter" in the search bar, Google assumes that, by association, a German interpreter is likely to be a translator as well. Thus, optimizing your page for both your main and associated keywords enhances the theme of your page. A stronger theme informs and encourages search engines to give your website preference over other websites for the keyword "German translator." Finally, keyword stuffing is a "no go" for search engines. Include "German translator" too many times on your page and Google will think you are trying to deceive its algorithms. And the reward may be lower rankings.

So what are the main tasks you will undertake in keyword research in addition to using Google's Keyword Planner? Well, you can start with an analysis of your top digital and your traditional competitors' organic and paid search results. You can continue by scraping the autosuggestion boxes of top search engines like Google and Bing. Thus, you will gain a very good understanding of the keywords that are being bid on. You may even want to go as far as performing keyword density analysis on relevant top-performing pages ranked by Google. And why not? You may scrape the top 10 ranked websites to obtain their relevant keywords and density. In the end, the aim of the game is aligning your keyword strategy, overall business strategy, and goals by optimizing your website for the right keywords, which will drive the right traffic with the right intent. After all, why would you put any effort or budget into ranking for keywords with no search volumes or driving the wrong customer behavior?

What are the best tools for Keyword Research?

There are many great keyword research tools on the market. Some of the most popular are Google's Keyword Planner tool, Soovle, Ubersuggest, KWFinder, SEMrush Keyword Research, Raven's Keyword Ranking tool, and Rank Tracker from SEO PowerSuite.

What is a Keyword difficulty score?

The keyword difficulty score indicates the amount of competition for a particular keyword. The more websites that are trying to rank for a keyword the more difficult it will be for you to rank your website on the first page in Google. And, when combined with a search volume analysis, keyword difficulty scores should provide a good indication of whether the keyword is worth pursuing.

I rank on the first page in Google for my keyword but I get no leads. Why?

There are many reasons why you may not get leads, even when your website is being ranked on the first page in Google. The reasons include technical errors, such as contact form errors. For example, visitors fill in your contact form, but the form is broken; hence, you receive no leads. Other problems can be related to conversion optimization. People may reach your website, but there are no obvious calls to action driving them through a sales funnel, e.g., no contact forms, no contact info, such as address, telephone number, email address; there may be too much text or not enough text. Wrong meta descriptions and meta titles can also impact conversion optimization. As an example, meta descriptions optimized for keywords rather than for click-through rates may discourage people from clicking on your website in the search results. The potential of the keywords recommended by your SEO agency could be yet another reason for low traffic; for example, the keyword that you naively suggested had no search volume in the first place, but they used it. Or people reaching your website may have a different intent than the user intent you are looking for. A simpler case could be that people are searching for an "online German translator." In this case, visitors are searching for a service like Google Translate, rather than for a "German translator," which you may be offering.

Should I optimize for the singular or plural form of my keywords?

Up to a point you should treat the singular and plural forms as two different keywords. Check the search volumes of both forms and optimize for both. If you have to choose to optimize one or the other, you should probably go for the plural form, though a word of caution is appropriate: Google is smart and will likely associate the singular with the plural form; hence, do not over-optimize either. In the end, it depends on your type of business: if you are an individual hotel it may pay to rank for the singular form, let's say "Hotel in London." By contrast, trying to rank for the plural form would put you in direct competition with larger online travel agencies who are more relevant to the query, "Hotels in London." Finally, make sure the text flows naturally, and optimize for both forms in a balanced way, avoiding over-optimization.

6.2 Keyword research – tools of the trade

As we've discussed, choosing the right keywords to deliver on your KPIs is the top priority in optimizing your website. You would be surprised to learn how often websites are ranked on the first page in Google but get no business. Keywords may be too broad, have the wrong user intent, or have very little search volume. A common problem is that inexperienced SEOs perform keyword research without paying attention to the local situation, negative keywords, keyword matches, and so forth. Specifically, a keyword can appear to have a high search volume internationally, but a closer inspection shows that it has very few UK searches. Or, the search queries may be in the wrong context. To sum up, get your keyword research wrong and all your hard work is in vain. Many tools are available to help you perform good keyword research. The obvious one is **Google's own Keyword Planner** tool. This tool used to be made available to everyone, but unfortunately this is not the case anymore; Google only makes it available via its Google AdWords Platform. That means that you will need to have an active AdWords account. Google's Keyword Planner provides a wealth of information and metrics on your targeted keywords, related keywords, monthly search volumes, and competition for the keyword. You can get really granular on user intent and location by adding negative keywords, locations or keyword matches.

Should you not have access to Google's Keyword Planner tool, then you will most often use third party keyword research tools. One tool providing similar functionality to Google's Keyword Planner is **SEMrush's Keyword Research**. Do keep in mind, though, that as with all third-party tools you will never capture quite the same results as you would with Google's own tools. That being said, SEMrush definitely offers some of the best SEO tools available at the moment. SEMrush is a market-leading SEO tool provider and offers some very powerful features. When carrying out keyword research, several features are available to help you make the best possible choices. The first feature is the organic search traffic overview. In this feature SEMrush provides you with the keywords your website is ranked for organically, their positions within Google, volume search, and more. You can now understand the impact of your digital marketing efforts by monitoring changes over time in your keyword rankings. You will also quickly understand whether your target keywords are relevant to your overall goals. For example, you may rank on the first page in Google for a keyword with a search volume of 20 searches per month. This may be sufficient for some niche markets; however, in general the volume will be too low for most businesses. Furthermore, you may run an analysis of your competitors' websites and businesses. Such analysis uncovers the keywords your competitors are being ranked for, the search volume of these keywords, the performance of your competitors' rankings over time and the general theme of their websites. You will often discover keywords you did not consider, and at times go as far as reconsidering your entire strategy. The second feature you will use for keyword research is the paid search section in SEMrush. With this feature you can run an analysis of you competitors, learn about their paid search strategy, budgets, keywords bid on, and search volumes. You can even see the ads they have running. The tool is simply to use; all you need to do is input the URL of a competitor's website and click Start. Another great feature provided by the tool is the keyword gap analysis. You can input the URLs of your top five competitors; the tool now scrapes these websites for the keywords they are indexed for, compares the sites against your website and recommends keywords you should be focusing on—a powerful option. In practice, you can start your keyword research with Keyword Chief or SEMrush's Keyword Gap analysis tool, understand the keywords a competitor is being indexed or ranked for, and the theme of their website. You can continue your keyword research in SEMrush by benchmarking the keywords your competitor is paying for via paid search campaigns. The Google Keyword Planner tool provides you with further data on volumes and competition. You can continue by cross-checking with Soovle, Keyword Tool and Ubersuggest against Keyword Chief, SEMrush and Google's Keyword Planner tool. Finally, should any new keywords be discovered via Soovle, Keyword.io or Ubersuggest. You can run new keywords via the Google Keyword Planner tool and repeat the process.

Yet another tool providing similar functionality to Google's Keyword Planner is **KWFinder**. You will often find some hidden keyword gems when running this tool. Both SEMrush and KWFinder provide information on the average number of searches for a keyword, average cost per click, keyword difficulty scores, and many other metrics. Other tools provide similar functionality, they include SEO PowerSuite's or Moz's keyword discovery tools. These tools are simple to use; simply input your keyword and click Start.

Another way of enhancing your keyword research is scraping the suggestion or autocomplete search bars of popular search resources, such as Google, Amazon, Yahoo, Bing, Wikipedia, Answers.com and YouTube. Let's briefly reconstitute your typical search experience. You start typing a query into the search bar and various autosuggest options are presented to you in a drop-down format. What you have been experiencing is the search engine attempting to predict and improve your search experience by recommending the most relevant results. Overall, scraping autosuggestion search boxes complements the historical trends approach employed by tools such as Google's Keyword Planner, SEMrush's Keyword Research, and KWFinder. Both methods should be used together. As an example, you can conduct research with Google's Keyword Planner, scrape auto-suggestion boxes, then cross-check the terms found through the two methods. You can now run new terms through the first set of tools to discover their potential, meanings, contexts, and synonyms.

One great keyword scraping tool is **Soovle**, which impresses through its simplicity, visual impact, and support for all main search engines. Simply start typing and the tool instantly autocompletes search suggestions from the top seven search engines, all on the same screen.

How does it work?

Type a character, and the tool starts the autocomplete process; type another character, and Soovle refines the results; type another, and it further refines results; and so forth. You can download results into a CSV file, upload the file to KWFinder or SEMrush, click Enter, and collect the relevant information on the potential of those keywords.

A similar tool is **Ubersuggest**, one of the most popular free keyword research tools. Simply type in your keyword, click Enter, and a list of keywords is generated. Furthermore, you can query Google Trends for every keyword from within the tool's dashboard. And if you are a more visual person, a cloud tab is available to highlight keywords with high potential. You can copy or download keywords as a list and upload the list to your favorite keyword research tool, such as SEMrush's tool or KWFinder.

The third tool I will introduce you to is **Keywordtool.io.** This tool is almost identical to Soovle; however, the information is presented in a different format. Both tools share the capability of scraping Google, Amazon, Bing and YouTube. Soovle supports Wikipedia and Answers.com, while Keyword Tool supports eBay and App Store. That being said, Keyword Tool is overall a more complete tool, as it also provides keyword search volume information, CPC, and AdWords Competition metrics, but this is not a free tool.

Keyword Chief

I often come across websites that lack an on-page optimization strategy, particularly at a keyword targeting level. I also often find that pages are optimized for one or two keywords, with little thought put into the theme of the page. It is not uncommon to find over-optimized pages, keywords being repeated obsessively on page, and no strategy to target synonyms or semantically related terms for the purpose of enhancing the theme of the page. Moreover, most SEOs optimize pages using a rule-of-thumb guideline provided by popular SEO plugins like Yoast SEO. However, experts agree that there are no clear-cut rules regarding a universal keyword density requirement, or indeed if keyword density still represents an SEO factor in the first place (it does, by the way).

We have discussed various tools that can be used to perform keyword research. The tools provide information on volume potential and the most popular terms. By contrast, these tools provide little information about specific keyword density in various niches. This is where a tool like Keyword Chief comes in. This tool scrapes the first 10 Google search results for your targeted keyword, discovers the most-used keywords on those 10 websites, and calculates the actual keyword density of these same top-performing sites. Hence, if you think about it, you are leveraging Google to assess the content it values, what the theme of the page should be, the keywords you should use, and the actual density you should apply to each of those keywords. Keyword Chief also provides a text analysis feature; simply input the text of your or competitor's page and press Start. The text is now analyzed and a result is returned showing the keywords and their density, based on the top 10 ranked websites. You are even told the number of times you should use the word on a page. It takes the guessing out of the equation, identifying keywords or themes you had not considered; and it leverages the knowledge and efforts of the competition. Ultimately, the tool provides the opportunity to optimize your website, based on what Google actually ranks, rather than on universal recommendations or advice that may or may not work in different environments. Finally, you can also use the tool to identify sales opportunities and provide value to your clients, by keeping them up to date on competitors' moves, i.e., product launches, new campaigns, and so on.

Google Trends

You will often use Google Trends to better understand changes in demand for a category of products, and the impact of the changes on traffic to your website. Is your traffic lower year on year? Are you looking to understand and assess seasonal trends in your area of business, or the performance of a product or a keyword over time? Looking to track trends over the years, or changes in demand between products? Maybe you are looking to understand the demand for a product in a specific context, e.g., business, education? Google Trends has it covered. Simply input your keywords, choose the category, period, comparison term, and the region, and click Enter.

CHAPTER 7.
CONTENT RESEARCH

Content creation is an essential part of delivering your SEO and your overall growth-hacking goals. It is no secret that search engines value quality content that delivers the best answers to users' queries. In a highly simplified way, the more visitors engage with and value your content, the more authority search engines allocate to it. Highly relevant and engaging content, created and tailored with your targeted audience in mind, will also naturally attract links. And, as backlinks are still a top SEO ranking factor, your content strategy is crucial for the success of your SEO campaign. Content writers must be involved in your project from the very beginning. They must gain a good understanding of your brand or company identity, its culture and values, its "voice", its strategies, and its short-term and long-term goals. Content writers must also fully understand your digital marketing strategy, including the keywords that are being targeted, your social media plan, and your content amplification and link building strategies. Unfortunately, far too often content writers are being asked to contribute, but have little involvement in the overall growth-hacking conversation. And too often irrelevant content is being produced, ending up on a webpage or blog that makes little or no contribution to delivering the campaign's goals.

Any growth-hacking project must start by providing all parties involved with a clear understanding of the brand's values and identity, its manifestations, history, long-term and short-term goals, and the strategies being used to deliver those goals. Equipped with this knowledge, the content writer carries out a comprehensive analysis of the current issues in the relative field and an analysis of the competitors, identifies the most-shared and most-relevant content on the web, semantically analyzes that content, and conducts a comprehensive keyword analysis. This ensures that your article is relevant, has potential to go viral, taps into a topic of interest, and is written with an SEO theme in mind.

Finally, every story, article, or blog must go through a thorough internal review process. You will need to answer four questions:

- Is the content relevant to your brand identity?

- Is the content original, current and interesting?

- Would you share it?

- Would you link to it?

If you answer Yes to all four questions, you are on the right track; otherwise you need to refine your article.

The lack of involvement of content writers on the one hand, and the lack of a strategic process in producing the content on the other, has some unfortunate consequences. We have already discussed irrelevant content that results in no action toward meeting your goals. In fact, the former point impacts the effectiveness of your campaign in two ways. One obvious consequence is that you are wasting budget on ineffective content; the second consequence is the opportunity cost you are suffering. What if your budget had been spent on effective content marketing; what would this have meant for your business?

Content writers themselves cannot be absolved from blame when creating irrelevant content, either. Too often content writers' ideas are brought forward with little or no research into their potential. Similarly, too often, content writers pick up ideas from the client and run with them. And when the content is not delivering the results expected, they explain it away...it was not their idea, it was the client's. To sum up, content writers must take responsibility for the impact of their content and its contribution to the overall delivery on the KPIs agreed with the client. They must put the effort in to researching relevant, sharable or current industry issues. They must benchmark and learn from successful content and practices in the industry. They must deliver the goals of their campaigns. We discussed in the keyword research section the foreseeable result of SEO professionals ranking irrelevant keywords and failing to deliver the goals set for their campaigns. We have seen how SEOs explain away their failures by placing the fault on clients who provided the keyword ideas. We have also seen how the delusion that experience must be right leads SEOs to overconfidence and to making decisions partly or fully based on gut instinct. Cognitive dissonance has driven these professionals to commit to the idea that failure of a campaign is not their fault, and polarizes their views, in order to reduce the stress created by this dissonance. Confirmation biases kick in, with SEOs only considering information that matches their point of view: the client asked to be ranked for these keywords; the SEO's experience dictated their choice of keywords; they could not have predicted that it would not work. The SEO may continue their line of thinking and polarize their views. In fact, they have done their job and ranked the keywords on the first page in Google; the problem must be that there is no demand for the services. Of course, the SEOs will not consider aspects of the situation that may disconfirm their point of view. Maybe they should have carried out more research and ranked keywords with better volume, user intent, and commercial potential. Maybe they should have challenged and educated their client in terms of their proposed keyword strategy, and so on.

Similarly, content writers cannot explain away their failure in reaching targets. They must take control and accept accountability for their content, the number of people it reached, the number of links it received, the number of shares or likes, the number of people who filled in a form after reading the article, the impact on SEO ranking, and any other relevant issues. Content writers must embrace the mindset that their content is not an end to their task, but rather a means of delivering goals and scoring high on KPIs.

Let's turn our attention to some of the tools that we can use to ensure that the content for our marketing campaigns is effective and delivers the best possible results.

I mentioned content writers who pick up the theme of an article with very little research put into understanding the most relevant and current issues in the industry in question, not reviewing the most popular articles, or simply missing out on other great content ideas. There are several tools that can support content writers in overcoming these issues. So let's get started!

Answer the Public

The truth is that Google is obsessed by user experience. Its algorithms are focused entirely on delivering the best possible answers to its users' queries. Hence, it pays to produce your content with that end result in mind, rather than starting with ideas about what you want to write. What questions are users asking? What answers do they need, and in what form? Answer the Public is a fantastic tool that will provide you with answers to these questions. You can think of Answer the Public as your very own, free, brainstorming team. Simply input your keyword and the tool will retrieve a massive amount of questions being asked on the Internet related to your keyword. You will find quite a few ideas, and get excited about going back to work answering some of those questions in your copy.

ContentGems

ContentGems is another tool you can use to brainstorm great content ideas. It offers both a free and a paid-for version. The idea behind the tool is identifying and curating the most relevant, popular, and current pieces of content based on your targeted keywords. This acts as a brainstorming exercise, allowing you to think of new ideas and titles; learn what works and in what form. ContentGems is by no means the only tool providing this functionality. However, what really distinguishes the tool is the level of granularity you can add to your search. For example, you may perform searches by specifying a keyword and adding negative keywords, excluding words that are not relevant.

BuzzSumo

BuzzSumo is one of the most popular outreach tools. It provides a free—though quite restrictive—version, which you can use it to get a feel for what the tool does.

So what does the tool do?

BuzzSumo allows you to search for and find the most-shared content on the Internet, based on platforms such as Facebook, LinkedIn, Twitter, Pinterest, and Google+ shares. You can use the tool to brainstorm new content ideas, titles, and strategies. You can also assess the best content strategies for each platform. For example, you may be interested in identifying the most-shared content on LinkedIn, based on your specified keywords, and likewise for other platforms. This is valuable information, as various types of content will perform better on some platforms than on others, based on factors such as user base characteristics.

Fresh Title

Prior to promoting your content, you must optimize the title of your posts for click-through rate. Having a great piece of content is not sufficient if you are missing out on the opportunity to maximize the click-through or opening rate of the article. Furthermore, from an SEO perspective, click-through rates have their role to play in Google's perception of your article, page, or website as being relevant to the searcher's query, hence contributing to higher or lower rankings. You should never launch an article without running it through a tool such as Fresh Title, Headlinr, Portent's Content Idea Generator, or Blog Ideas Generator by Hub Spot. You can compile two or three headlines, A/B split them, pick the winner, and repeat.

So what does Fresh Title do?

Fresh Title provides access to a massive database of blogs on proven titles, and to a large database of email headlines. Another feature is a thesaurus, which can help with suggestions and synonyms related to the words within the titles. For example, you may want to rejuvenate your email marketing campaign by generating new title ideas for existing blog posts and email headers, A/B split test them, refine them, and start again.

Headlinr

To re-emphasize: regardless of how good your content is, how brilliant your amplification and conversion optimization strategies, it will all amount to nothing if people do not click on your post. Headlinr includes a large database of the best-converting titles ever written, and you will appreciate its delivery as a Chrome extension. If you are in the middle of writing your blog post, article, or page, simply click the extension, input your keyword, and get instant access to great, inspiring, and proven titles that are sure to get your creative juices flowing.

Portent's & HubSpot's Blog Ideas Generator

We have discussed the paid-for browser extensions and tools that you can use to generate great topic ideas and titles. Two free tools are also available to aid your search for great topics and titles: Portent's Content Idea Generator and HubSpot's Blog Ideas Generator. Simply input your keyword or keywords and generate quality title ideas for your posts.

CoSchedule's Headline Analyzer

You have used those tools to find great blog ideas and titles; what next? Most marketers leverage the functionality of these tools but often fail to complete the final step in the process—preparation for launch. This final step makes all the difference between a good title and an exceptional title. Input your title in CoSchedule's Headline Analyzer, click Analyze Now and the tool will provide a detailed analysis report on your title, starting with an overall Headline score. A wealth of information is provided, including data on common, uncommon, emotional, and power factors. Feedback is also provided regarding the length of the title, the number of words, sentiment analysis, and snippet previews.

CHAPTER 8.
BRINGING YOUR IDEAS TO LIFE

You have been researching for and have found great topics and titles for your content. It is now time to bring your ideas to life. This is one task that entrepreneurs, business owners, and marketers often feel anxious about. You see all these great articles, well written, with plenty of special effects to capture attention: images, inspiring videos, presentations, GIFS, infographics, and so on. How will you ever create content of similar quality? You may start asking for quotes from digital marketing agencies and consultants, but these services are expensive. You may settle for lower quality content, but then again, this content will never help you deliver on your ambitious KPIs.

Video content, presentations, characters and animation, scenes, and more.

You would be amazed at how little many multimillion-dollar businesses actually say about their business, or engage visitors on their website pages. Too often, ignorance creates large gaps between the content expectations of their websites' users, and the actual input of the companies to their websites. Many times a website includes a couple of paragraphs on its pages, describing the company, rather than answering the questions of the visitor. But what do visitors want? Visitors generally want relevant content, FAQ, infographics, PDFs, videos—anything that keeps them engaged and answers their queries.

On the other hand, smaller businesses point to the challenge of their low budgets as one factor to explain away the inadequate quality of their website content. Indeed, producing a video, infographic, or a professional presentation can be expensive. For example, a lower-cost alternative to a video is an animated presentation, and even that cost up to $70 for a one- to three-minute clip. And most presentations on offer online are templates; you input the text, which is then added to the template presentation. In fact, providers of these services generally use a library of hundreds of customizable templates. The library has been purchased for a ridiculously low price, and they have built a business model around it, charging prices that are outrageous when compared with their one-time investment.

We will now talk about various low cost tools and video libraries that are available. These libraries will enable you to improve the content of your website, bring many of the assets we have spoken about to your fingertips, and save you lots of money in the process. Below you will find a collection of professional videos, animated characters, scenes, royalty-free blockbuster type music, and more. Really simple to use, intuitive, and no programing skills required.

http://www.videomakerfx.com/specialpt/

http://viddyoze.com/backdoor/

http://easysketchpro.com/

http://viddyoze.com/club/

http://www.videopal.io/special2/

http://www.videomakerfx.com/specialvpfx/

http://vidstory.co/mega-discount-member-only/

http://digiproductmusic.com/massif/

http://digiproductsound.com/v1/

http://videoowide.com/vol3/jv/

Royalty free images

Another challenge you may have when creating content is finding good royalty free images. Some popular online sources are Shutterstock, Google Images, Getstencil, and Canva.

Getstencil & Canva

There are two tools you can use to help you create and edit blog posts fast; work with images; edit images; retrieve free and paid-for images; add overlay text; find vectors; create logos, icons, and backgrounds; and more. You may feel some anxiety in using complex tools like Adobe Photoshop. Rest assured that Stencil or Canva will provide you with the capability of performing advanced editing tasks via easy-to-navigate, intuitive dashboards, with no prior editing experience needed. Moreover, Stencil also provides 10 free images a month; simply input your keyword and choose an image; add your text, the size, and the format, all on one screen; save, and download your image.

Easel.ly and Piktochart

We have already reviewed various tools, both free and low cost, that enable you to create professional videos, sketches, presentations, images, audio, sound effects, and more.

One particular type of content that is often acknowledged as a top strategy for driving engagement and link-building is the infographic. In addition to their positive impact, engagement, and time-on-site metrics, great infographics attract links to your website when embedded or shared on other websites. Of course, great infographics are shared a lot, hence your content reaches more people and audiences, as well. Tools like Easel.ly, Piktochart and Canva make it extremely easy for you to build your own great infographics. Create an account, choose a template from the large selection available, edit the text, add your great content, and your very own infographic is ready for use. And, if you feel the template does not quite do it for you, you can customize it by adding your own images.

Camtasia

Camtasia is a popular video creation and editing tool that you can use for most video-related tasks you might need to perform.

What does Camtasia actually do?

Camtasia's main feature is that it will record your own screen and let you edit the result. You can use Camtasia to record your training sessions, webinars, or one-to-one Skype calls. Furthermore, Camtasia provides an enviable degree of customization of video assets. The tool provides the functionalities to edit, to cut, and to add video and sound. You can add backgrounds, arrows, special effects, transitions, and so forth. You can edit videos created with Camtasia or import and edit your own videos.

Snagit

Snagit is a tool developed by the creators of Camtasia. Snagit provides similar functionality to Camtasia's, but focused on capturing your screen image, and performing in-depth editing tasks quickly and easily. Compared with the complexity of Adobe Photoshop, Snagit's simplicity is an obvious advantage. You can also upload and customize images from your computer, record your screen, upload videos, and perform simple video editing tasks.

Lumen5

Lumen5 is a tool offered by the creators of Sniply that I have been using regularly since its introduction. It provides an easy way of creating a very professional video from your blog post or from any images, media, or text you provide. Input the URL of your page or blog post, add your story text and an image for each of the panels/steps to be displayed in your video, then choose your audio background, preview, and generate your video. You can add images from a very large royalty free image library or upload your own image, and there is a large library of background sound available as well. A really-easy-to-use, yet very powerful, tool.

WP-GraphicWhiz

You now have various alternative sources when searching for royalty free and paid-for images and editing tools, with Getstencil in particular allowing you to download up to 10 free images a month. If your website is being built on a WordPress platform, one plugin you could use to speed up the work is WP-GraphicWhiz.

How does it work? Imagine writing a blog post, and finding yourself in need of images. Simply input a keyword, right there within your dashboard, choose an image, and that's it.

Other similar plugins and sources of royalty free images you may decide to look at:

- http://alluneed2succeed.net/wpimageplus/ , another WordPress plugin similar to WP-GraphicWhiz

- http://digiproductimages.com/high-impact/ Over 3,000 high-quality images, all royalty free for a small onetime fee.

TTS Sketch Maker

TTS Sketch Maker is another great tool; it enables you to build whiteboard videos like a pro, while using text-to-speech technology as an overlay voice. It includes a large variety of inbuilt templates and is very cost effective. It's very simple to use for any non-technical person, and text-to-speech voices sound natural in most cases. You can add your own images, animations, and music. You can put the tool to work when creating training videos, reviews, sales pitches, SEO matter, and lots of niche-related videos—you name it.

GifBuddy—Amazing GIFS

GIFs are one type of content that have the potential to greatly increase your social media engagement. One example of a large and affordable collection of GIFs is GifBuddy. GifBuddy makes it superbly easy for you to find popular GIFs based on a specified keyword, customize them, and deploy them to your Facebook, Twitter or WordPress project. Think of GifBuddy as the Shutterstock of animated GIFs, but significantly upgraded, with the power of full customization and syndication. It's a really great asset, proven to increase conversions on social media and on personal websites.

Meme generator

Another type of content that attracts social media engagement is memes. Meme Generator, from imgflip.com, is one cool free little tool; you can easily create and customize meme with it, and there's no technical skill required.

Intro-video creation

Many psychology studies have investigated the impact of first impressions in human behavior. We have already discussed the concept of confirmation bias and its manifestations. Confirmation bias also applies to your content, whether your videos, sales pages or the look and feel of your website. Moreover, as we saw in the psychology section, making people "feel" your content will help to increase your conversions. One example of a tool that can help you build great first impressions is Intro-video creation, an inexpensive tool that makes adding professional, inspiring and customizable intro-effect to your videos as simple as it can be.

Viral Content Creator

I had always thought interactive content to be beyond the competence of SEOs, until I found this really cool tool. First things first...what do I mean by interactive content? Well, some examples of interactive content are quizzes, games, and trivia questionnaires. Of course, as I have learned during my career, there are very few skills that cannot be commoditized nowadays, and the WordPress Viral Content Creator plugin is yet further proof to that. The tool can create a large variety of quizzes, beyond the traditional text-based quizzes you might be used to. Imagine you are a lifestyle magazine looking to launch a contest. The contest is surveying your audience to determine their choice of Man of the Year. You begin with a headline making a simple request, such as "Choose six celebrities that should be shortlisted for our Man of the Year award." Below the headline the reader is presented with 20 images. They pick six people. They are now asked to choose from the six celebrities left in the competition those that best match the award title. They can pick four. Next, the four remaining celebrities are served in two pairs, and another question will determine the two finalists. Of course, this is just a simple example to point out the granular level of customization you can apply in your quiz.

Video Remix

One benefit of working with clients is exposure to a large variety of content and the crazy prices consultants often quote and charge for various types of content assets. Take 360-degree videos. As a business owner you might not consider trying to save yourself a lot of money by doing it yourself. It is far too complicated, you may think. Or the thought, "I am not a professional video editor," comes to mind. However, you might be pleasantly surprised to learn that there are tools out there that will enable you to create such a video. With VideoRemix, for example, you can import your own 360-degree video, or choose from a database of over 360 templates. You can customize the video's audio, text, and headings; add images, logos, photographs, and links; trim the video and the audio; and add call-to-action buttons. Finally you can connect the tool to your email marketing partner, be it AWeber, MailChimp, or GetResponse. Many other integrations are available, allowing you to quickly and easily share your new video with the world.

Graphitii

Remember those images that display continuous flows of water, lights, or traffic? These are called cinemagraphs. You look at it and wonder at the years of experience required to achieve this level of mastery as a professional video editor. You would not even consider a DIY approach. And yet, the process is much simpler than you might think. Graphitii enables marketers to build engaging assets in the form of cinemagraphs. Log in to the dashboard, search through the large variety of templates available in literally any niche you can think of, trim the video to your required size, add any customization from the many options available, and personalize by adding your logo. Finally, color in the area you would like to apply the flowing effect to. Once you have done all that, everything around the colored area freezes. You now have a cool, expensive-looking cinemagraph, and you have done it all by yourself in no more than a couple of minutes.

Up to now, we have been reviewing a variety of tools that can empower you in creating your own professional-looking content. But what if you are lacking the time or inspiration to build this great content? You may be a great entrepreneur, business owner, or marketer, but this does not make you a great content writer. Most of the time the solution is either to outsource or to automate your content creation.

CHAPTER 9.
CREATE ORIGINAL CONTENT

Copify

One of the challenges you will face when running your digital marketing campaign is generating great content quickly. Outreach is an essential part of SEO, and quality of content directly impacts the success of your outreach campaign. You may decide to search online for content writers, but mostly they are expensive. Here's where Copify comes in.

What is Copify?

Copify is an outsourcing content creation platform, at the time of this writing charging a flat $0.04 per word. The type of content you can request includes blog posts, press releases, email content, articles, and website pages. Copify has a very strict delivery process in place; the article is delivered for you to review. You can provide as much feedback as you feel is necessary. And, every time you accept an article, you are required to provide feedback and rate the writer. Based on the writers' scores, future requests for articles are directed to the most suitable ones, securing great quality articles at all times. The people writing for you are all experienced bloggers and journalists, so the low cost is not a reflection of the quality you receive—the quality is great. The bottom line is, you do not need a freelance professional writer to get great content. And if you consider that a typical content writer may charge you around £80–£100 for 800 words, you will appreciate how paying £38 for the same article could benefit you and your business.

Alibaba, Konker, PeoplePerHour & Fiverr

I am a big fan of Pareto's principle. This simple but powerful concept applies in most aspects of life. The principle states that 20 percent of your efforts deliver 80 percent of your results, which implies that 80 percent of your efforts will deliver only 20 percent of your results.

How many times have you heard the sentence, "Work smarter, not harder"? You may have heard it from your boss or your colleagues, or read it in the myriad of management and leadership books you have been reading. This is a highly misunderstood concept, and it wrongly implies that by working smarter you don't need to work harder. So, let's re-write the concept on something like these lines: "Work smart by working really hard on the 20 percent that will deliver your 80 percent." In brief, work as hard as before, but focus on the right things.

Your first task when working on a project is assessing where that 20 percent is, what the tasks are that only you can perform and which can be neither outsourced nor automated. Then, simply outsource or automate the 80 percent. Now, you will stay focused and deliver your project on time. Furthermore, professionals will most likely perform the outsourced tasks faster and better than you would do them yourself.

One of the biggest challenges I hear from most entrepreneurs and small business owners is controlling costs. Somehow, when outsourcing tasks, costs seem to spiral out of control. Worry no more; there are many good websites connecting freelance professionals to clients, and the fees are, most of the time, well below the prevailing market price. Most importantly, the wide range of services offered by these platforms means that, whatever service you may need, it will most likely be available. You will of course have to do a bit of research, such as reading the ratings of the freelancers, or their reviews. And yes, it is likely that at times freelancers may not really be up to the job. Overall though, the ratings and reviews are a great indicator of the quality of service you can expect to receive.

Several suitable websites are available if you are looking to outsource your work and projects. Fiverr is a big one; the $5 minimum cost is simply ridiculously low. A similar platform is Konker. Overall, these two platforms should cover any task of a low to medium difficulty level.

Sometimes, you will need to perform a more complex task, requiring the skills of a developer or a more specialized professional. You can use Freelancer.com, SEOClerks or PeoplePerHour. And, as mentioned earlier, when I am looking for original content creation, Copify links me to low-cost professional bloggers, journalists, and other writers.

A particularly great platform is Alibaba. You can build an entire business for a fraction of the cost you would incur by launching the business in the traditional way. Think of Alibaba as your outsourcer of choice for pretty much everything. Do you want to develop a tea business and brand? Go to Alibaba, search for tea, chose the product, the branding, pay the ridiculously low fee and that's it—you have your very own brand of tea. You don't need to interact with any tea producers or branding companies. This applies to any product you can possibly think of. Alibaba is best suited to entrepreneurs who are looking to build a product, and market it afterward. This is a classic example of focusing on the 20 percent—marketing—and outsourcing the 80 percent—the product.

CHAPTER 10.
CONTENT AUTOMATION

SEO Content Machine

The scramble for unique content can be costly these days, not to mention time consuming, so coming across SEO Content Machine is a welcome discovery. Not only does it allow you to find content from all over the Web, based on your keyword preferences; it also provides a way of rewriting content so that it is unique. So, two pretty big boxes ticked straight away. Its compatibility is a big plus, allowing you to manage PBNs clearly and easily through automated drafting and posting, be they Blogger or WordPress based. It comes with a package called Content Toolbag that includes all the essentials, such as Tier 1 content creation and scraping Google Suggest.

In terms of its ability to turn content around, there are few plugins which rival it. If you've got some keyword-relevant content in Spanish, but want to present it to an English-speaking audience, SEO Content Machine will let you do just that, offering a translator which supports all the main Western languages. You also have an article downloader and what they call a content combiner, which can be used to capture content that you like and make it your own. There is something very significant about that—it means you can widen your SEO-focused content campaign across borders, thanks to the ability to use several languages. For someone with an internationally focused service, this is almost priceless, and beats hiring a translator or grappling with Google Translate. Combine that with an ability to focus themes on a certain region, and the power of SEO Content Machine becomes clear.

And, if you are worried about receiving a load of spammy content, which you don't need, fear not: SEO Content Machine algorithms are generally quite efficient in removing the irrelevant stuff. As for integrations, it supports GSA,

SEnuke, and Ultimate Demon. For the modern day marketer, keywords are so vital to overall objectives that in many cases they inform the overall direction of the online marketing campaign. For this reason, Kontent Machine really stands out from the crowd, offering a very useful way to base your content on keywords, without having to trawl the Web for hours on end. It ticks all the key boxes of an auto-blogger tool, such as content sourcing and article scheduling, but it is the extra bits that make Kontent Machine very efficient. If you have massive PBNs to attend to, the backlinking support offered by Kontent Machine is one feature that could help you become more efficient. The tool provides capability to create a huge number of pieces in a short space of time, while also giving you the full complement of backlink varieties to choose from.

As any backlinker knows, being and staying unique is vital, and the way in which Kontent Machine lets you vary anchor texts, eliminating footprints, comes as a welcome feature. If you see backlinking as being a slow and mind-numbing process, Kontent Machine actually makes your life a lot easier, and allows you to devote time to other methods of charming the Google algorithm. A couple of tools are included with Kontent Machine, including an option to work from locally saved files and blueprint settings, which means you can leave the same campaigns running or tweak them to your heart's content. Finally, all information from your Kontent Machine campaigns will sit neatly in the cloud, providing you with flexibility in terms of where you initiate your campaigns from. Now, this is an old-school black hat practice so as a word of caution you must pay attention to what you actually use the tool for. The submission to hundreds of directories for example is in fact not recommended as we discussed in the SEO section. Ultimately, you will need to pick and choose the "safe" bits that will positively improve your workflow.

We have already discussed the significant impact that backlinks have on ranking your website on the first page in Google. Indeed, one of the main SEO tasks you will need to perform is placing content on external websites; examples are guest blogs and social media. And, creating all these pieces of content can be both time-consuming and challenging. You may take the view that you create one great piece of content and then share it on all available channels. This practice will of course help you to grow by reaching a wide audience, but it may hurt your website from an SEO point of view. Indeed, Google has made it known that backlinks gained by placing identical content on a variety of websites may be perceived as spam and damage your rankings. One of the many solutions available is to spin your already existing content, generate an increased number of original articles from your content, then amplify the content. This way, the content you have amplified is original, and if you have put the time in to proofreading all the articles, you will keep the visitor base as well. Of course, it is more complicated than this, and often spun content may not be of the same quality as your original article. Practice makes better, if not perfect, and often your article will only need to be good enough, depending on your goals.

Now, let's turn our attention to one of the many spinning tools available on the market, to provide an example how this works.

The Best Spinner

Few digital marketers are unfamiliar with the concept of spinning articles. But how does spinning work?

You write an article, run it through spinning software, and the software generates as many variations of the article as you set it up to generate. To spin an article, each spinning tool has access to a thesaurus—the traditional term is "dictionary"—built into the tool or accessible via integration with a third party, or both might be available. It is important to point out that the process is not as simple as just pushing a button, although most tools will advertise it as being so. You must put in the time to choose the right synonyms from the lists of suggestions, variations of phrases, and so forth. However, this does become a very easy process as you work with it more and more. And it's worth the effort, if you think about it—one article becomes 500, a task that could have required a significant amount of money and time. And, most tools include an inbuilt originality checker, ensuring that only highly original articles are being deployed for outreach purposes. As already mentioned, many tools are available that offer the same functionality; another one I know of is SpinnerChief. Kontent Machine and SEO Content Machine are two more tools you can use for this purpose. Of course, as I have shown in the section on the future, spinning is not yielding the results it used to do years ago...Google's algorithms have been catching up and are much better at recognizing that even though the content is 100 percent "original" the semantics is 100 percent duplicate.

WP Robot

We have discussed various ways of producing your own content: outsourcing your content to Copify, employing freelance writers, generating content via tools such as Kontent Machine, and spinning content to improve your outreach efforts. Another way of building quality content into your website is content curation. Content curation is a model deployed by many well-known platforms; Scoop.it. is one such. Content curation will not work well when the goal is for your website to deliver organic SEO results. Specifically, as you will duplicate content from other websites, Google will award "authority" to the websites hosting the original articles. However, automated content will work well on a website that is already blessed with high traffic and is seeking to build brand identity, authority, and improved conversion levels.

Marketing experts constantly tell us that content is king, and our business will sink or swim according to the strength of the content we distribute across our website and social media. The problem that some of these self-appointed gurus have not addressed is that many of us, particularly those of us with small businesses, cannot afford to spend all day writing blogs, posting blogs, and replying to comments on blogs; nor do we have the resources to hire a blogger.

This is where WP Robot comes in, offering an automated drip feed of quality content from around the Web, matched to your requirements. After all, who really cares whether content is being produced directly by you or is garnered from YouTube, as long as it is engaging and interesting? Among the most impressive elements of WP Robot is its flexibility. You're not confined to a single platform for your blog, as the plugin allows you to build a new autoblog, even as a satellite site if you wish. That means you can have WP Robot supply content to a new site or blog while also acting as a refresher to update your existing blog or site, with new images and videos to augment the existing content. It comes with an RSS Feed aggregator and PLR label importer, as well as a WordPress site monetizer and enhancer.

Finally, for those who wish to monetize their website by getting involved with affiliate marketing of products, WP Robot provides this functionality as a feature set, meaning it is suitable for webmasters who are already enjoying a fair amount of traffic and want to cash in on the fact.

CHAPTER 11.
LINK BUILDING AND OUTREACH

11.1 Concepts

One of the top three ranking factors for SEO is the number and quality of backlinks to other websites. Regardless of all the talk about content being king, the truth is that you will find it very hard to rank your website in search engines without a very strong backlink profile, particularly when your keywords are highly competitive. Yes, Google is getting smarter, and this translates into a more comprehensive understanding of the quality of links pointing to your website vs. relevance to your content. Indeed, content relevance has won out over many earlier practices such as optimization of title tags, meta descriptions, URLs, and headings, although quality and relevant backlinks are still a high ranking factor. There is no doubt that Google's aim is to develop its algorithms to a point where backlinks will lose their supremacy and quite likely become just another minor ranking factor, as the history of meta titles and meta descriptions shows us can happen. When this does happen, you will truly be able to say that SEO is dead and content will be crowned the new king. This is, of course, good news for users, bad news for SEOs.

What is a link?

Content writers place a link as a reference and a connection to another document or resource on the Web. It is generally highlighted in a different color, making it distinguishable from the rest of the text. Click on that text/link and you will be immediately teleported to the resource you have linked to. Think of a link as a bridge between two resources.

What is the difference between internal and external links?

Internal links connect various resources on your website. Internal linking is important for SEO, as search engines travel around your website by crawling links connected to other pages of the site. Think of a link as a bus taking search engine crawlers from one resource to another. A good internal linking architecture enables search engines like Google and Bing to crawl more pages, discover more relevant content, and get more information about the theme of your website. By contrast, external links connect your website to resources external to your website. For example, you may quote an article in a magazine and link to that specific article, providing readers with the opportunity to read the article in full. It is thought that linking externally does carry some SEO value, though very little, and only when you provide links to resources relevant to your page and content, hence offering more value to the user. The argument is that linking externally to a relevant resource is yet another indicator of the theme of your page, and improves user experience.

What is a backlink?

We have learned that internal links and external links are links you place to other resources. By contrast, backlinks are placed by someone else who links to your website. For example, an article about your company is being published in an online magazine and a link is placed within the article taking readers to your website—you have just earned a backlink. You register your company in a directory of services, fill in the section about your website and add its address. Now, when people view your profile on the directory they can click the link and access your website—another backlink. Just as with internal and external links, backlinks are an important SEO factor. In fact, backlinks are a far more important ranking factor than internal links. The reason for this is simple: Google values internal links less, as you have control over them, and values backlinks more, because in theory you have no control over them. Hence, when someone else links to your website Google perceives the link as a vote of confidence. Thus, the more high-quality, relevant backlinks that point to your website, the better your chances of ranking in Google. The reality is far more complex; however, for the time being you should just remember the importance of gaining quality backlinks.

What is link-building and why do I need to build links?

You have fixed your technical SEO issues, conducted keyword research and optimized your website pages. Surely Google will now acknowledge your great content and rank your website? Not quite so, actually. Remember the internal vs. external links debate? Google's crawlers discover your website pages and content by following internal links between the pages. I have made the analogy of a link being like a bus taking the crawlers from one page to another: the more buses, the more pages Google discovers and travels to. You can apply the same analogy to backlinks: the more buses/backlinks are pointing to your website the easier it is for Google's crawlers to discover and reach your website. And, as Google perceives backlinks to your website as votes of confidence from other websites, the more votes you have the more chances to rank highly. Please keep in mind that this is an extreme over-simplification, as I will explain. Overall, for the time being, what you need to keep in mind is that the more good-quality and relevant backlinks from websites within your specialist ecosystem, the more chance you will have of winning the SEO race. Thus, building backlinks is the process of proactively working on gaining more and more votes of confidence/backlinks from other websites relevant to yours, whether they be directories, social media sites, online publications, or other relevant online resources.

What are domain authority and page authority and why do they matter?

Domain authority is a metric used within the SEO community to measure the value that Google assigns to a website based on known SEO factors. As an example, a website with a large number of good-quality, relevant backlinks would have a higher domain authority than a website with no backlinks at all, or with lower-quality links. By contrast, page authority refers to the authority allocated to a specific page. Most often your website will have a high-authority domain with a mixture of high- and lower-authority individual pages. Various third-party providers calculate website authority in different ways, based, for example, on the number of relevant and quality backlinks pointing to a specific page. However, the most popular tool is MozBar; I use it all the time. If truth be told, no one really knows how Google calculates page authority, or even if this metric is a consideration at all. Tools like MozBar calculate the authority, based on the static factors that are best known to influence rankings. Given the advancements in machine learning, it is more than likely that these factors are far more changeable than any tool available out there can calculate. So, for the moment we will have to be content with tools like MozBar, and consider authority to be related to the score allocated by such tools.

Should I focus on quantity of links or on quality?

In ancient SEO times the more links you had, the better you were ranked by Google, whose search algorithms were basic when compared with current machine learning algorithms. It seems needless to say that webmasters could easily abuse this ranking factor. Millions of websites appeared overnight, with one purpose and one purpose alone: to serve as link farms for clients who were willing to pay to increase the number of backlinks to their websites, with no regard to user experience. Too many creative approaches to be named here were used to increase the number of backlinks, and it really worked for a while. Many websites were being ranked based on SEO creativity rather than on value provided to the user, and the user experience was impacted negatively. Google brought an abrupt halt to these practices with the launch of several algorithms that tackled both on-page over-optimization and the madness created by the entire link-building industry of the time. The result was devastating: millions of websites lost their ranking overnight, never to recover it. Entire businesses providing link-building black hat solutions also disappeared overnight. The winner here was the user, who now experienced improved suggestions to queries faster, better, and more accurately than ever before. And of course, companies that really invested the time in optimizing their websites properly were equally winners, seeing their efforts rewarded with higher rankings, more traffic, and more leads.

So, quantity or quality? I will have to say undoubtedly: Quality. But what is quality? Well, if the backlink appears on a high-authority website, then this is a quality backlink. If the website operates within your industry ecosystem, then the link is of greater quality and value. If the same high authority website offers the same services as you do, then the link is of even better quality, and so on. The idea is that the more difficult is to get that link, and the more relevant it is to your industry, the more the link is valued by Google. In the end, a genuine vote of confidence is far better than one you can control. It has often been rightly said that a good quality backlink from a high-authority relevant website can equal or beat 10,000 lower-quality links, and I have personally ranked websites in competitive industries with significantly lower, but more-relevant links, than the competition. Thus, definitely focus on quality over quantity. Even better, let's aim for quantity and quality at the same time—the more quality backlinks pointing to your website, the better.

What are Follow and Nofollow links and why do they matter?

Webmasters have the option to follow or nofollow links on their websites. A follow link is a command that tells search engines something like: "Please take this bus to the resource I link to; I trust the resource and I vote for it!" A nofollow link, by contrast, tells search engines: "OK, I am linking to this resource, as it is relevant to the user, but I am closing this bus stop. So, do not travel to the resource." The distinction between follow and nofollow links is very important. Follow links allow search engine crawlers to follow the link and discover the resource linked to. For example, if another website links to your website via a follow link, Google both discovers your website faster and assigns it authority, based on the confidence vote received from the website linking to you. By contrast, when webmasters nofollow links to your website, they instruct search engines like Google and Bing not to crawl that link, hence Google and Bing will not be able to follow and discover your website via that particular link. What this means in effect is that you should really focus on obtaining follow links rather than nofollow, which will help search engines to discover your website more often and allocate it authority derived from the quality of the confidence vote. Similarly, the proportion of nofollow links from the total backlinks to your site should be kept low; the higher the proportion, the more search engines may question the relevancy of your site. This is not to say that you should pursue a strict no nofollow links policy; on the contrary, a mixture of follow and nofollow links looks more natural. The key is to ensure that nofollow links are relevant to your website and drive traffic to it. In simple terms, the nofollow links should be used to drive traffic to your website, and as they are placed on relevant websites the assumption is that visitors will increase your time-on-site metrics and lower your bounce rates, thus indicating that your website is relevant and should be rewarded with higher rankings.

What is a backlink strategy and why should I pay attention to it?

When an SEO consultant or agency pitches for a contract, you will hear quite a few jargon terms thrown around in an attempt to impart expertise to their services. One of the terms you may hear is "backlink strategy." You should really pay attention to their approach to the acquiring of backlinks, as these assets are, as I have already explained, a top three ranking factor.

You have to focus on obtaining links from high-authority websites that are from, as far as possible, within your industry ecosystem. If you are a translation agency, then you should aim to build as many links from translation-related publications, websites, blogs, and other relevant online resources as possible. High-authority, trusted websites, even if unrelated to your industry, can help too. However, you should focus on relevant links, as in the long run Google and Bing will place more and more value on the relevancy of backlinks. You should also keep an eye on your follow/nofollow approach to link-building. Of course, the more follow links, the better the opportunities for your website to be discovered by search engine crawlers, and the better the value assigned to the link vote. Nofollow links are good too, if on relevant websites, driving traffic to your website and helping your website to improve time on site and to lower bounce rates. The larger the dis-proportion between follow vs. no-follow links the more your link profile may look suspicious to search engines. Still, the more domains that link to your website, the better. Ten backlinks from 10 different domains will always be more valuable than 10 links from two domains, all other things being equal. Links within text are more valuable, and the higher on the page, the better. Diversity of backlinks is important too, so focus on acquiring links from a variety of sources, such as social media, relevant directories, publications, and relevant blogs.

Of course, there are many other factors to consider, and entire SEO books have been written on link-building strategies. However, overall, the points mentioned above should enable any non-SEO webmaster or business owner to plan a link-building strategy with confidence.

My competitor performs negative SEO on my website...

A PR agency recently redeveloped its website, re-launched it, and rapidly lost rankings. The people at the agency contacted the developer, who conducted an investigation and concluded that some "toxic links" were pointing to the website and, the developer concluded, Google had penalized the website. Furthermore, the developer explained that someone, possibly a competitor, was performing negative SEO on the website, and he forecast further loss of rankings if the situation continued. Obviously, this top PR agency became concerned and asked me to have a look at their website. I immediately identified the issue as human error at development stage; I rectified it and within 10 days the website regained its rankings.

With regard to negative SEO, it is highly unlikely that such practices still have an impact on rankings. That being said, as best practice you should still perform regular toxic links analyses and disavow any suspicious links, in the same way that you optimize headings and meta tags as best practice. Google is far smarter than it used to be, and will simply disregard toxic links; it will not confer any value or authority to them, and Google will certainly not penalize you for them, either. The only reason why toxic links are disavowed as best practice is not as obvious as some SEO consultants believe: if negative links are placed on unrelated websites, then visitors land on your website, understand the website is not relevant to their query and leave your site. Search engines now assume that you have large numbers of visitors to your page but low time-on-site metrics. That is why those links should be disavowed. Your website is not relevant to those visitors' queries. But, again, your website is not relevant to what? Most likely, as the traffic comes from unrelated sites, Google analyzes the backlink and the website it was placed on, and concludes that your website is not relevant for that industry and keywords. Which is perfectly fine. How would this look in practice? You are a translation website and someone who is performing negative SEO, places a large number of links pointing to your website on online betting websites. Google assumes you are not relevant to betting-related queries.

I don't have time to build links...should I buy links?

No, no, no! I could relate from first-hand experience far too many horror stories of business owners who have let themselves be talked into SEO practices that have had a catastrophic impact on their website's performance. Let me make it very simple: SEO is earned, not bought; it requires a clear backlink strategy, focus, and hard work. There really is no easy way to get your website ranked, and if you are one of the few people who have managed to deceive Google, it will quickly figure it out, you will lose rankings, and very often you will never, or you will find it very hard to rank your website again. Do not misunderstand me here; there are many white hat link-building services out there, and they work. But these services are expensive, and if you decide on a mainly DIY approach, I assume that is partly because your budget will not allow for this expense. Equally, there are also many bad practices available; private blog networks being one example. You should be wary when a link comes at too low a cost—it usually does so for a reason.

Which page should I focus my link-building efforts on?

In the on-page SEO section, I explained that when optimizing you website, you allocate specific keywords and variations to specific pages, and optimize each page for a theme that is in line with the targeted keywords. You should avoid keyword cannibalization by not optimizing multiple pages for the same keywords. The same strategy applies to link building, as well: you build links to your target pages, with a clear link-building and anchor-text strategy to support each page and its theme.

Ok, enough theory. Let us now turn our attention to some of the tools and technologies available to support your link-building efforts.

11.2 Tools for Link building and outreach—step 1

Many marketers miss one vital but obvious step before publishing and promoting content. You must make it easy for people to share your great content, and this goes beyond simply providing sharing bars and buttons. You must make your content available for downloading or sharing in as many formats as possible. In doing so, you will improve your reach on multiple online channels, present information in easy-to-read, professional formats, and build your brand identity.

WP Coursify

WP Coursify provides functionality that allows you to build your very own online courses with a similar look and feel to Udemy, Khan Academy, or Coursera. You can easily set up courses, add unlimited chapters and modules per course, and accept payments via PayPal or offline payments. WP Coursify has a great, user-friendly dashboard and a large variety of course templates, and it is very easy to use. You can use the plugin to build lead magnets, provide a free course to deliver traffic to your website, or maybe to form part of a funnel...the possibilities are endless.

Audello

If you are looking to run a podcast, Audello is the only platform you will ever need. It has too many features for them all to be mentioned here; however, they include: podcasting, audio pages, audio gateways, playlists, timed events, audio bars, and A/B split testing. The analytics are particularly impressive and include heat maps, geo analytics, traffic sources, and interaction metrics.

WebinarX

One powerful lead magnet, conversion optimization and sales asset, and education and engagement tool is a webinar. WebinarX is an easy-to-use platform, should you decide to choose this route for amplification purposes. It takes less than two minutes to set up a webinar; WebinarX is very user friendly, it can accommodate an unlimited number of attendees, and you can run as many webinars as you want at no extra cost. Some of the many other features included are: live streaming, automated webinars, email notifications, built in live chat, autoresponder integration, live stats, and a voting system. A Professional version is available, which allows you to use and customize your own logo and hold unlimited monthly webinars. It also provides a developer license, Facebook comment integration, and an incredibly smart and powerful feature: re-targeting. Yes, you can actually re-target people who have attended your webinar.

AppMakr

One of the many benefits of having a mobile app is that it makes your services and content more widely available. But building a mobile app is hard, expensive and stressful, right? You must be able to program in Java or C++ maybe? I am sorry to disappoint you but up to a point you will need no coding skills to build your very own app. There are many companies providing DIY app software; however, you will find that most of them are expensive and that you pay for each app built. This, of course, means that if you want to build two apps, your cost doubles. AppMakr is one platform you may want to use to build your app; it requires no prior knowledge of the process. It has an easy drag-and-drop menu and its prices are highly affordable, with the highest-priced package for developers at only $25 per month. An option is also available to publish your apps for $9 month. And, if you don't need it after you have built your app you can simply cancel your subscription.

AppInMinutes

Another tool you may use is AppInMinutes. This tool has the advantage of a one-off low fee of $9 for the first year, and then up to $37 per year, at the time of this writing. The tool provides the same functionality as AppMakr and is very similar to your familiar WordPress builder elements. It comes up with over 100 templates built-in. Besides the templates, a further advantage over AppMakr is that you can build professional contact forms within the app. AppMakr also offers this option; however, you would need to create an account with Wufoo, which would incur a further monthly cost.

RefferalCandy

Another tool you can set up prior to launching your content marketing campaign is RefferalCandy. This tool provides the functionality of setting up your own referral programs, encouraging website visitors to share your article or product with their friends in exchange for a gifts or a reward. Various professional templates and custom features are available.

Magazzine Style

One area in which you should be very particular is the brand identity of your website. Your website must reflect and be congruent with the identity of your business. We have discussed the importance of variety and quality of content in keeping your website visitors engaged. High engagement with your website impacts on both your SEO ranking and the reach of your content. Hence, the more relevant the resources on your website are, the better the engagement. Videos, FAQ, lists, PDFs, and presentations are only few ideas for the type of content you should be thinking about. Magazzine is one type of tool that can transform your content into your very own professional publication. Content assets such as FAQ, articles, and newsletters can become highly sharable and professional assets when transformed using the large variety of templates offered by this tool.

Ultimate eBook Creator

You have great content, you've worked very hard on it, placed sharing capability on your website, and you have your very own magazine. Why not make it into a book? Why not publish it on Kindle, iBooks Store, Smashwords or Lulu? Ultimate eBook creator is a tool that supports you in doing just that. It includes an inbuilt editor and a spellchecker, and you can import your book from various formats such as a Word document or a PDF. You can insert media, such as images, audio, video, bookmarks, and more. And, in addition to books, you can create lead magnets, checklists, and articles, with a very professional look and feel.

Post Gopher

I keep emphasizing the importance of great, engaging content. You can make use of many automation tools to work your way around the task of creating such content. Curating, re-purposing, personalizing and scheduling, spinning, automated content creation, and outsourcing are only few of the examples we have discussed. And, as I mentioned, too often marketers work hard at building their content assets but fail to maximize the reach of the content.

Another tool that can help you built your email subscribers lists and build links back to your website is a WordPress plugin called Post Gopher. What this smart plugin does is allow readers to transform your blog post or page into a PDF and save it for reading at a later time or simply share it. To download the article readers need to input their email address. They are now into your funnel...auto-responders, email marketing, remarketing and so forth.

One final point to re-emphasize, though: the objective is not to manipulate the reader into providing their email address, but to engage people with your content. Why else would they want to download your post, share it, or embed it? And why would you need an email from a person that is not interested in reading and sharing your content? Again, we have been discussing this idea at great length in the section on psychology.

Vyper

You can use Vyper to run highly targeted contests, growing your email lists and social media following at the same time.

How does it work?

The tool works on the principle of a scoreboard. The more points your visitors get the higher they go on the scoreboard. Maximum points are awarded for sharing your content or following you on social media. Points are also awarded for downloading a PDF or any other action of your choice. The more attractive the giveaways are, the better the results. The contest's look and feel is professional, and the tool integrates well with the main email service providers.

VidSkippy

VidSkippy introduces another fantastic growth marketing practice, distinguishing itself through ingenuity and simplicity.

What does it do?

You can take any video, including from YouTube or Vimeo, add an in-stream link to it, and distribute it to your target market. The link is in the form of a "play" button. Really professional and indistinguishable from the overall video, it is in fact part of the video. You can set up the link to be made visible 10, 20, or 30 seconds into the video, or after any period of time you specify.

How does it look in practice?

You discover a viral video—Van Damme's Volvo commercial is a good example. You download the video, then add your link to it. You now share this already proven, viral content with your groups, add it to your email marketing, and so forth. How many views will this viral video receive in your niche? How many people will click the link? How much traffic will be driven to your website? The tool provides a good dashboard, and you can share the video from within the tool.

Videelligence

Just when you thought you had learned everything there is to know about easily creating a video, along comes Videelligence. This software enables you convert any webpage to a video. Yes, you read that right...to a video. And it does this in several very simple, intuitive steps: pick up the URL, drop it into the tool, choose the template you would like to use, customize or accept the calls to action, titles and prices scraped by the tool from within the page, tick the images you want to use, and add sound from the tool's library. You are now at the stage where you can fully customize your video, e.g., add text, headlines and even video background. Finally, upload your logo and create a highly professional video. Furthermore, if you are looking to promote one of your products using a video, Videelligence has a section which provides the option to select a template, add your own image, customize the calls to action, prices and text, and—voila! Your very own professional video presentation of your product.

WP Viral Payments

WP Viral Payments is a WordPress plugin that will support you in your efforts to achieve many of the commercial goals you have set up for your website. Its features are powerful and all packed into one single plugin.

So what does it do?

One of the features provided by this tool is the creating and fully customizing of one-click upsell order forms, just like you would experience on Amazon.

How does it look in practice?

You have a product, maybe a book, and are looking to upsell a similar book. The plugin provides functionality to add a "people who bought this also bought this" form. You can add two, three, four, or as many similar products as you like. Tick boxes are available to enable buyers to add products to their cart. Of course, you can be as creative as you want with the content of your message, e.g., buy these products now and save £5, and so on. The plugin integrates with payment processors such as PayPal and Google Checkout. It also provides the ability to lock your product page and place a "Share on Facebook" button, or to offer visitors a discount in return for sharing the content on Facebook. The downside is that the plugin allows only Facebook shares. WP Viral Payments also provides a coupon discount option, enabling you to create discount coupons for your products. You can even add, "requires opt-in" before allowing people to reach the checkout—another feature to support your list-building efforts. You can combine the "share" and the "requires opt-in" features. Do ensure that you plan your strategy though. It may make sense to ask people to subscribe when promoting a popular product; but this may not be the best idea when your product is of average functionality. People may abandon their cart.

11.3 Tools for Link building and outreach—step 2

OK, so you are now happy with your content and its format. Now, you are looking to amplify your content across multiple organic media channels—social media, blogs, and mainstream. Paid amplification strategies are available should you decide to take the paid-for route: pay per click, remarketing, social media advertising, and content discovery platforms. Depending on your goals, you must maximize ROI for every piece of content you create: likes, engagement, visits to your website, sales funnels, backlinks, leads, shares, goal completions, and conversions. There is one final step you will need to consider before amplifying your content: on-page growth strategy and its setting up. Specifically, you will need to decide on the right mix of amplification strategies available to your readers on page.

BuzzSumo

BuzzSumo is an amazing outreach tool; it is in fact one of the most popular tools for outreach purposes. It offers a free version that, although it's quite restrictive, you can use to get a feel for what the tool does.

What does the tool do?

BuzzSumo enables you to discover the most-shared content on Facebook, LinkedIn, Twitter, Pinterest or Google+. Think of all the great growth-hacking tools we've discussed: how could you leverage the most popular content in your niche for driving people back to your website? How could you use those articles to brainstorm new content ideas, titles, or strategies? How about assessing the best content strategies, assessing, for example, the type of content that works best on each platform. And why stop there? BuzzSumo also offers a list of all backlinks pointing to any popular article, and a list of people who have shared it. All you need to do is put together your content, and start your outreach campaign from within the tool.

Another powerful feature provided by BuzzSumo is the Influencer area. Simply input your keyword, start the search and discover a list of top influencers in your field or niche: their biography, page authority, domain authority, number of followers, retweet ratio, reply ratio, and average number of retweets. Save the Influencer in your project dashboard and start working with it.

The tool also provides the option of Monitoring, which provides the functionality of monitoring brand mentions, content strategies, and the performance of your competitors, benchmarking information on them, and more.

Bloggers and Journalists Outreach

I emphasize over and over again throughout this book that no matter how strong your growth-hacking or SEO actions, they will be wasted without great content. To use the well-known cliché again: content is king. As we have seen, one of your top SEO tasks as a business owner is building backlinks and traffic from high-authority domains.

But, how will you reach these bloggers, influencers, or journalists?

Many outreach tools are available, and the more you research, the more confused you become. I will try to bring some clarity to this area and present four main platforms specializing in reaching journalists, in addition to Buzzsumo.

Pitchbox, ResponseSource, and JustReachOut

Pitchbox and ResponseSource are two great outreach platforms that will empower you in taking control of your outreach process. The disadvantage of these tools is their recurring high monthly prices, which are most likely out of the reach of a freelance digital marketer or small business owner. Nevertheless, Pitchbox and ResponseSource are two of the top outreach tools available. A more affordable tool is JustReachOut; the cost in this case is still a bit high; however, you will not find a better-value tool than this.

HARO

HARO (Help a Reporter Out) is a brilliant idea that helps to illustrate the future trends and impact of technology on professions such as journalism. HARO is a platform where journalists submit queries on subjects they are interested in, and members of the HARO community reply with the best possible answers. Of course this support is far from disinterested; the helper will hope that the final article will include a traffic-generation asset of some sort, e.g., a mention of the author and a link to their website. The publications involved generally carry high website authority, and a link from such a website may boost both your traffic and your SEO rankings. Simply register, provide your field or fields of expertise, set up your alerts, and contribute.

Social Locker

You have been putting a lot of work into creating your content, amplifying it, optimizing it, building links to it, and so on. People are now visiting your article, your analytics indicate high engagement rates with the page, and yet a trend begins: an initial surge in visitors occurs when you post a new blog, but the surge is soon followed by traffic drying up. Social Locker is one WordPress plugin you may want to consider to tackle this problem.

What does it do?

You have published and amplified your blog post. You have put in the time to ensuring that the first half of the article is highly engaging. Visitors are driven to your post and engage with the post. Halfway through the post, a pop-up locks the page, asking the reader to share your post, which action will unlock the page. So now the reader is in a dilemma: should they stay or should they go? In the section on psychology, we discussed at length various concepts confirming that when things are presented in the right way, people will complete the action you require, in this case sharing your article. Now, let's think for a moment. How many of their connections will now translate to visibility of your post? Let us perform a simple math calculation as an example. Take 100 visitors and multiply them by a couple of hundred connections each. Does that equal the number of pairs of eyes on your content? Of course, this a simplification; we already know that your organic reach is greatly diminished by social media giants like Facebook, which is looking at pushing paid search. The Social Locker plugin supports all main social networks: Facebook, Twitter, Google+ and LinkedIn.

Other aspects to consider when optimizing your website for SEO are: hidden content, visibility, and the crawlability of your website. When SEOs think about locked content, their first thought is: you may amplify the content, but as the page is locked, search engines like Google will not see, or crawl, the content. Social Locker includes an option to make the page content visible to Google even when the page is locked.

Pay with a Tweet

A variation of the Social Locker plugin functionality is Pay with a Tweet. This is a great idea and one of the most well-known tools in its category. It offers both a free and a paid version

What does it do?

Imagine you browse a website and come across a really good offer or a great piece of content. You can access the offer by paying with a tweet. Click on the button, login to your social media account, share the offer, and gain instant access to the offer. How many people will then be reached by the offer? How many people will the offer reach if 50% of the second wave of sharers also share the offer? I trust I made my point. The name of the tool is misleading, as Pay with a Tweet supports Google+, Twitter, Facebook and LinkedIn. However, where the tool really distinguishes itself is the option to pay with a share on Xing and VK. Thus you may deploy different growth strategies and KPIs for Xing and VK when compared with LinkedIn. You may go as far as translating some of your articles into German and Russian if you want to further customize your funnels.

GoViral!

GoViral! is a really cool growth-hacking application that you can use for driving people into your sales funnel by offering something of value to them. The application supports Facebook, Tweets, Instagram and 16 other services, so it's a bit restrictive compared with other platforms. However, its unique features are its two-step "bribe" system and its powerful bribe funnel customization feature.

How does it look in practice?

Someone is browsing a website, discovers a great offer, and is prompted to "Share for instant access." They go ahead and share. They are now presented with another bribe in return for sharing the offer on another platform or emailing the offer. You could set up a first step asking people to share on Facebook and a second step asking people to share on Twitter. So, thinking about it...how many people have you reached up to now?

Sumo.me

SumoMe will support your growth by engaging people that have already reached your website. It provides the capability to place a share bar on your pages. You can customize it and brand it, and in-depth analytics are available, as well.

What else does it do?

The tool also provides capability to set up various pop-ups. You can ask your website visitors to download a free guide or gift of some sort by providing their email address, to share an article, accept a special offer, sign up to a newsletter, and more. You may add a sticky bar at the top of your website, a pop-up that appears after scrolling three-quarters of the way down the page, and another one after reading the whole page. Trying to leave your website? The mouse movement is tracked, the tool concludes that the visitor is looking to close the window, and another irresistible offer pops up in an attempt to bring the visitor back into the funnel. All pop-ups and templates are highly professional, easy to implement and easy to customize.

Another great feature is heat mapping. You can gain a good understanding of where your website visitors clicked, how often, when, and where from. Finally, the tool includes great analytics, image sharing capability, contact forms, and list builders.

AddThis

This is another great set of sharing tools offering features such as share buttons, follow buttons, related posts, list building, and link promotion. I use this tool all the time.

Pushengage

People receive quite a few emails in their inboxes every day, all very interesting. The reality is that they simply do not have the time to read them all, so what they generally do is skim through the list. Another type of amplification strategy available to help you improve the reach of your posts is push notifications. Of course content is essential, and must add value for the reader.

How does it work?

You visit a page, read an interesting article, and a message appears on the screen asking for permission to send you notifications with new content. You like the content and the website, so you click "allow." The webmaster can now send you push notifications every time they decide to promote content, products, or special offers. A small banner with their brand and the name of the post slides in from the right side of the screen, giving you a preview of the new post. In most instances push notifications are more effective than email marketing and other amplification channels. This is because recipients have allowed for push notifications from your website, and they have given you permission to market your content to them. Think about it as a remarketing exercise.

Pushengage is one tool that enables you to set up push notifications. Simply copy a piece of code, paste it into the header of your website, and customize your notification by adding your photo, logo, or URL.

I cannot stress enough the fact that high-quality content is essential. After all, what else would make people accept push notifications from your website? On further reflection, people will only allow a limited number of websites to send push notifications. They allow these websites to send them notifications as they are likely to provide original points of view, products, offers, or new and innovative ways of looking at and approaching work practices within their industry. Setting up Pushengage is simple; it takes five minutes to register, get a piece of code, and place it on your website.

LiveCaster

Facebook Live and You Tube Live place high value on live stream. We know this already. LiveCaster provides the capability of uploading and scheduling your videos as live stream events. This works even when you are not really streaming live. You can make comments and customize your videos. You can connect the tool to any of your Facebook pages or groups.

IFTTT and Zapier

We have discussed focusing on the 20 percent that will deliver 80 percent of your results. You must identify what the 20 percent actions are, and then outsource the remaining 80 percent of your tasks. We have also discussed several choices to meet your outsourcing needs. Platforms like Fiverr, Konker,

Freelancer, PeoplePerHour, Alibaba and SEOClerks provide literally any service you can think of, and for a fraction of the cost of traditional specialists.

Let us now talk about the second type of opportunity available for improving your workflow: automation. Throughout this book we have or will be covering many tasks that are open to automation. Some of these tasks are: social media auto -posting, content curating, and growing social accounts. If you are to make the best use of your time, be more efficient, and focus on your 20 percent, you must obsess about either automating or outsourcing all tasks falling outside of that 20 percent. Zapier and IFTTT are two market-leading tools that can improve your efficiency by automating many tasks you would normally perform yourself. These tools support integrations with almost every application you can think of: social media platforms, MailChimp, Evernote, WordPress, Gmail, Google Drive, Salesforce, Dropbox, Google Sheets, HubSpot, Gravity Forms, Zoho. In brief, anything you want, they've got.

How does it look in practice?

You have an email list, and are looking to send an email via Gmail to every contact added to the list from now onwards. Zapier can do it; this task also complements well your email marketing campaigns. Auto-respond to emails on Gmail? That is provided as well. The truth is that if you are looking to automate a task, it is likely that the app is within Zapier's arsenal. IFTTT and Zapier are two tools that will streamline your workflow and you may end up considering them to be indispensable to you and your business.

WikiGrabber

If you are a savvy growth hacker, continually looking for new ways of driving relevant traffic and powerful backlinks to your website, then you will appreciate the functionality provided by WikiGrabber.

What does it do?

Input your targeted keyword into the tool, and a list of all Wikipedia broken links related to your keywords will be generated. Click on any broken link and you will be directed to the Wikipedia page that is hosting the broken link. In the search box at the top right-hand side of the screen write, "dead link"; this will take you to the broken link. Edit the broken link and input your own link. The catch is that your link must be very relevant; indeed, you must provide an even better answer than the page the Wikipedia article was linked to previously. We are not talking about a black hat practice, just pure, genuine hard work to provide the best possible answer. Try anything else, and you will quickly get yourself banned. The process is not as easy as it sounds; however, as you get more experienced it does become easier, and the effect of the strategy is massive if you put the time into it.

WikiGrabber is a great tool and you should really work hard on perfecting this strategy. The traffic it will bring to your website, the links, and the authority will be worth it.

Web 2.0 Sniper

You often hear people talking about how old-school SEO is dead, and this is true to a large degree. However, one thing still works...backlinks are still a top-three ranking factor.

We have discussed old-school link-building practices: link farms, irrelevant websites, low authority, not in the same ecosystem as your business, and so on—practices that don't work anymore. Nowadays, all that matters in backlinks is the quality, and blogger outreach within your industry's arena is still a top link-building strategy.

I can empathize with you when I think of the large number of emails received in your inbox or on your LinkedIn profile from people offering placements on various blogs for astronomical sums. Unfortunately, at times we will need to pay for good, white hat backlinks. Very recently, one link-building specialist reached me via LinkedIn introducing a link-building method leveraging the authority gained by expired domains hosting high authority websites. The link builder scrapes the Internet, discovers an expired domain with high authority that is relevant to your niche, and runs it through a comprehensive analysis, ensuring that the expired website was not highly spammed or banned. They then register the domain, build a new website, and now they have high authority blogs—instant links, follows, high authority, and relevance. Or they simply redirect the newly purchased domain to your website. This is all for a fraction of the cost you would pay for a regular blog post and its placement on another. As an entrepreneur or business owner you can go as far as creating an entire new business model by providing this service, or build these websites into real businesses.

How do they do it?

One tool you can use to perform this action is Web 2.0 Sniper, simply input your keywords and proxies and search. The tool discovers the most relevant expired domains, and provides authority metrics by leveraging Mozscape API. Free domain registration for the expired websites is also provided. A word of caution: building your blog network is not as easy as it may seem; there are many pitfalls you will want to avoid to get the best out of your newly acquired blogs. Overall, it is not very difficult, but you must do your homework before you start. And Google will fully dismiss this practice as well sometime in the future.

CHAPTER 12.
SOCIAL MEDIA

12.1 Intro

In the section on Future from my previous book HACKING DIGITAL GROWTH 2025: Exploiting Human Biases, Tools of the Trade & The Disturbing Future of Digital Marketing I argued that organic social advertising is doomed, and pointed to several studies with findings such as the one from Facebook, which found significant limiting of the organic reach of your posts. We also discussed the innovator's dilemma and learned that as social media companies grow, it becomes harder to achieve growth in revenue and profit, or even to maintain their levels. This explains why social networks must generate profit to prevent loss of shareholder backing and loss of market share. Twitter is one example where lack of profit generated panic on Wall Street. And, as social advertising represents the main revenue source for most social media networks, in the future we will see more and more of it. What this means, for marketers and small business owners in particular, is that organic social media is becoming less and less viable as a growth strategy. This places SMEs and low-budget businesses at a great disadvantage against businesses with high social advertising budgets. What can be done about it? Well, 53 percent of people recommend products in their tweets; social media influences 93 percent of buyers' decisions; and 90 percent of customers trust peer recommendations. (Marr, 2015) Your goals? To increase your reach you will need to achieve two particular goals, both obvious. The first goal involves paid social advertising; there simply is no way around it. In this section, I will present various social platforms you can leverage for growing your business, some popular, some with high potential but less popular. If you are in the SME category, or simply on a low budget, you may find that trying untapped advertising platforms may be more beneficial than competing against high-budget advertisers on popular platforms such as LinkedIn and Facebook. I certainly encourage you to consider your options very carefully. Your second obvious goal: to achieve a high number of social media followers and contacts. The greater their number, the more people you can reach organically; after all 16 percent of 1,000 is far better that 16 percent of 100. In the section on psychology we discussed at length the nature of social networks. In this section I will focus on providing you with tools you may use to confidently employ a DIY approach, save time, and grow your social media channels organically. My intention is to provide a quick overview of the type of platforms and concepts available, and open your mind to the various types of tasks that can be automated. Specifically, I am looking to give you the confidence to employ a DIY approach to building and running your own social media campaigns, whether paid or organic. That being said, you should keep in mind that new tools appear all the time, old tools disappear, and social media advertising settings and offerings change all the time as well. For those reasons, taking a UDEMY course prior to launching your social media advertising campaign will certainly pay off and provide you with a better understanding of the concepts, processes, terminology, and strategies on each channel you would like to employ. Similarly, a thorough review of the tools presented in this book will maximize its benefits to you, help you to avoid mistakes, and indeed help you to determine whether any particular tool is right for you and your business.

Let's get started!

12.2 Facebook Advertising

Facebook is the most widely used social media platform, with the largest user base and most interaction. The company is investing heavily in artificial intelligence, and its machine learning algorithms are improving at exponential rates, driven by billions of daily interactions between its users. Its fanatic focus on delivering the most relevant content and experience to its users is one reason why the platform has remained the undisputed social media market leader for so long. Social advertising on Facebook is the first step you should consider in delivering your goals. Its advantage, in addition to the large user base, is the high level of data and granularity you can apply to your audiences. You could target users that liked your competitor's Facebook page, or who have an interest in certain people or influencers, or who have specific job titles, or—why not?—people who have three children, a low income, like baseball, and are divorced. Call it creepy, but Facebook is, of course, every marketer's dream.

What is Facebook Advertising?

Facebook is by far the largest social advertising opportunity available, with over 1.7 billion people using the platform every month. Of course, marketers have figured out a long time ago the benefits of advertising on Facebook, and they most often include it as a default option in their social media plan. The large user base, high engagement rates, its flexibility in tailoring the goals of your campaign and its far lower cost per click compared with Google AdWords and Bing ads makes Facebook the go-to social advertising platform.

How many types of Facebook advertisement exist?

You can choose between three macro-marketing goals in Facebook: brand awareness, local awareness, and reach. You are then prompted to choose the goal of your campaign from a variety of options. These options, such as traffic, engagement, app installs, video views, leads generation, change all the time, so you shouldn't really be surprised to find different options each time you log in. Finally, you can set up your conversions and start tracking results. Several ad formats are available: Photo, Video, Carousel, Slideshow, and Canvas, and these formats can be served as Lead adverts, Dynamic Adverts and Link Adverts.

How do I boost a Facebook post?

Boosting a post is one of the fastest ways of promoting your post to people interested in your Facebook page. This is also the easiest way to share updates, posts, videos, and special offers with a larger audience. Simply choose the post you are looking to boost, click the Boost Post button at the bottom right-hand corner of the post, choose your audience and budget, and decide the duration of your social campaign. Add or change your payment method and boost your post. Done. While this is a fast way to advertise on Facebook, you will most often not use it, mainly because its targeting settings are limited compared with Facebook Ads Manager or Facebook Power Editor.

What is Facebook Ads Manager and how does it work?

You will most often create and manage your campaign within the Facebook Ads Manager. Here you can choose your campaign objective (brand awareness, local awareness, reach), state your end goals (traffic, engagement, app installs, video views, and lead generation), and set up your conversion pixels (conversions, product catalogue sales, and store visits). You can set up your new campaign, target audience, placements of your ads, billing, and the actual ads. I think you will really like the Facebook Ads Manager; its high level of targeting options and ease of use make it ideal for marketers with various levels of expertise.

What is Facebook Audience Insights?

Facebook Audience Insights is one of the best social media audience-targeting tools available. It makes available too many targeting options for them all to be discussed here. However, as an example, you can target people by age, location, or gender. You can also target audiences by interests (e.g., people who have an interest in translation services), connections (e.g., people who are connected to your competitor's CEO), behaviors, language, income, relationship status, education, work, and much more.

What is the Facebook Text Overlay tool?

Facebook allows a limited text-to-image ratio on your images; if you have too much text than Facebook will reject your ad. To help users in evaluating text-to-image ratios, Facebook provides the Text Overlay Tool. Simply upload the image and the Facebook Text Overlay Tool tells you whether your image is within the text-to-image ratio limits, and whether it has too much or too little text.

How do I create a Facebook ad?

Three options are available to you when creating social ads on Facebook. The first option is boosting a post; this is the easiest and fastest option, although the targeting options are quite limited. You will most often create your ad using Facebook Ads Manager or the Facebook Power Editor, due to their higher flexibility and targeting options.

How much do Facebook ads cost?

As with any pay-per-click model, the cost of an ad depends on several factors. In Facebook's case one factor impacting the cost per click is your bidding strategy. Your cost will differ depending on whether you are setting a manual bid or an automatic bid. The idea behind the automatic bid is that Facebook optimizes your bids to drive as many clicks as possible and, as you have probably already figured out, this option increases your costs. Other factors are ad quality and relevance. Facebook focuses obsessively on user experience for two reasons: first, bad ads damage its brand identity and its image and causes it to lose users. And second, bad ads don't get clicked on; hence, bad ads do not make Facebook any money. So, when optimizing your cost per click it really pays to focus on ensuring that your ad is relevant and optimized for your target audience. Another factor that can increase or decrease the cost of your Facebook ad is the accord between the action you set up and the intent of the audience. Let's assume that you set up purchases of your translation package as your campaign goal. Simply because your audience shows an interest in translations or in other particular pages, it doesn't mean that they are looking to buy translation services. Hence, the higher the gap between your goal and the audience intent, the lower the cost will be for you. Facebook will assign a lower value to an audience that is less likely to buy. Conversely, the closer the match between your goal and your audience's goals, the greater the value Facebook places on that audience; hence, higher costs will obtain. And, of course, an ad with a lower bid per click but higher quality and relevance may be shown at the expense of other ads with higher bids per click but poorer quality.

How can I A/B split test my ads?

Facebook's ability to A/B split is somewhat limited when it is compared with Google AdWords. Google AdWords provides functionality to set up as many ads as you desire within an ad group and optimize based on performance. Facebook does not provide this option. There is, however, a way around it when setting up your campaign in the Power Editor. The Power Editor has a very handy option to Duplicate. You can simply create another ad group by duplicating the first ad group. You can then make your changes and use the two ad groups for your A/B split test.

12.3 Twitter Advertising

Twitter advertising is aimed at increasing the engagement rates of your tweets, reaching more people, and starting conversations with your audience. You can grow your followers on Twitter, drive people to your website, drive conversions, encourage people to download and engage with your mobile app, and extend your email database.

Twitter advertising?

In spite of growing worries in the Wall Street financial community, you cannot deny the power and reach of Twitter advertising. Twitter boasts a varied user base of over 317 million, which includes business leaders, celebrities and, of course, President Donald Trump. You can use Twitter advertising to achieve goals, such as increasing traffic to your website, gaining more followers, promoting specific tweets, and promoting your mobile app. If you instinctively assume that advertising on Twitter is a very competitive arena, you may be surprised to learn that that is not always the case. In fact, you may be even more surprised to learn that a great many social media professionals do not include Twitter advertising in their paid social media plan. Their clients are missing out, thus providing you with a great opportunity to get ahead and beat the competition.

How much do Twitter ads cost?

Like most other social advertising services, Twitter uses an auction-based system to determine the placing of your ad. You can choose between two types of bidding strategy: automatic bidding and manual bidding, or CPC (cost per click) bidding, as the latter is better known. With an automatic option you will most likely experience increases in your CPC. The great feature of Twitter ads is that you are only charged for clicks to your website; you will not pay for any other actions or engagements, e.g., impressions, replies, and retweets. And, of course, your cost varies depending on the level of competition: the more competition, the higher the cost per click of your ad.

How can Twitter advertising services help my business?

With a base of over 317 million active users, Twitter is a preferred communication channel for most celebrities, business leaders, opinion writers, and the general public. Advertising on Twitter is a major growth-hacking opportunity. In fact, it is a much under-used opportunity, in spite of most marketers acknowledging its importance as an organic social media strategy. Why would you advertise on Twitter? Twitter provides several routes to supporting the growth of your business: increase traffic to your website, increase engagement via your tweets, promote your app, and gain more followers. You can promote accounts, tweets, or trends; hence, it offers a variety of online advertising opportunities.

Finally, I would like to challenge you to research any digital marketing agency or digital marketing consultant that is highly ranked by Google. On their social advertising services page look for the Twitter social advertising section. You will quickly notice that most of them do not advertise or provide this service, as they mostly focus on just one or a few social media platforms, such as Facebook, LinkedIn, and Instagram. What a great online advertising opportunity is being missed—and what a great opportunity for your business!

How can I create a Twitter ad?

Sign in to your Twitter business account. Next, click the Get Started button. You are now prompted to choose your target audience based on interests, geography, gender, device, users similar to your followers, or certain keywords in people's tweets. Choose from the type of ads available (promoted account, promoted trends, promoted tweet), set your budget and your bidding strategy (automatic or CPC), and you are good to go.

Should I advertise on Twitter?

It really depends on your business goals and objectives. Most people, while acknowledging the power of Twitter, have little knowledge of its paid advertising option. This situation is not necessarily caused by ignorance—most marketers are not running Twitter advertising, as they focus entirely on Facebook, Instagram, and sometimes LinkedIn. Implicitly, their clients are not aware of the benefits of Twitter advertising and are missing out on it, which offers another great social advertising advantage to you.

12.4 LinkedIn Advertising

Quite often conversions- to-leads metrics vary on LinkedIn vs. Facebook, depending on factors such as time of day, day of the week, and the purpose of your message (e.g., branding, selling, lead generation). The main advantage of LinkedIn over Facebook is the professional nature of the network and the mindset of LinkedIn professionals while they are navigating their way around the platform. Specifically, LinkedIn users are more receptive to business messages, as opposed Facebook users, who display a more relaxed, social, non-business behavior.

What is LinkedIn Advertising?

LinkedIn is a great opportunity to leverage the power of over 450 million users, mainly professionals. LinkedIn members are more likely to include within their profile information such as title, company, demographics, and many other relevant pieces of occupational information. This means that you can really get value from your LinkedIn advertising budget by reaching a highly targeted professional audience. And finally, as LinkedIn is a professional network, its people are more likely to pay attention to business messages than are Facebook users, who display a more social mindset.

How many types of LinkedIn ads exist?

One of the options provided by LinkedIn is sponsored content. Sponsored content is a great option for promoting your updates to a large, highly targeted audience base. Two bidding strategies are available, a cost-per-click (CPC) option and a cost-per-thousand-impressions (CPM) option. Conversion tracking is available to assess the impact of your LinkedIn-sponsored content ads. LinkedIn also provides Sponsored InMail, an option providing the ability to reach a highly targeted audience directly via their email inboxes. You can also A/B split test various parts of your InMail messages, thus improving the conversion rates of your campaign. Finally, with Text ads you can reach a highly targeted audience within minutes. The main advantage of this is that you can quickly create your own social ads, set your budget, choose your audience and bidding option, and launch your campaign. By contrast, to set up an InMail campaign, you would need to contact LinkedIn's sales team.

How much do LinkedIn ads cost?

The cost varies according to several factors, but overall it revolves around your bids and the historical performance of your campaigns (CTRs). Two bidding options are available. With cost per click (CPC) you only pay when your ad is clicked on, and with cost per thousand impressions (CPM) you pay based on the number of impressions your ad receives. You will most often use the CPC option for lead-generating campaigns, but may find the CPM option more appropriate for brand awareness campaigns. Finally, LinkedIn ads are generally more costly than Facebook ads, presumably due to LinkedIn producing higher conversion rates and the more professional, action-driven nature of the audience it offers.

Should I use LinkedIn's or Facebook's social advertising services?

You will often find that LinkedIn delivers both great results in terms of conversions (i.e. leads) vs. Facebook, mainly due to the nature of its audience. Specifically, on Facebook users tend to be more open to social interactions, while on LinkedIn the professional nature of the audience means that users are more likely to engage with your ad. That is why LinkedIn ads are more expensive than Facebook ads—LinkedIn assumes that its leads are more valuable, more likely to result in action. You should always consider trying social advertising on both LinkedIn and Facebook, assessing results against objectives, and refining your social media strategy, accordingly.

How do I create a LinkedIn ad?

Three options are available to you: Sponsored Content, Sponsored InMail and Text Ads campaigns. To run an InMail campaign, you need to contact

LinkedIn's sales team; they do not currently offer a DIY option. If you are looking for a quick DIY option, then Text Ads and Sponsored Content are available; you can launch your social advertising campaign in minutes. The interface is intuitive, as well, which helps. Log in to the Campaign Manager, identify the account in which you will create your text ad or click "ad account" if you are new to LinkedIn advertising, choose "Click campaign," then "Select text ads." Fill in all fields and then click "Next." Choose "Destination", write the text of your ad and Save. Add any further creatively, then click "Next." Choose your target audience, click "Next," choose your bid type (CPC or CPM), input your bid, and click "Launch Campaign.,"

12.5 Instagram Advertising

Instagram advertising is another option you should consider including in your social media marketing strategy. With a base of over 500 million users, Instagram is ideal for brand campaigns, sharing stories, launching new stories, and reaching highly engaged audiences. As a Facebook company, Instagram benefits from all the advantages, know-how, and systems developed for Facebook social advertising. In fact, Instagram adverts are created via Facebook's Ads Manager and Power Editor; hence, the same level of segmentation is applied to both Facebook and Instagram ads.

What is Instagram Advertising?

Instagram is another platform with a lot of potential for promoting your brand to highly engaged audiences. How do you assess the social advertising potential of Instagram? Well, Facebook did buy Instagram—not a bad vote of confidence.

So, where will your Instagram ads appear? To quote Instagram itself: "Instagram adverts appear in a bold, linear format at the center of visual inspiration"...cheesy but really powerful, particularly for brands looking to develop a strong identity and reach creative and savvy audiences. And, as Instagram ads are set up via the Facebook Ads Manager or its Power Editor, all the relevant benefits described in the Facebook advertising section are there, including the exceptional targeting opportunities.

What do Instagram ads cost?

The same cost principles that apply to Facebook advertising apply to Instagram advertising. The costs depend on the relationship between your bid, your CPC strategy (automatic or manual), and the quality and relevance of the ad.

How can I create an Instagram Ad?

You can create Instagram ads via Facebook's Ads manager or its Power Editor, in the very same way you would create a Facebook ad.

Should I advertise on Instagram?

Instagram ads are an excellent social advertising opportunity, particularly for companies looking to build and develop a brand, enhance brand identity, or re-launch a brand to a highly engaged, savvy, and creative audience.

Should I advertise on Instagram, Facebook or LinkedIn?

Your decision of whether to run advertising on Instagram, Facebook or LinkedIn depends on your social media strategy, and goals. Instagram works well for brand awareness campaigns, and for building distinctive brand identities. However, it may not work as well for more-commercially-focused goals such as generating sales or enquiries, unless of course when you leverage the power of Instagram influencers. By contrast, generating sales and enquiries is something that LinkedIn is ideal for. Its large pool of users and granular targeting options, the professional nature of the network, the more commercially engaged audience, and the ability to target professional audiences based on factors such as job titles or companies are ideal for lead-generating campaigns. You would use Facebook advertising to get a bit of both worlds. Facebook's large user base and the social nature of the audience it offers can be suitable for brand awareness campaigns. Facebook can drive traffic to your website and move potential leads to the first stage of your sales funnel. Most often, you will use a combination of these platforms, depending on your social media strategy, and goals.

Other Social Advertising Services

Too many marketers use only Facebook, LinkedIn and Instagram for driving their online goals. Indeed, these three platforms are very attractive, given their large user bases, quality of interactions, highly targeted audiences, and know-how, together offering fantastic targeting options. However, keep in mind that other social advertising solutions are available and are seriously underutilized.

What other social advertising services are available?

You can run online advertising campaigns on Tumblr, Reddit, Pinterest, StumbleUpon, Foursquare, Yelp, Xing, VK, and Snapchat.

Should I really advertise on other social media platforms?

You should really be considering running campaigns on less-popular paid social media channels, depending on your target audience and goals. As mentioned, a large proportion of digital marketing professionals are either not aware of or do not offer social advertising services on most of these networks. And if you asked them why, they would most likely dismiss the opportunities and justify their ignorance by stating that it was not worth it. In reality, in most cases, these marketers have never tried these paid social media channels, and they will swiftly shift the conversation to what they know best: Facebook, LinkedIn and Instagram advertising. You should not let yourself be misled; be sure to explore all opportunities available. These social advertising platforms also have large audiences, less competition, lower costs, higher interaction at times, and more niche markets. In many industries you will have the opportunity to be a first mover, so get to work; there are leads to be had, new growth-hacking platforms to be tested, and lessons to be learned.

12.6 Tumblr Advertising

Two hundred million blogs and 80 million posts a day should give you some idea of the potential of this platform. You can test Tumblr advertising against Taboola and Outbrain Amplify, and on quite a few occasions find that your articles will drive more visitors, better CPC, and more links via Tumblr.

So what are the types of services available on Tumblr? The most common ad is the Sponsored Post, which in effect is a normal post but far more visible. The targeting options of Tumblr sponsored ads are quite limited: you can target audiences based on location, gender and interest. Sponsored video posts are also available, being very similar to sponsored ads. Video ads include further, video-related, analytics, such as views and engagement. And then there is Sponsored Day, this provides you with the option to tag your logo and tagline at the top of the dashboard for one day, with links to the high-traffic Explore page, which can include your posts or posts you have selected—a very smart social media marketing idea indeed.

12.7 Reddit Advertising

If you know a bit about Reddit you will vouch for the high level of engagement displayed by Redditors. In fact, dare I say, Reddit users are sometimes far too engaged, and they are very passionate.

Now, 234 million active users and more than 10,000 communities of highly engaged users; and so many of your competitors are not leveraging Reddit's potential. Is that an opportunity or what?

What do you need to create a Reddit ad? Well, you need a Reddit account to start with. You can now click on the "advertise" link at the bottom of any Reddit page. Create your ad copy—there are two ad options available: link and text. Link ads are used to drive traffic to your website, while text ads are used to engage audiences in conversations. Optionally you can add a 70 x 70-pixel thumbnail and a 1200 x 628-pixel card image. After creating your ad you will be progressed to the "edit promotion" page. You will then preview your ad, select targeting options, set your maximum bid (Reddit uses a CPM model) and schedule; and you're good to go.

12.8 Pinterest Advertising

With Pinterest having 150 million users each month, Pinterest ads are a viable alternative to test against Instagram ads. Just pick the pins you want to promote, set up your target audience, choose your goal—engagement or visits to your website—and launch.

You can split test results against Instagram advertising on metrics such as visits to your website, engagement, cost, or conversions.

12.9 Xing Advertising

You can think of Xing as LinkedIn's very little German brother; they are very similar. Both are professional networks, though Xing has a far smaller user base at around 12.5 million. The same benefits of advertising on LinkedIn apply to Xing. When it was first formed, the search intent of Xing's users used to be quite different than LinkedIn's. As opposed to LinkedIn, whose user base is made up of professionals, mostly in full time employment, on Xing, an estimated 50 percent of users were initially searching for a job, and around 750,000 users were students in German-speaking countries. However, Xing has successfully developed its user base to emulate many of the characteristics and features of LinkedIn. Xing's audience nowadays consists primarily of professionals; hence, it offers a great opportunity to leverage that audience in reaching your goals, particularly when your strategy involves targeting German-speaking audiences. You can promote your website, your business, news pages, your company profile, or even a job ad. Xing also provides the option of promoting your Xing event, Xing profile or Xing Group. To build your campaign, start by choosing your goal, then set the metrics of your target group, such as location, age, gender, career level, industry, and so forth. You can now set your bidding, build your ad, and click "Post."

12.10 VK Advertising

Just as you can think of Xing as a German version of LinkedIn, you can think of VK as a Russian Facebook. VK is in fact the social media leader in Russia. Hence, if your strategy involves social advertising in Russia, you should really consider VK as part of your social media plan. This is also true when your advertising strategy is focused globally and includes Facebook advertising. As Facebook advertising has a lower market share in Russia, advertising on VK will complement your Facebook advertising campaign. You can create VK ads to promote your website, promote a special project, or target particular groups. To build you campaign, simply pick one of the three goals available, define your target market, create your ad, specify the type of ad you will run—newsfeeds or VK pages—set up your bidding and launch.

12.11 Snapchat Advertising

Snapchat advertising is one of the first options you may want to consider when promoting to young audiences. Some statistics proudly shared by Snapchat: 173 million Snapchatters on an average day; Snapchatters who use the site daily open the app on average 18+ times a day and spend 30+ minutes on Snapchat each day (https://forbusiness.snapchat.com/, 22 Sept). Snapchat provides three goals: raise awareness, increase consideration, and drive action. Again, it's easy to set up, with a very intuitive interface; and it offers a great opportunity to reach a targeted audience for some of the lowest cost per click available.

12.12 StumbleUpon Advertising

Stumble Upon is a platform you can leverage to amplify all kinds of content, such as articles, videos, slideshows, and basically anything that has a URL. It has a considerably smaller user base than other social media platforms we have talked about, with "only" 25 million users. That being said, a study published in an article by searchenginepeople.com shows that StumbleUpon usually drives more traffic than Reddit does, which in itself is quite impressive, given Reddit's significantly greater user base. StumbleUpon is all about content; the platform represents yet another content amplification opportunity to split test against the mighty Outbrain Amplify and Taboola. You will love StumbleUpon from an SEO perspective, i.e., building links to your website, driving traffic and improving time-on-site metrics, achieving lower bounce rates, and recruiting loyal followers.

12.13 Foursquare Advertising

With over 60 million users and its smart business model, Foursquare provides an exceptional opportunity to drive local people to your shop, restaurant, hotel, or any other bricks-and-mortar business.

How does it work?

Suppose I'm a Foursquare user and find myself in your neighborhood looking for a good restaurant or a hotel. Generally, the most relevant local businesses would be served up to me in the usual way as Google would be applying its local SEO algorithms. With a Foursquare ad, however, your business would appear at the top of my Foursquare listings, bypassing your competitors; hence, it has a far higher potential to convert searchers to customers. Foursquare can complement your Google local SEO and paid efforts, and get you ahead of your competitors, particularly when you have a bricks-and-mortar business. You really do have a competitive advantage here, as most businesses in your neighborhood will be unaware of Foursquare advertising.

How can I get started?

Set your monthly budget, write your ad and launch your campaign. You will only pay when Foursquare users interact with your ad, either by visiting your business or by tapping on your business information. Analytics are provided to assess your ROI.

12.14 Yelp Advertising

Yelp offers yet another advertising opportunity often missed by business owners at a local level. A great opportunity to leapfrog larger brands and competitors, Yelp shows ads for your business on search results and mobile apps, but most importantly, it also shows them on the business pages of your competitors—a very powerful feature. Setting up Yelp ads is extremely easy, once you've created your Yelp business page. Click on Yelp Ads; Continue; Choose your budget. Input your card details and you are good to go. One note of advice: ensure your Yelp business profile is completed as comprehensively as possible.

CHAPTER 13.
SOCIAL MEDIA AMPLIFICATION

Up to this point we have discussed the main paid social amplification channels available to you as a marketer or business owner. Let us now turn our attention to some of the tools you may use to increase the organic reach of your content on social media. Some of the tools presented next are labeled "white hat" by digital marketers, and some may be considered to be "black hat." Collectively, the tools presented in the next session will provide you with a good understanding of the wide range of social media amplification practices and strategies available. As always, do be sure to research more deeply before using some of the tools, particularly given the changes to the GDPR standards that came into play starting May 2018. This is important both to ensure you are using the tools correctly and to make the best use of the features and functionality provided.

High Proxies

As an innovative and driven marketer you will often try new practices that would not technically be thought off as "white hat." You will sometimes venture outside the limits of the White Hat Kingdom, across the Grey Kingdom and deep into the Black Hat Kingdom. The point is, if you feel happy to live within the White Hat Kingdom's borders, you will never get to meet people of different cultures (Grey Hat and Black Hat Kingdoms), learn new practices, get ideas, and indeed innovate. If, however, you acknowledge and embrace innovation, learning new things, and trying new things, then you must learn to travel incognito between these worlds. If truth be told, the Google god does not have people like you at heart. But how will you travel incognito, without attracting the attention and the rage of the Google god? Well, this is where proxies enter the game. Let's try to gain a somewhat simplified understanding of what proxies are and what they do. Assume you go online and browse around some websites. You leave footprints. Online platforms such as Google, Facebook, and Twitter collect data about the online behavior of the person or persons located at your IP address. And, when these companies suspect the use of black hat practices, they ban your location. This is bad of course. You need a way of travelling incognito, avoiding placing your IP address at risk. Proxies are the solution most often used; these can be purchased from many providers, such as High Proxies. Proxies are in effect IP addresses you may use to mask your own IP address. In fact, once you enable a proxy, Google will not see your real IP address. Instead, Google reads the IP address of the proxy. You stay safe while traveling incognito.

How does it work?

In a normal non-proxy situation, you start your search online; there is no intermediary between your server and your URL destination. Google knows exactly who you are. A proxy, by contrast, acts as an interface; you send your request, which is directed to a third-party proxy server. This server transfers your request to the proxy IP address, and sends your request from this proxy address. When the search engine server responds, it sends its response to the proxy IP address you purchased, and the request is subsequently sent to your real IP address. You leave no footprints, as any request you send is perceived as coming from the proxy IP address. Please keep in mind that this is a significantly oversimplified explanation. Using proxies is one of the very first skills you will need to learn; I encourage you to do this almost before using any tools that necessitate the use of proxies. It may sound complicated; however, using a proxy is simple enough: buy it, drop it into the designated area in your software, and go. The truth is that you will probably use proxies with most of the social media growth tools I describe in this book, and with any software built around the idea of using bots for the purpose of automating tasks. So, get on board with proxies; this is important!

If your website is built on a WordPress platform you will want to consider using the following two social media amplification plugins to increase your reach and considerably improve your workflow.

Blog2Social and NextScripts

Blog2Social is one of two social amplification plugins that you will find very useful on your website. The other one is NextScripts. Both plugins offer free and paid versions.

So what can Blog2Social and NextScripts do for me?

These plugins provide the functionality of amplifying content on over 25 social media platforms at the touch of a button. Of course, you might already be using various other tools we have discussed or will be discussing—SocialPilot, Board Commander, or Post Planner, for example. Linked with Sniply, you can use Blog2Social and NextScripts to amplify and automate part of your content on the main social media platforms, such as Facebook, Instagram, Twitter, LinkedIn, Pinterest, VK, Xing, Google+, and a few more. However, SocialPilot and Post Planner will not offer support for many other high-profile social marketing channels, such as Medium, Torial, Flikr, Diigo, Delicious, Reddit, DeviantArt, Instapaper, LiveJournal, Plurk, StumbleUpon, Yo, 500px, Blogger, Flipboard, Scoop,It, vBulletin, Weibo, and even WordPress blogs. To sum up: you may use these two plugins to complement tools such as SocialPilot, Instamate, Board Commander, and Post Planner, and amplify your content on almost 30 social media channels and hundreds of groups (LinkedIn, VK, Facebook, Xing, etc.).

SocialPilot

SocialPilot is one of the best social amplification tools you can use for social media automation purposes. You can use SocialPilot to automate your workflow on a variety of social media platforms: Facebook, Twitter, Google+, VK, Xing, Pinterest, and Tumblr. SocialPilot can be pretty much a set-it-and-forget-it tool that will maintain a flow of high quality content to your social accounts. It provides three posting options: on profiles, pages, or groups. Which you use depends on the plan you have chosen. You could do a bit of research before choosing SocialPilot, and look at tools such as Hootsuite and Buffer. However, you may find that these tools are far too expensive. In the end, SocialPilot will do for you what Hootsuite or Buffer do, and more, for a fraction of the cost. You will find that at $100 per year for the Individual package you can amplify your content to up to 10 accounts.

So what does SocialPilot actually do?

You can amplify and schedule a post on up to 200 profiles, groups and pages depending on the payment plan you have chosen. SocialPilot also provides a great section with curated content. Simply choose your area of interest, then browse through the news and if you like something then schedule it. You will never run out of content ideas, and you will save time. You can share great content on your social media and build a personal brand and social media signals (e.g., likes, shares, and profile views), and you can drive people to your website when integrating with Sniply. Moreover, every post that is curated comes with social metrics in the same way that BuzzSumo displays the number of shares on various social media platforms.

Another great feature of SocialPilot is retrieving and scheduling content from an RSS feed. You can easily set up one or more RSS feeds within the tool, and allow SocialPilot to automatically pick up and post articles to as many social media channels as you care to specify, and as often as you like.

How does this look in practice?

Each day, SocialPilot picks up posts from your specified feeds and posts them on your social profile; no action is required on your part after the initial set up. Simply copy the RSS feed URL of the website into SocialPilot, indicate how many posts you want picked up, when they are to be posted, e.g., the day and the time, and how often; then just forget about it. Other features include the ability to set up teams and groups of posts. Suppose you are running social campaigns for hotels, dentists, and hairstylists. You can create specific groups of posts for each campaign and tailor your content strategy to the various audiences. You can set up groups for Facebook alone, or maybe a group of social accounts that receive posts at 7 AM, and another group that receive at 10 AM. The possibilities are endless. Integration with VK (the Russian Facebook) and Xing (the German LinkedIn) can provide additional opportunities to reach audiences and niche markets. You can set up and share projects with clients or anyone else. This really does help from a client engagement perspective, building trust and transparency.

SocialPilot also offers a Chrome extension, which you can use to pin and schedule items on the go. You may read a lot of very interesting articles during the day, and you can schedule many of them at the push of the button. After all, if you find content valuable, innovative, and informative, your audience should find it so, too—which only helps to improve your engagement rates.

SocialPilot also provides an easy-to-read analytics dashboard. You have full control over the content you post, when you post it, and where it is posted to.

Post Planner

Post Planner is a tool similar to SocialPilot, with the difference that it focuses its efforts on Facebook, Pinterest, and Twitter only. It is, however, working on integrating with most other social media channels accommodated by SocialPilot. You can use Post Planner to manage your Pinterest, Twitter, and Facebook profiles, pages and groups. Its strength is in the quality of curated content; and in addition to curated articles, a large variety of quotes, popular and funny content, and top news is available. And all this at a fraction of the cost of more-established tools such as Hootsuite or Buffer.

Other such tools are available, including market leaders Hootsuite and Buffer; however, overall most tools will provide similar functionality at higher pricing levels.

Sniply

We have been discussing automating your social media marketing using SocialPilot and Post Planner. A short reminder: these tools provide you with the ability to select and schedule high-quality curated content, to schedule from the feeds of your preferred blogs and magazines, or to schedule your own posts, while also posting to various social media accounts, profiles, pages, or groups. The tools are very valuable to any serious growth hacker, and inexpensive when compared with other more established tools such as Hootsuite and Buffer.

So where does Sniply fit in?

Sniply allows you to create snips of content that include an image and a call to action, which in turn drives traffic back to your website. Whenever a person visits and reads an article you have shared from another blog, this person will also see a professional-looking snippet overlaying the article and promoting your offer or your call to action. You can tailor your snippet to include your brand logo, a message, and a call to action. For example you could overlay a popular article by Neil Patel with the following call to action "Would you like to read more articles on SEO? Click here. " Now, whenever you share your or someone else's article via SocialPilot or Post Planner, your audience will also see a cool, modern, and discreet snippet that will drive them into you funnel. And most importantly, the tool leverages the principle of association perfectly, as your overlay is on this article of such high authority that surely you too must be an influential figure—a great example of piggybacking on the authority of another influencer or publication.

What will I use it for?

You will most likely have various social media automation strategies in operation. You might use Post Planner for a highly customizable experience on Facebook, Twitter, and Pinterest, or you might simply use SocialPilot for all platforms: Xing, LinkedIn, Google+, VK, Facebook, Twitter, Pinterest, Tumblr, and all the others. You may complement these tools with the Blog2Social and NextScripts plugins, to increase the reach of your content. From a content marketing perspective, you will likely use LinkedIn and Xing to reach a more professional audience, and Facebook or Twitter for a more social audience. You will curate and create content to match the specific intent and interests of every platform, and customize your snips to each audience. As an example, one snip may be personalized to drive leads for your business on LinkedIn, and another snip would encourage Facebook users to visit your blog to read similar articles. To take the example further, on Xing you might translate your articles and snips to German; on VK you could replicate the strategy with Russian.

Sniply also offers the capability of creating RSS feeds, though you may prefer to do this via SocialPilot and Post Planner directly. The tool also includes an analytics function, and data is available measuring KPIs, such as clicks on your snips, conversions and conversion rates. A Chrome extension also allows you to schedule posts and create snips on the go, which is a really powerful option.

Finally, one of Sniply's biggest competitor advantages against similar tool is its large base of integration options: Buffer, Hootsuite, SocialPilot, Edgar, Facebook, Twitter, LinkedIn, Scoop.It, MailChimp, HubSpot, AWeber, Salesforce, Google Chrome, and many more.

Speedleads

You should by now love Sniply's idea; it really is innovation at its best. You may also like their free plan—don't we all? However, when you have to apply this strategy to high-traffic websites, or if you finally manage to build a steady high-traffic website, Sniply's various plans can become expensive. Furthermore, as a cost-conscious entrepreneur or marketer, you may prefer to avoid recurring fees. Indeed, you may prefer to keep your fixed costs low and search for one-time-low-payment tools.

Should you decide to look for cheaper alternatives to Sniply, the truth is that there are not many great alternatives out there. Moreover, Sniply has a significant competitive advantage with its numerous integrations and partnerships, something that not many tools currently provide. In fact, one main reason why you may choose to use Post Planner and SocialPilot for your social media growth-hacking strategy will be their integration with Sniply!

One great tool that partially emulates Sniply's functionality is Speedleads, a powerful Chrome extension with a great dashboard interface. Speedleads provides you with the capabilities of adding calls to action and sharing your favorite article while still reading it. And this is for a one-off payment, as well. You can use it for most of your clients without recurring monthly costs. The tool also has several upsell packages; you may want to purchase the Scheduling option, which allows the scheduling of posts on social media.

Overall, Speedleads is a great alternative to Sniply, and requires a once only low payment, as well. There are two things on the downside, which may not concern you if you use both SNIPLY and Speedleads in parallel. It all depends on your needs and budget available:

-        Speedleads lacks the powerful integrations that Sniply excels at, which is why Sniply is still part of most marketers' arsenal. If you rely heavily on social media automation and integrations with tools like Post Planner, SocialPilot, Buffer, and Hootsuite, then Sniply will be your weapon of choice.

-        Speedleads was constructed as an upsell model. The more functionality you need, the more the upgrades will cost. And yet, it is a one-time financial outlay, and if your traffic is very high, it will work out cheaper than Sniply.

ClipClap

CliClap is another alternative to Sniply; in fact it provides similar functionality to Sniply's, but with a twist—it was completely free at the time of this writting. For the time being, the founders continue to offer this great tool free, most probably up to the point when they have managed to grow and develop their user base to a particular level. One disadvantage of ClipClap is its lack of the numerous integrations offered by Sniply; this is one area where I expect the ClipClap team will focus their efforts next. Overall, the best value available if integrations are not part of your content marketing strategy and you prefer to curate posts manually. I do however expect that this tool will soon be monetized and the attractive "free" pricing option will be dimissed.

Social Jacker

Another Sniply-like cool tool is Social Jacker. The difference between this and Sniply is that the overlay added to the article you are emulating has a social media call to action: "Continue with Facebook." Assume you are running a contest. You are deploying Social Jacker on a popular article and you share it online. People reach your page, your offer is displayed as a pop-up chat at the lower right-hand corner of the screen, with an enticing image, text, and a call to action. All the visitor needs to do is click on "Continue with Facebook," then click on "Continue as [user's name, e.g., Jack, etc.]." Now, a Thank You message is displayed, informing the user of the notification they will receive via Facebook with details of the contest. And, what type of information do you get once people "Continue with Facebook"? Well, you get email address, name, profile photo, gender, and even age range! And all you need to do is pick up the URL of the article you are looking to emulate, drop it into the tool, and receive the output. The amount of customization that the tool allows is fantastic; it includes the position of the chat box, its size and font, images, and much more. The tool also provides bot support, which you can fully customize. Assume that instead of a competition you are asking the audience a question like, "How can we help?" Your website visitor answers with something along the lines of, "I am looking for training tutorials." As you have been setting up your bot to answer with a phrase such as, "Please follow this link to reach our tutorials section," every time someone types in "tutorials," they are served the pre-programed message.

Birdsong

If you are looking for innovation in your marketing, growth hacking, and email-list-building efforts, this is one tool you may want to look at. You already use various tools to leverage the power of great curated content and drive traffic to your website (Sniply, Speedleads, CliClap, to name just three). Birdsong is another example of ingenuity in digital marketing.

So what does Birdsong do?

Think about a great article you have recently read within your field of interest. The article captured your attention, and as it happens, half way through the article, or after 10 seconds, 20 seconds, or whatever the Webmaster has decided, a pop-up appears asking you to subscribe. You are asked to join an email list, and most likely offered a special discount, a download, or something of interest in your line of business. You would love to continue reading the article, and the offer is irresistible as well. Perhaps the author is an authority in the field, or you may simply love his content. You offer your email; his email list gets bigger and he now has a lead. This is of course a very good article; the sign-in rate is most likely high. But what if you could use this great article to your advantage by replacing the pop-up window with one of your own? By replacing the sign-in form with your own, all those emails will now build your email list. How powerful would that be? Birdsong does just that.

How does Birdsong work?

It all starts with a great article, video, or white paper. You input the URL of the article or whatever into the Birdsong software. The software will then duplicate the original article page, place the duplicate on their domain, and include a dozen highly professional pop-ups. You now have an exact replica of the article, with a set of highly customizable pop-ups. You can set a pop-up to appear at the beginning of the article, or within the article at any time you specify. You may decide to allow readers to spend 30 seconds on the page, allowing them to engage with the article, then lock the screen with your pop-up. Follow the same process as the actual author of the article and grow your email marketing list. Finally, link your project to your autoresponder and you can start your email marketing campaign! By now you should have realized that you are not really hijacking the subscription form of the writer. In effect, you are simply duplicating the page and adding a professional sign-in form linked to your autoresponder. You will still have to do the ground work of sharing, promoting, and so on, but what you need to realize is that when accessing the Birdsong link, nine out of ten people will not even realize that they are reading a duplicate page. In fact, to them this is the original article, the real thing.

As a driven marketer or entrepreneur you have probably already thought to yourself: I can share on social media, share on groups, share via email marketing, and so on. Maybe I could check out one of my competitors' social media profile, or a great blog by my favorite writer, run it through birdsong, and share it as a comment posted on their very own social profile, or maybe in all the groups I am part of? And every time the post gets accessed, a proportion of the readers will subscribe to my list. There is also the aspect of social proof provided by the author and article; most often, the article will not be ignored and your email list will leverage the reputation of the author. I have used this extreme example so that you can further understand the power of this tool. Black hat? Yes! Smart? Yes again!

Another feature is on offer, as well. During the process of creating your first link, Birdsong automatically builds a very-professional-looking profile page hosted on their servers. Every time you share a birdsong link, this will automatically be added to your profile. You can think of this page as a version of your Paper.li or Scoop.It profile. But what can you do with your profile link? You can place it on your Instagram profile, social accounts, email signature, and so on. And, every time someone visits you profile and clicks on that high-quality article you have been sharing, you will further increase your chances of growing your email list. The truth is that you may not use this option generally, but it may be useful at times. One word of caution, though: this is in my opinion a black hat tool; you are deceiving people and persuading them to join a totally different email list than that of the author. I have presented this tool not to encourage its use but to show how thinking outside the box will often lead to innovative ideas. And this strategy may work well in some niches and not so well in others, as I have shown in the section on psychology.

CHAPTER 14.
SOCIAL MEDIA AUTOMATION

I will describe two of the follow/nofollow tools as representative cases. Once you have grasped the principles and functionality of these two tools, you will have an understanding of all other similar tools and how they can support your social media strategy.

Social media is often an integral part of any growth-hacking strategy. By now, you will be aware of various strategies and tools you can use to grow your social accounts and gain targeted audiences. You can use SocialPilot, Post Planner, Board Commander or Octosuite to curate content, schedule from RSS feeds or find content by keywords, and post to hundreds of profiles, pages, or groups. You may also use Sniply, Speedleads, or CliClap to drive targeted traffic back to website.

Now, let's assume that you will be using a combination of curated and own content to reach your audience. You have great quality content and yet no one seems to discover it or to interact with it. In fact, the content makes no contribution to your overall digital marketing strategy; it drives no traffic, no leads, and no business. You are also a very busy entrepreneur or marketer, juggling quite a few tasks every day. Prioritizing your time is key, and you would want to focus on the 20 percent of the tasks that will deliver 80 percent of your results. Implicitly, you will outsource, automate, or offshore the remaining 80 percent of the tasks. Marketers will always find innovative ways to improve their workflow, while getting best value from their social media activity. And, when successful, innovative tools and ways of working become established, they are widely adopted. Many of these tools and practices will be perceived as white hat, grey hat, or black hat, and it will be up to you to decide your level of comfort when adopting various practices. I am a strong believer that as a driven entrepreneur or marketer you must be open-minded, learn, adapt, try and try again, and eventually succeed. Let us now learn how you can grow your social accounts on autopilot, while also promoting your content to a large and relevant audience. You could think about this as Step 2 of the process of growing your networks, while also maintaining your network relevance. The concept in that statement is crucial, as the goal is to grow your social media follower base and connect with like-minded people, relevant contacts who will be interested in what you have to offer, whether it be content, products or any other assets. The truth is that most often you simply don't have the time to manually search for contacts, invite them one by one, and repeat the process on every social media network you are active on.

The tools I shall describe will emulate and automate the process you would normally follow in manually managing your social media activity. So, let's get started. Add your proxies to the tools, link your social accounts, adjust your settings, start the tool, and automatically perform actions such as auto-follow, un-follow, follow back, like, unlike, pin, comment, share, add friends, view or comment on video, send messages, and more. Social media automation tools have the capability to perform most tasks you would perform manually, but do it faster, better, and on a far larger scale. And once you get your settings right, you can think of it as a set-and-forget action; though you should really monitor performance, test various settings, and thus maximize your benefit from the tool. An essential point to keep in mind, though, as with many tools described in this book, is that you must perform in-depth research before using these tools. It is the only way you can decide for yourself whether the tools fit in with your strategy, business, and personal values. Your research will also allow you to get the best out of any tool you use, and avoid a number of mistakes that most people make when first starting to use these tools. Far too often, business owners or marketers excitedly set up their tools, create accounts, and wait to get rich, with very little effort to develop their profile to be attractive and interesting, a profile worth following. And, far too often, entrepreneurs set up their tools driven by the desire to win quickly and easily—and have accounts banned by various social media providers. This will not work. Tools like SocialPilot, Post Planner, Board Commander, and Octosuite will help you build and tailor your profile with high quality curated or original content by automating the process. Whatever tool you use, keep in mind that people will not follow you if you are of no value to them.

Another skill you need to master is using proxies; it is, actually, a skill you will need for most of the current innovative digital marketing tools, as already discussed earlier in the book.

Nevertheless, the tools you learn about will provide you with a significant advantage over your competitors, improve your digital marketing productivity and workflow, save you significant amounts of time, and support the delivery of your business goals and KPIs. Most importantly, it will allow you to focus on the 20 percent of the tasks that will deliver 80 percent of your results, as your time is, of course, put to better use on research, innovation, and networking, rather than manually following people and creating or curating content.

Two tools will now be described to enhance your understanding of how you can grow your following on the main social media accounts through the follow/nofollow approach. There are, of course, many other tools available that operate on the same principle and provide similar functionality.

Social Zen

The first social media automation tool I will introduce is Social Zen.

So what does Social Zen do?

Well, there are perhaps too many things it does to include them all here; however, let's give it a go. The tool automates your whole social media growth on the seven main social media platforms: Instagram, Facebook, Google+, LinkedIn, Pinterest, Tumblr and Twitter. The tool is built around the idea of modules. Let's look into it more closely.

The Social Automation module

You can post to groups, grow fan-page likes, auto-like, follow and un-follow, grow followers, comment, and re-blog. You can also auto-join, and you can do so based on keywords or number of members or followers, a highly targeted approach. Another great feature is auto-adding friends, based on your specified keywords, a great feature for networks like LinkedIn.

How do you set the tool up?

Input your proxies, fine-tune your settings, and input your keywords, targeted locations, groups, or any other relevant attributes. Click "Start" and you're done. In reality, you will of course have to monitor your campaigns, which should take not more than 10 minutes a day. The principle behind the tool is simple: you set up great social profiles and you auto-invite people to your network; or you follow people and they will follow you in return on the principle of reciprocity. This is in fact the principle most social media automation tools are built on.

How does it look in practice?

Assume you are looking to grow your LinkedIn network. You are an IT specialist specializing in hotel services. You would like to connect with hotel managers and decision makers. Simply connect your account to the tool, input keywords, such as Hotel Manager, Marketing Manager, or any other relevant keywords. Push the button and the tool begins sending the invitations; it is that simple.

The Social Tracker module

Another great module, very similar to SocialPilot and Post Planner. You can view the trending content on social media, search for viral content, such as images, posts, and videos; you can re-post content, edit images, add special effects, add your text, your hash tags, or your logo. You can really tailor it to your own specifications. At this point, the tool has already improved your workflow on two tasks: content quality and growing your social following.

The Auto-poster module

The functionality provided by this module is identical to SocialPilot's; you can search for great content and schedule it in advance. Simply set the tool up a month or two in advance and forget about it.

At this point, it may be tempting to think that Social Zen could replace SocialPilot or Post Planner. That would be a mistake. Social Zen is great for curating social media stories, but it lacks the flexibility of SocialPilot and Post Planner when it comes to variety of content. For example, Social Zen does not currently include a section for curated content, and it has no support for RSS feeds, either. This means that you cannot schedule and automate content from industry-leading RSS feeds. Finally, the lack of integration with Sniply means that you cannot drive people back to your website. You will, therefore, use Social Zen in conjunction with SocialPilot to automate your growth, provide value to your audience, build a brand identity, tailor content marketing strategies to different social media channels, and leverage the integration with Sniply to drive traffic back to your website.

One gap filled by Social Zen is Instagram automation, which is not a facility provided by SocialPilot. The main reason for this omission is Instagram's obsession with cracking down on bots-driven automation tools and fake community builders and improving user experience.

So what automation options are available for Instagram?

Within the content discovery area of Social Zen you can quickly assess trends on Instagram, helping you to judge what is the most relevant topic to write about. You can discover what is the most-shared content based on your target keywords or hashtags. You can provide a keyword and retrieve popular images based on it. From these, you can select as many images as you want, post them, edit them, schedule them, and more. Another helpful option is the ability to find the most popular hashtags relevant to your specified keywords and the number of posts in each category. You can browse different hashtags and schedule as many posts as you want.

In addition, a section is dedicated to popular hashtags, continuously comprehensively updated. This really is the cherry on the cake; it allows you to ensure the best hashtags are being used to maximize the reach of your content.

You can upload, edit, and schedule your own images. An image-editing area allows you to search for popular images and edit and customize them. You can add your own text, logo, and so forth. The Video Editor replicates the functionality of the Image Editor; you can customize any video to suit your requirements.

How does it look in practice?

Suppose you decide to manage your Pinterest account within Social Zen. In addition to the follow and no-follow options, Social Zen also provides the option to find and post in popular Group Boards. You can also automate and schedule posts from these popular Group Boards. Now, you can curate content and schedule and automate amplification to profiles, boards, and groups. And, the follow and un-follow option is great as well. Set up and forget...

FollowingLike

An alternative tool to Social Zen is FollowingLike. This tool can be used to grow and manage the following social media networks: Instagram, Facebook, LinkedIn, Pinterest, Reddit, Tumblr, Google+ and YouTube.

So what will the tool do for me?

You can set the tool to auto-follow accounts based on specific keywords, specific profiles, pages, or other relevant attributes. You can set the tool to un-follow people after a specified period of time. For example, you may decide to un-follow people who have not, within a certain time, followed you in return.

You can set the tool to follow people, communities, groups, blogs, or companies, and you can do so by specifying keywords, followers of certain accounts, and other criteria. You can set the tool to find and automatically invite people, groups, and communities to join you, based on various specifications. You will often use keywords as an attribute.

You can set the tool to auto-like, share, comment, or post to your own or other social profiles, based on keywords, followers of other accounts, and other attributes. You can manage multiple accounts and use proxies; and many other features are available.

Let's now shift our attention to tools of a different type, more specialized and tailored to a particular social channel. These are tools that do one thing but do it really well. All-in-one tools are great, until networks such as Instagram decide to make changes. All of a sudden, the tool you have been using for years becomes redundant. There is no better example than the recent legal stand taken by Instagram that led to the closure of two main players in the field, Mass Planner and Instagress. Even tools like Instamate became unavailable overnight, with no warning given. From another perspective, very often, your social strategy will be limited to specific social media channels, and you will need the best and most network-specific automation tools to deliver your goals.

Tweet Attacks Pro

TweetAttacksPro is one of the tools you may use to grow the number of your followers and manage your Twitter account on autopilot.

So what will the tool do for me?

Tweet Attacks Pro has some commonalities with Social Zen: follow, un-follow, follow back people based on keywords or followers of other people, and follow imported lists. For example, if you are in possession of an email list for your targeted audience, you can upload it to the tool and automatically follow your audience and connect with them on Twitter. One of the most advanced features is the ability to Tweet and Mention people based on keywords associated with your target audience. This is a way of building a relationship— remember the Ben Franklin effect? And it's another reason for people to check out your profile and reciprocate by following you in return. Similarly, another module provides the capability of retweeting tweets based on keywords associated with your target market. For example, you can set up the tool to retweet automatically tweets by people having the keyword SEO included in their profile; you can also specify how often the retweets should happen.

There are many more options you can use: send direct messages, auto-reply to new tweets, add mentions in a reply, spin content, search tweets and "favorite" them, and back up data automatically. There are also powerful filtering and search capabilities.

As with many other, similar tools, Tweet Attacks Pro doesn't necessarily look the part; however, this is one of the most complete tools available for managing Twitter. And yes, the name sounds very "black hat"; however, innovation is all about trying new things and keeping an open mind.

AutoSoci

AutoSoci is another Twitter automation tool providing various capabilities to manage your twitter account on autopilot. The tool helps you to find highly relevant and popular content; and it allows you to auto-schedule and automate your Twitter-content marketing, with the options to customize each tweet, add your own message, and more. The tool also provides the functionality of finding and joining high-performing lists based on keywords of your choice. Furthermore, follow and un-follow, mentioning, and retweeting are all options available, as well. In a nutshell, AutoSoci provides capability to both find great content and automate the growth of a highly targeted, relevant follower base on autopilot.

FanInviter

When people like one of your posts, that particular like is not converted to a like of your fan page. Basically, what this means is that someone has liked your great post, but the next time you post something, your new post may not be delivered to their timeline. The explanation is very simple. If you like my post it doesn't mean you also like my page. Facebook is obsessed with user experience; hence, it will not deliver my next post into your timeline, because it obsesses about keeping irrelevant stuff out of your timeline. In brief, for Facebook "less but more relevant" is better, and if you want more, then you should pay for it! Things are different when you like my fan page; in this case you will most likely get my next post into your timeline, as well.

So, the challenge is to convert your post likes into likes of your fan page. And what you will need to do to achieve this is invite people who like your post to like your page as well. You can of course do this manually; however, let's remember Pareto's law: focus your efforts on the 20 percent of the actions that will deliver 80 percent of your results. And of course, manually inviting people to like your page is not part of the 20 percent you will want to focus on!

Fan Inviter automates the task by bulk-inviting people who like your post to also like your page, so that your next post will reach and engage more people.

LinkedEngine

LinkedEngine is one of the most complete examples of LinkedIn social media automation software on the market. This tool will significantly improve your workflow, increase the reach of your LinkedIn content, and grow your account's follower base.

What does it do?

LinkedEngine provides you with the capability of finding groups and automatically sending join requests, based on a set of specifications you provide, keywords being one example. You will also have the ability to automatically search for and send invitations to people, based on attributes such as keywords, company, employer, or location. Auto post, spinning functionality, and many more features are available, as well.

One area where LinkedEngine excels is in speeding-up your email-list-building efforts fast. How? you may ask. LinkedEngine provides an option to download all the email addresses of your contacts. You can then upload them to your email marketing software of choice and launch your email marketing campaign. You may also use the list for remarketing purposes in Facebook, Google, or Bing, send messages to your contacts and your group members, and so forth. And, with a Premium membership you can send InMail messages to anyone on LinkedIn. Furthermore, you can download lists of group members and send them messages and invitations to connect. And of course, once they connect with you, you can download their email addresses as well. As mentioned, the features provided by the tool simply emulate the tasks you would normally perform manually. The invaluable benefit is that LinkedEngine does it faster and better, and it saves you the social media consultant's fee as well. It also enables you to focus on your 20 percent.

Octosuite

If your social media marketing plan includes Facebook, then Octosuite is one tool you can use to deliver your Facebook strategy. Octosuite provides many of the features already provided by SocialPilot, Social Zen, and Post Planner. It offers a content discovery area, where you can research Instagram, Pinterest and Twitter trends, thus focusing your efforts on creating relevant, engaging content. You can discover the most-shared content by keyword; and you can simply input a keyword and retrieve popular images from the relevant category, choose as many images as you want, customize them, post them, or schedule them. A copyright-free Images section is also included—very helpful when writing your blogs, posts, or creating or updating your website. You can also upload, edit and schedule your own images and posts. In the Image Editor section you can curate images, edit them within the tool, ad text, add a logo, and so forth. You can also add your comments and repost the image. The Video Editor section provides the same features as the Image Editor.

Two areas you will really find useful are Webinar replays and Training, providing great insights into how to maximize the usefulness of the tool and social media strategies in general.

Board Commander

If your strategy includes Pinterest, Board Commander is an all-in-one, easy-to- set-up tool, very similar to Octosuite. Like most other social media automation tools, Board Commander includes a follow/nofollow option, using attributes such as keywords, boards, or accounts. Board Commander also provides the option to search and post in popular group boards, set up RSS feeds, and schedule posts on autopilot. A set-up-once-and-forget tool. With the Graphics module you can edit and customize images, add text or logos, brand the images, and more.

If, for whatever reason, you decide against a DIY approach, then you can still save yourself a significant amount of agency fees by approaching some lower-cost companies. One example of such a company is https://socialupgrade.co/, which helps companies grow their Instagram network with targeted audiences; it offers packages from $39 per month. Similar services are available for most other social media networks, including Facebook. All you need to do is Google for a keyphrase such as "Get more Instagram Followers."

Finally, in the section on Psychology I proposed that sometimes you may want to purchase likes and followers, as a way of conferring social proof and trust on your profile. Also, I have argued that most people would not follow or connect to a profile which does not display evidence of social proof, such as number of connections or number of likes. You may have great content, yet people will not give you a try; after all, if you do not have connections or likes it must be for a reason, right? Thus, buying likes and followers can sometimes be a solution, as long as it is not abused. In order to buy fake likes and followers all you need doing is search in Google for "Buy Facebook Likes, Followers etc."

CHAPTER 15.
PAY PER CLICK ADVERTISING (PPC)

15.1 Google AdWords

When running paid search campaigns you will most likely use Google AdWords to deliver your commercial goals. This is because Google's market share within the paid search market is by far the largest. Furthermore, Google AdWords' smart algorithms improve by the day, driven by billions of interactions and observation of user behavior. And, if truth be told, Google is working hard on helping you to optimize your campaigns—after all, paid search revenue represents its prime source of income. Google's ability to profile audiences at the most granular level has often been thought of as creepy. However, for a marketer or business owner looking to grow their business, the amount of data held by Google on your potential audience members is a heaven-sent gift.

So, what is AdWords?

AdWords campaigns generally refer to two main paid search platforms: Google AdWords and Bing Ads. Due to their having the largest market shares— Google AdWords in particular—these platforms represent the de facto choice for marketers. They are also proven to provide the highest return on investment.

What is Google AdWords?

You will often run a Google AdWords campaign to complement your SEO efforts. As stated, Google has by far the highest market share of visitors, which by default makes Google AdWords the undisputed choice as a paid search platform.

How much do Google ads cost, and how does Google determine the cost per click (CPC)?

When Google AdWords was first introduced, marketers were able to run PPC campaigns at ridiculously low costs. As Google AdWords went mainstream and more marketers adopted the services, competition increased to the point where Google AdWords has become a highly competitive game. Nowadays, Google AdWords' costs can be quite high, but if your campaign is set up and managed in a professional manner the cost will worth it. The cost of Google AdWords depends on many factors, but generally revolves around the quality score of each keyword. You could easily assume that the more money you put in, the better your paid ranking position will be, but this would be a wrong assumption. While Google does generate most of its revenue via paid search, its model is sustainable only by maintaining and increasing its user base. That is why Google's primary goal is to deliver the best user experience. This is where keyword quality scores come in. When optimizing for keyword quality, you need to consider three areas: your ad text relevance to your targeted keyword, the bid per click, and the landing page's relevance to your keywords and ads. The more relevant these three pillars are, the lower your cost per click will be, and the better your ranking position in paid search results. In simple terms, the more your ad answers the query of the user, the more Google rewards you with better ranking and lower costs. Conversely, lower quality ads are placed lower down the paid search rankings, even though the bids per click may be higher. The idea is that, regardless of how much you may bid on a keyword, if people are not clicking on the ad, you earn no money for Google. In brief, you should obsessively work on improving your click-through rates and lowering your cost per click. Monitor and test various factors, such as ads text, CPC levels, devices, locations, and modifiers. The aim is to achieve optimal CTR for the lowest CPC. Of course, the more competition for the keyword, the more costly the keyword will be.

How does Google AdWords Work?

Before setting up your Google AdWords campaign, you must fully understand your company strategy, macro and micro, the long- and short-term goals. You will need to consider how paid search integrates with your overall business objectives, and how these objectives translate into digital marketing KPIs. You will need to conduct keyword research to discover keywords that will best match your digital marketing KPIs. In brief, your research will identify the right keywords, with the right search volume and the right potential to drive conversions to your business. For example, a translator offering German translation services would target a keyword such as "German translation services," as most people querying this term are searching for a German translator. By contrast, it would make no sense to bid on "online German translator," even though it may have a lower CPC and a higher search volume, as the intent of users is to find a Google-translate type of software. As with SEO, choosing the right keywords, with the right search volume and user intent is paramount in building your Google AdWords campaign. The same process and thoroughness you applied to your SEO keyword research must be applied to your paid search campaign, as well. After deciding on your keywords, you can proceed to set up and structure your campaign. This process includes setting up campaigns for your top-level goals, services or products, followed by setting up different ad groups within each campaign. Think of ad groups as representing the products, services and micro goals linked to your main campaign goals. If your campaign concerns translation services, then your ad groups would be "German translation services," "French translation services," and "Italian translation services." Within each ad group you would add your keywords and ads. Thus, in the "German translation services" ad group you could include keywords such as, "German translation services," "German translation solutions," and "German translator." You should set up at least two, but preferably three, ads per ad group, as a way to A/B split-test the group's efficiency and ensure that modifiers are being set for each keyword (broad,

272 | DIGITAL MARKETING MADE SIMPLE

exact match, and phrase match) and are relevant to the campaign goals. One task that is often overlooked is a comprehensive analysis of negative keywords. By adding negative keywords to your campaign, you will inform Google about the keywords you do not want your ad to be triggered for. Taking the example of the German translation services further, you would like to ensure that your ad is not being triggered for a query such as, "Free German translation services." Hence, you will set "free" as a negative keyword. Finally, please keep in mind that it is beyond the purpose of this book to provide in-depth training on using any of the tools presented. With regard to Google AdWords, providing a full training session on setting up the campaign is beyond my purpose. Entire books have been written on that subject alone. I would, however, like to point out that setting up and monitoring your campaign is not highly complex and is definitely within your DIY skills, once you have taken one of the many courses available on Udemy.

Is Google AdWords worth its cost?

Google AdWords is worth its cost. The key is in ensuring that your Google AdWords campaign is set up, monitored, and managed in a professional way. Far too often, campaigns are set up either by inexperienced business owners or marketers or by members of their families, under a DIY approach, and turn out to be unsuccessful. And, when the campaign is not delivering its KPIs, these business owners and marketers conclude that Google AdWords is not worth bothering with. The main point to remember is that choosing the right keywords with the right search volume and the right intent is essential in delivering your campaign goals. Obsess over the structure of your campaign, the settings, keyword modifiers, and negative keywords. Reach your target audience at the right time and you are a step closer to success. Improve your quality scores, test, refine, test again, and you will have a successful Google AdWords campaign. And, remember it is OK for you to take a DIY approach, but make sure you first take a Udemy course to understand the principles. Afterwards, the sky's the limit.

How to use Google AdWords

Too often, business owners looking for SEO services assume that SEO will guarantee first page placement of their website, and that this can be switched on and off at the push of a button. However, SEO is a long-term strategy; it takes time, hard work, continuous focus, and commitment. And it definitely is not a switch-on-and-off option. By contrast, Google AdWords is a switch-on-and-off alternative to SEO. In fact, Google AdWords should be part of your overall digital strategy, complementing SEO efforts. Google AdWords provides your website with instant presence and visibility, reaching your short-term goals of selling, getting more leads, and so forth. Google AdWords also provides the opportunity to target keywords your website is not being ranked for, and tailor your campaign to the user intent you are looking for. We have also seen that the top four positions in Google get more visibility and clicks than all the other positions on the page. Finally, it is common knowledge that well-run Google AdWords campaigns have far higher click-through and conversion rates, mainly due to an ability to tailor campaigns at a very granular level.

15.2 Bing Ads

One alternative to Google AdWords is Bing Ads. In spite of Bing's far lower market share of users, distributing your budget between Bing Ads and Google AdWords generally makes sense at an initial stage in a campaign. This enables you to split test results on key metrics, gain insights on various performance metrics, and refine, improve or change your paid search strategies and assess which search engine works best for you.

What is Bing Ads?

Bing Ads is Microsoft's alternative to the Google AdWords platform. Bing advertising is generally deployed as a second choice by marketers. This is attributed both to its lower market share of users, and to a perception of a less-action-oriented user base. It is a widely believed that action-oriented users, providing sales, enquiries, and leads, are mostly using Google, while Bing users are perceived as information seekers.

Does Bing Ads cost more than Google AdWords or less?

Many business owners and marketers believe that due to Bing's smaller market share of users, the costs of running a paid search campaign will be lower. This belief is a myth. The cost of Bing Ads is determined by similar factors to Google AdWords: keyword quality scores, bidding strategies, competition for the keyword.

How does Bing Ads work?

The principles described in the Google AdWords section apply to Bing advertising as well. A smart feature distinguishing Bing Ads from Google AdWords is the Import function provided by Bing. With this feature you can import your current Google AdWords campaign into Bing Ads with just a few clicks. The obvious benefit is that less time is spent on building your Bing campaign. Another benefit is that you gain the ability to A/B split the results of your campaign at search-engine level. This could in turn lead to a change in your paid search strategies, should Bing deliver better results than Google. You could, for example, decide to optimize your campaigns based on discovering that some campaigns deliver better results in Bing, while other campaigns may perform better on Google. We have to acknowledge the spirit of entrepreneurship displayed by Bing; it could have been ruled by pride and made no reference to Google AdWords. Instead, it decided to be humble, acknowledge Google's paid-search dominance and make it easy for marketers to import their Google campaigns, and it stole market share in the process.

How should I use Bing Ads?

You could run Google and Bing advertising simultaneously, thus gaining an extra level of A/B split testing at search-engine level. While running such testing, you will most likely identify opportunities to improve your overall paid search results. Possible examples are: lower costs on one or the other search engine; or better click-through and/or conversion rates and lead generation on various campaigns, perhaps using different ad groups, keywords, or demographics. This provides opportunities to further optimize your overall paid search campaign—by picking the winning campaigns or ad groups on each engine, for example. There really is no reason why you should not give Bing Ads a try, along with Google AdWords, unless you have a low budget and you would rather focus your budget on either Bing or Google advertising exclusively.

15.3 Amazon Advertising

You would be surprised at the number of digital marketing agencies and companies that overlook the opportunity to advertise on Amazon. Amazon has grown to be a search engine in its own right, and with an active base of over 285 million customers, it represents an untapped opportunity to both grow market share and create new business models. On Amazon you can run product-boost advertising campaigns, brand identity campaigns, and advertising campaigns for increasing the number of app downloads.

What is Amazon advertising?

The Amazon Advertising Platform (AAP) is one of the most overlooked PPC platforms I have come across during my career. Many digital marketing agencies, consultants, and business owners do not see Amazon as a search engine. However, with over 285 million active users, Amazon is beyond any doubt a search engine in its own right. Amazon advertising works on the same principles as Google AdWords and Bing Ads. It uses a pay-per-click business model, enabling Amazon sellers to reach searchers on Amazon websites and through mobile apps. A highly effective way of placing your products in various areas of Amazon's website, such as at the top of the results for a relevant query, in side bars, at the bottom of the page, or even inside your competitors' product pages.

How does Amazon advertising work?

Amazon advertising provides the opportunity to achieve the following goals: increase your product sales on Amazon; drive traffic to your website; and increase mobile application downloads. Various types of ads are available, as well. Product display ads appear on the product detail page, on the right rail of search results, at the bottom of search results, on the customer-reviews page, on the "read all reviews" page, at the top of the offer-listing page and in Amazon-generated marketing emails, such as follow ups and recommendations. Headline search ads, in contrast, appear at the top of search ads on Amazon's first page every time you win the auction for your targeted keyword. Sponsored product ads are keyword-targeted ads placed throughout the Amazon website and are designed to draw attention to your product from visitors searching for your keywords. This is the closest thing to Google and Bing advertising.

How much does Amazon advertising cost?

The cost differs depending on the type of ad you want to run. The criteria for determining your ranking position are similar to those for Google and Bing. On Amazon advertising, however, the focus is more on the bidding. Specifically, when bidding for a product, you enter into an auction, and your ranking position depends mostly on whether you win the auction. Of course, keyword and ad relevance are also important, but generally, the higher you bid the more chance you have of outbidding your competitors, winning the auction, and achieving a higher ranking. Different costs are associated with the different types of ads you can run on the Amazon advertising platform. If you are running an Amazon display ad, then the minimum CPC accepted for product displays is $0.02 with a minimum $100 budget for all campaigns and a minimum of $1 per day. For a headline Amazon ad the minimum CPC accepted is $0.10 and a minimum $100 budget per campaign and $1 per day. There is no minimum CPC cap for sponsored product ads and the ads are served depending on your daily and monthly budget.

Why should I use Amazon advertising?

Amazon is a highly untapped paid search opportunity, compared with Google AdWords or Bing Ads. For this reason, advertising on Amazon offers both competitive advantage and fantastic opportunities to improve your sales. If your goal is personal branding rather than profit, then you are in the right place at Amazon—the more you bid, the more exposure your book, product, or service will get.

15.4 eBay Advertising

eBay advertising is yet another untapped opportunity to grow your business or create new business models. As in the case of Amazon advertising, you will find that many marketers are either unaware of or dismiss the opportunities created by advertising on eBay. Most marketers prefer to focus on what they know best, that is, Google AdWords and Bing Ads.

What is eBay advertising?

eBay advertising is an overlooked opportunity for brand owners and companies to place their products in front of over 159 million potential customers, targeting the right people, at the right time, with the right behavioral intent. It offers promotion via ads and via programmatic display. As with Amazon advertising, search online for digital marketing agencies and you will quickly find that their services are mostly limited to Google AdWords, Bing Ads, Facebook advertising, and LinkedIn ads. Hence, a great opportunity for you to leapfrog the competition and steal market share via Amazon and eBay advertising.

How does eBay advertising work?

As opposed to Amazon advertising where a pay-per-click model is employed, eBay uses a pay-per-sale model. This means that you only pay a commission, which is based on the total price, when one of your items is sold. The obvious benefit is that you only pay per sale rather than paying on each click. The downside is that you pay a higher unit rate than you would pay in a cost-per-click model. That being said, the seller can set their own rate of commission at anywhere between 1 percent and 20 percent, depending on the amount they are willing to pay. Depending on the ad rate set by the seller, the ads may appear on the first page in 4th and 5th positions, for example, and then lower down as the ad rates set by the seller decrease. As the commission is a percentage of the sale, you can easily calculate the impact on your margins before setting up your bid. Another factor influencing the cost of eBay ads is the level of competition; the more companies with products similar to yours, the more pressure to raise your ad rate, and the higher the cost. Conversely, less competition means lower ad rates and lower costs.

15.5 What to expect from a PPC agency

You will often find that digital marketing agencies launch paid-search campaigns with little involvement on your part as a client. They will then report back to you the results in a weekly or fortnightly call, and the truth is you will have little visibility of your campaign or understanding of whether it is maximizing your ROI. You should not accept the situation; you must be involved directly with the agency in building your campaign; ask questions, understand details, such as keywords, bidding strategies, A/B split test practices, reporting, and the search queries that are bringing clicks to your website. A rough outline of the process of setting up your paid search campaign is presented below.

Agree Strategy

Your paid search strategy must align with your short- and long-term goals. Combining long-term strategies such as search engine optimization with immediate results via paid search will deliver both short-term and sustainable results. At this stage you decide on the paid search channels most relevant to reaching your KPIs, or whether paid search is the right strategy for you in the first place. You conduct a comprehensive keyword analysis and decide on the most relevant terms to bid on. When choosing your keywords you will consider factors such as user intent, volume potential, competition, and cost. Equally important, you will also determine what your negative keywords are, ensuring your ads will not be served to irrelevant queries.

The nitty-gritty

The time has come for building your paid search campaigns. Whether you will be running advertising on Google, Bing, Amazon, or eBay you must define the right audience with the right intent, and the right time to reach it. You will build audience segments, create campaigns, ad groups, ads, and keyword match types and extensions. You will set up bidding strategies and landing pages, research for negative keywords, set demographics rules, and so forth. You must ensure that comprehensive tracking is set up to measure results. This will include traditional tools, such as Google or Bing analytics, but also heat mapping, live user behavior recordings, events, A/B split tests, and some of the other third-party tools we have discussed in the Data Insights chapter.

Launch and refine your campaign

Once the preparation work has been completed, it is time to launch your paid search campaign. You must monitor the performance of your campaigns, ad groups and keywords regularly. Some metrics you will want to keep a close eye on are: number of clicks, click-through rates, costs per click and per acquisition, bounce rates, time on site metrics, market shares, quality scores, ad rankings, A/B split testing results, and funnels. Most importantly, you must also review your search queries regularly; a high number of clicks will not deliver leads if the queries are not relevant to your goals. Thus, you want to make sure that your budget is not being wasted on irrelevant queries. This generally occurs when a comprehensive negative keyword analysis has not been performed prior to launching the campaign, or keywords and settings are too broad. Hence, monitor your search queries regularly, and optimize your campaign by adding new negative keywords to your list. No stone should be left unturned if you want to ensure that your campaign is optimized for maximum clicks, relevant results, and the lowest cost per click possible.

Overall, reviewing these areas is really not a difficult process, but I guarantee that if you are employing an agency and you keep them on their toes, you will see beyond the fog of pretentious jargon and get more leads and conversions.

CHAPTER 16.
NATIVE ADVERTISING

Native Advertising is one type of ad that has been growing massively over the years. For practical purposes in this section I will focus on one of the six categories of native ads you will are most likely to use, which is sponsored content. To best explain sponsored content let us consider your experience of reading an online article in a highbrow newspaper. Specifically, focus on reaching the end of the article. What sort of content is served below the article? The answer is that you will most often see several sponsored articles relevant to the theme of the article you have just been reading. This is sponsored content, and in this section I will be providing you with information and tools to assist you in placing this type of content in many online magazines and newspapers, with no help from a digital marketing agency or consultant. The process is simple and intuitive, and you can save you the consultant fees. As always, I recommend a bit of research; viewing a YouTube video should be sufficient for you to familiarize yourself with any of these tools. Finally, let me point out a couple of things that make sponsored content so powerful. Firstly, in the section on psychology we discussed the principle of association. In our case, sponsored content piggybacks on the authority of the hosting publication, as people associate the quality of the publication with your article. Think about the publication as social proof, extending its authority to your sponsored content. Secondly, given the high authority of the publication, people label your content as being of good quality prior to actually reading it. Expectations change perceptions, and subconsciously people will have already decided that your article is of high authority; after all it wouldn't have been in that publication if it weren't. And, given this perception, confirmation bias kicks in, with people often confirming their expectations. So, there you go...three powerful principles you can leverage through Native Advertising.

So, how do I start?

Outbrain Amplify

Outbrain Amplify is the leading sponsored-content marketing platform, providing the opportunity of tapping a target market that, while not displaying a commercial intent, does have an interest in your industry and the theme of your article.

How much does Outbrain sponsored content cost?

The cost per click (CPC) in Outbrain is determined by two factors: competition and the performance of your campaign. When a high number of articles compete for the same space, industry, or related pages then your cost per click increases. If the CTR rate for your article is high, then you will often be able to optimize your CPC and lower your overall costs, as you are making money for Outbrain. Outbrain recommends a starting CPC of £0.5, and running the campaign for couple of weeks before optimizing it based on results.

What content can I amplify on Outbrain?

As your content is being recommended on premium publisher platforms, it must by written to a professional standard. Outbrain has a very strict system in operation to ensure that the content being published is of high quality. Most content amplified via Outbrain is articles and blog posts.

Which sites will my content appear on?

Outbrain partners with a large number of publishers; too many to name them all here. As a guideline, some publishers working with Outbrain are Fortune, The Daily Telegraph, Sky News, The Washington Post, Rodale, CNN, ESPN, Spiegel Online, Mashable, Le Monde, Fox News, and People.

Why should I use Outbrain Amplify?

The obvious benefits of amplifying your content on Outbrain is higher traffic and the promoting of your brand in front of people with an interest in your industry. Some of those people may seek your services at a later date. Access to premium publishers is another reason for using Outbrain; you would normally find it very difficult and expensive to reach such publishers' audiences in an organic way. Moreover, as more people discover your content, the more opportunities there are for people to link to your website, if your content is relevant for them.

Why should my article be optimized for SEO?

To begin with, by optimizing your article for SEO you will have a greater chance of ranking your content for SEO and helping search engines to understand the theme of your website. You will most likely experience an increase in relevant traffic and time-on-site metrics—overall, a positive SEO impact for your website.

To further understand the reason for optimizing your Outbrain-sponsored article, simply consider how Outbrain's algorithms work. Outbrain promotes your sponsored content on pages where it will be similar to or relevant to the other content on that page of the publisher's website. Specifically, Outbrain's algorithms match your article to the theme of the publisher's page by taking into consideration factors such as keyword density and backlinks. Of course, this is an oversimplification of the metrics considered by Outbrain's algorithms. Now, just as in the case of Google AdWords or Bing Ads, Outbrain is in the business of making money. If it serves your content, but people aren't clicking on it, Outbrain concludes that your content it is not relevant and reduces its visibility, or simply stops showing it. Similarly, let's assume that, for whatever reason, people click through to your website, but find your article to be irrelevant to them. Visitors leave your website, impacting negatively on your time-on-site and bounce rates. This may in turn signal Google that your website is not relevant to the keywords associated with the industry, the theme, or the keywords on the publisher's page. So you must ensure that your article is relevant, has click-through-optimized titles and content, and has the potential to act as a "link magnet" to your website. Of course, quality is key, and your article will not get past a moderator if the content does not meet the quality standards of the publisher.

How does the Outbrain platform work?

Outbrain Amplify is a pay-per-click content-discovery platform, allowing readers of material from premium publishers such as CNN, The Telegraph, and Sky News to discover content related to the content they have already been reading. But why do premium publishers allow sponsored content on their websites? Well, as you have probably guessed, it's partly because people don't read as much news in a paper format as they once did. This situation impacts directly on the advertising revenue of the publishers. Moreover, in digital form, the advertising space is far more flexible and there is more of it available compared with the paper version; hence, a good source of advertising money for the publishers. Finally, machine learning algorithms enable publishers to tailor their ads and improve ROI by harnessing the power of hyper-targeting, segmentation, and A/B split testing, then utilizing the huge amount of data gathered on the performance of campaigns.

How does it work in practice?

You start by writing an article that is relevant to your goals and optimized for SEO. You publish it on your blog. You set up an Outbrain campaign which includes the URL path to your article, the title of the article, and the image to display when your sponsored content is served. You can now set your CPC bid and hit Start. After launching your campaign, Outbrain matches your content to relevant pages on the website of its partner publishers. At this stage, it is important that your article is optimized for the target keywords and theme.

Well-optimized content delivers relevant placements and higher click-through rates.

You will also A/B split test the performance of your article. Some changes you can split test are: the name of the article, the text, images, videos, location, and platform targeting. You can try different URLs and new articles and Outbrain recommends split testing around 10 different URLs. You could also test different CPC points; this involves duplicating your current campaign and changing the CPC in line with your split-testing strategy. Throughout your campaign, Outbrain monitors the performance of your content. If your sponsored post is often clicked on, you make Outbrain money; hence, it will show your content more often. You will most likely be able to reduce your CPC, as well. If, on the other hand, your content is not being clicked on often enough, then Outbrain may reduce your article's visibility or stop serving it, as you are not making them any money.

How do I ensure that my finance article doesn't end up on a sports page?

Write a finance-relevant article and optimize for SEO. Outbrain crawls your page, learns what your content is about, and serves it on the most relevant publishers' pages related to your subject.

Can I shut off some of the publications?

Currently, Outbrain allows you to exclude up to 30 publishers per account via their dashboard. Outbrain advises against shutting off publications, as this affects the performance of your campaign, limiting the number of impressions. In brief, they argue that their content-marketing services will be made inefficient by reducing exposure. In reality, the main reason revolves around the potential of not getting your budget spent. While you care about where you traffic comes from, Outbrain is also a business, and they need to make money. Following this line of thought, the more clicks to your article, the more money they make. You should regularly monitor the situation and shut off various publications in order to optimize your campaign and get more clicks from websites that are more relevant to your content, targeted audience, behavioral intent, and brand identity.

Taboola Content Discovery

Taboola Content Discovery is the main native advertising competitor to Outbrain Amplify. The benefit of using both Taboola and Outbrain is that they partner with two different sets of premium publishers. Hence, your sponsored content will be more visible and reach more publishers when using both Taboola and Outbrain. You should run native advertising campaigns on both Taboola and Outbrain, compare the results at a platform level, and optimize accordingly.

How much does Taboola Content Discovery sponsored content cost?

The CPC for your piece of content depends on answering one question—to state things in a simplistic way, of course—are you making Taboola money? In a more technical manner what this means is that the higher the click-through rate to your article, the more money you make for Taboola; hence, the more Taboola will show your content. A popular article with a high click-through rate is a great opportunity to split test lower cost-per-click rates—Taboola prefers more clicks for lower cost per click to content generating more revenue overall. Another piece of the puzzle is the amount of competition for the space relevant to your targeted audience—the more competitors bidding, the higher the cost.

What content can I amplify on Taboola?

Taboola works with premium publishers, hence your content must meet the quality standards of those publishers. Very strict editorial policies are in force to ensure that only the best content is served. After all, the publishers would not approve bad content. Even assuming that it were approved, bad content would not attract clicks, and, hence, it would not make Taboola any money.

What publishers does Taboola work with?

Taboola works with a wide range of premium publishers, too many to list them all here. As a guideline, some of the many publishers working with Taboola are MSN, BBC, USA Today, and The Boston Globe.

How many variations of the title and images should I A/B split test per piece?

Taboola recommends a minimum of 10 variations of titles and images. I find this excessive; 3 or 4 variations should be fine.

Can I run sponsored content campaigns in specific locations?

Demographic targeting is a feature provided by both Taboola and Outbrain; hence, you can refine target audiences based on location specifications such as country, town, or postcode. Both platforms are looking to extend targeting options to a programmatic level, an exciting opportunity indeed.

How do Taboola algorithms decide which page my content appears on?

The same process that happens in Outbrain operates in Taboola. Taboola crawls your article, discovers the theme of the content, the keywords and contexts, and other on-page factors. In a nutshell Taboola figures out what your article is about, then matches your content to relevant pages on the publishers' platforms. You should not worry that your article might appear on irrelevant pages. In fact, Taboola's best interest is in ensuring that your content is relevant to the page. After all, if readers of a finance page are served an article on sports, nobody will click on it, and Taboola makes no money.

Should I use Taboola Content Discovery or Outbrain Amplify?

You should use both Taboola and Outbrain. Taboola and Outbrain have exclusive contracts with premium publishers; hence, you will increase the number of publishers you reach. Moreover, you can split test the performance of the two platforms based on various KPIs, such as CPC, number of visits, conversions, time on site, bounce rate, visitor intent, and so forth.

CHAPTER 17.
REMARKETING

What is Remarketing?

Remarketing, or retargeting, is the process of reaching customers who have visited your website but may not have taken the action you intended them to take. Examples of actions you may want visitors to take are: buying a product, buying a service, and submitting an enquiry. To understand remarketing in practice, simply reflect on your own browsing experience. How many times have you visited a website and navigated away from it, only to be followed around the Internet by a banner advertising the product that you have seen on that earlier website? Have you been looking for a pair of earrings on Amazon, then logged in to your email account or visited a sports page? Do you see an image of the earrings on your screen, even when you are not logged in to Amazon? You have just been remarketed.

How does it work?

It starts with someone visiting your website when you are running a remarketing campaign. They reach a page, and a cookie—a small piece of code—is dropped into their browser. Yes, they have just received a cookie, and you are going to remarket to them, using a well-established procedure. Remarketing works by gently, and sometimes not so gently, reinforcing a brand message, always there, always reminding a person to take action. The great benefit is that at the remarketing stage, users have already visited your website and they know about your product or service—you don't need to promote it to them. Your aim is not to raise awareness but, rather, to nudge previous visitors to your website into taking an action.

Google and Bing display advertising

Google is the undisputed leader when it comes to remarketing services. It has both the world's largest user base and the world's largest display network. This means more eyes on your website, more cookies, and more re-targeting opportunities. Google AdWords is also the most comprehensive paid search platform, giving you the ability to tailor your campaign down to the most granular level. Google is also a leader in the field of advanced machine learning technology. This technology is being developed for one purpose and one purpose only: to provide great user experience; and that implies making your campaign successful. In the end, happy users + happy advertisers = more money for Google. Bing advertising emulates the service provided by Google, though as we showed, it is most often a second choice.

Facebook remarketing

Facebook remarketing works on similar lines to Google AdWords, while also simplifying the process of building your campaign. Simply create your custom audiences, place your Facebook remarketing pixel on your website and start collecting "cookies." You can then retarget those cookies to convert them into leads. It hardly needs saying that this a powerful option, providing access to the biggest social media user base and to Facebook's partner websites. However, where Facebook excels is in the granularity you can apply to defining and selecting your audiences, and the high level of insights into their behavior that you can acquire. Facebook's Audience Insights tool is a gift brought to the whole of humanity... or shall we just say, to digital marketers?

AdRoll remarketing

AdRoll Retargeting is a market leading platform offering another alternative to remarketing services offered by Google, Bing, and Facebook. It works in the same way as the Google and Facebook tools: a visitor reaches your website page, a cookie is dropped into their browser, the visitor exits your website, and they are subsequently followed around by a bespoke remarketing ad nudging them to take action. What makes AdRoll really attractive for remarketing services is the variety of platforms that this company partners with: Instagram, Facebook, and over 30 other platforms. AdRoll provides a lot of flexibility and can be used in split tests against the remarketing services of Google, Bing, or Facebook. I particularly like their integration with Facebook, which enables remarketing on Facebook.

Native Ads Remarketing

We have previously discussed the power of native advertising. As a reminder, native advertising enables webmasters to reach the audiences of premium publishers, and it works on a pay-per-click model. Outbrain and Taboola are two content marketing platforms we reviewed in the paid search section. Both platforms offer the opportunity to remarket to people that have been reading your sponsored content. In practice, you amplify content via Taboola or Outbrain, and your content is then placed in publications such as The Daily Telegraph. John is reading your content, a cookie is dropped into his browser, and he is then subjected to remarketing.

CHAPTER 18.
EMAIL MARKETING

Email lists are one of the most important assets you can build for your business. Many opportunities are available for building your lists; your existing clients are one example. The following practices and tools will enable you to take advantage of innovative ideas, targeting specific markets and building highly targeted lists. Sure, they are not perfect; you will need to work on them, sort them, split them, or combine them. Some of the tools presented may of course fall within the grey hat or black hat area. The important point to remember is that the descriptions of these tools are targeted at raising your awareness of the ideas behind them. And, as with many tools presented in the book, do ensure that you undertake in-depth research, in order to maximize the impact of the tools and to avoid unexpected surprises. OK, time to turn our attention to the tools and ideas behind them.

MailZingo

MailZingo is a piece of email marketing software that boasts a large number of features, including easy campaign creation, unlimited emails and subscribers, A/B split test campaigns, and customization of emails, along with great analytics and a really-easy-to-use dashboard. Moreover, in contrast to MailChimp, AWeber and other similar software, there is only a one-time low charge, meaning no recurring costs.

SendinBlue

There are two main features that MailZingo does not offer if you are looking to run larger and more-complex email marketing campaigns. The first feature is the ability to create "If This, then That" segments and funnels; that is, create different funnels depending on the actions taken by the audience. For example, you may need to run a campaign and set up 10 different funnels: if a person opened the initial email, you would follow with another email within one day, offering an "Ultimate Guide"; if the initial email was not opened, you would follow with a great article, driving attention to the blog. If the person opened the initial email, then downloaded the guide, you would send another email, introducing your newly launched product. If, however, the person opened the first email but did not open the "Ultimate Guide" email, you might decide to send another email, including a very interesting article about the impact of AI in their particular industry. To sum up, setting up "If This, then That" campaigns is one advantage SendinBlue has over MailZingo.

The second feature offered by SendinBlue in contrast to MailZingo is the ability to set up SMS campaigns for highly affordable prices. With prices as low as £15 per month for up to 40,000 emails, SendinBlue is by far the most affordable email-marketing provider available.

The two tools I have presented have the advantage of being both cost effective and efficient. They are, however, at a disadvantage in one particular area compared with the larger, more established services: lack of integrations. Indeed, if integrations is something you are looking for, e.g. with Salesforce, Eventbrite, Google, Twitter, Facebook, Shopify, SurveyMonkey, or any one of many more, then you will most likely want to consider MailChimp or AWeber. Moreover, if your email list is not extensive then MailChimp offers a great free plan that includes up to 2,000 subscribers and 12,000 emails per month. It is, in fact, why most SMEs I work with use MailChimp for their email marketing services.

Rapid Mailer

Another great email marketing software option for WordPress websites is Rapid Mailer. To begin with, it installs as a plugin on your website, allowing you to manage your entire email marketing campaign on autopilot from within your WordPress website. You can import lists, add leads automatically, and great quality templates. Granted, the library of templates is not as extensive as with MailChimp or AWeber, but it is sufficient to run highly professional campaigns for a very low one-off fee. There is a great analytics dashboard, which includes information on metrics, such as open rates, clicks, bounces, unsubscribes, and so on. Another great feature of Rapid Mailer is its integrations with third-party senders like SendGrid and Amazon Web Services. In fact, this feature ensures that your inbox deliverability rate is optimized at all times, and your emails are delivered to the inbox, rather than the spam folder, of your target. Rapid Mailer also provides powerful integration with social media channels and various landing page providers.

Content Nitrous plugin

You will appreciate the Content Nitrous plugin if your website is built on a WordPress platform.

What does it do?

Well, it allows you to build a three-step funnel that aids the success of your email marketing, The first step in the funnel is whitelisting your email address; then the second is registering for a free webinar; and the third step is inviting people to join your Facebook group.

Let us briefly review the three steps and the ideas behind them.

Step 1 - Whitelisting your email address ensures that every time you email your subscribers the email reaches their inbox, rather their spam folder.

Step 2 - By encouraging people to sign up for a free webinar, you capture emails, build rapport, provide value, upsell, retarget, and so forth.

Step 3 – Inviting people to a Facebook group builds a community of like-minded people who actively signed up to receive your content, and creates peer support. You will find this step creates a dozen other great advantages, I am sure.

Content Nitrous is easy to use, and having the functionality to access it directly within your WordPress website is a real time-saver.

Let's now turn our attention to some of the more advanced email marketing platforms and tools available. There is no doubt that there are several contenders for market leader when considering your email marketing options. MailChimp, AWeber, Drip, and GetResponse are some of them. Most of these platforms offer free and paid plans, though free plans are quite restrictive. And when looking to purchase a paid plan, it can get fairly expensive.

Hence, if you are a price-conscious marketer or entrepreneur you may want to consider some of the more affordable options.

ColdLeadz

ColdLeadz is a piece of software that can significantly boost your email list in highly targeted niches. Input your keyword, choose your preferred search engine (Google or Bing), choose a social media network from the nine choices provided, the email provider (e.g., Gmail or Outlook), the location, and the range of pages you would like the tool to scrape (e.g. pages 1-5, 6-10, or 1-10). Click "Get Prospects," and your screen is populated with thousands of emails relevant to the keyword and settings you have chosen. Repeat the process for Outlook and other email providers. How many emails will you have at your fingertips? Remember, these are emails of people or businesses that are relevant to your targeted keyword. The tool has a module allowing you to scrape one or multiple websites for email addresses simply by inputting the URL of the website. And, an option called Email Validator ensures that all your emails are valid, preventing low delivery rates. Finally, access to over 40 different SEO tools is provided, encouraging you to use these tools as lead magnets for your audience.

Discover

Another fantastic tool, which works on the same principles as ColdLeadz, is Discover. Input your keyword to the search bar, choose the social media platform you intend to scrape, and the location, and select all results displaying website addresses. The kind of information you can get is email addresses, email profiles, number of backlinks pointing to the website, mobile responsiveness, and the number of keywords in the top 20 results. Take as an example LinkedIn. Let us assume for a moment that you are targeting marketing managers as the audience for one of your products. You type "Marketing Manager" in the tool, choose LinkedIn as an option, run it, select some or all of the results and click Run again. You will now be served with email addresses of the target companies or people. OK, so you have all these details....what next? The tool has an automation module incorporated, as well, a really helpful feature. Simply select the companies or people you would like to target and add them to a pipeline/list. You can now create your funnel—the tool provides the ability to create different steps and automation rules, driving people through the funnel. The tool integrates with the main autoresponders or with automation software such as Zapier. But what is really powerful is that once your pipeline is set up, you can automate your search; the software crawls the net and adds new email addresses based on the settings you have specified and moves the contacts through the pipeline funnel.

Mobile Lead Monster

You will recall my example of Hotel Sales Managers walking the car park of competitor hotels looking for leads or attending networking events with very little commercial impact on the business. The truth is that far too many outdated and inefficient commercial practices are still being used today. One tool you can use for local lead generation is Mobile Lead Monster. Its interface is not great, but its simplicity is. We have already discussed competitor-benchmarking practices such as competitor-backlink analysis and social-media and brand-mention monitoring. Simply input your location, the keyword best describing your target market—e.g., doctor, dentist—set up the radius of the area you want to prospect and click Start. The tool generates a list of all local businesses relevant to your keyword, their websites, business addresses and even email addresses. And it performs all tasks by leveraging the API of Google Places. You can also preview your competitors' mobile websites from within the tool, export lists, remove duplicates and build your email lists. Two other modules provided within the tool are Citation and Online listings, which can enhance your understanding of strategies employed by your competitors or prospects at a local level. Finally, another great feature that will simplify your workflow is the ability to email your prospective clients from within the tool.

Biz Lead Finder Ultimate Edition

Another tool similar to Mobile Lead Monster is Biz Lead Finder, This is a more complete solution than Mobile Lead Monster. The tool provides the following information on local businesses:

- Businesses with Google Maps errors

- Whether a business has a website or not

- Business name, website URL, email address, physical address, phone number

- Whether a business has a mobile-friendly website or not, and if the website ranks well

- Information on a business's reputation score

- A business's Facebook, Twitter, and LinkedIn pages.

If you are looking at prospecting potential local leads then this is one tool you will often use. You can use these tools to gain a top-level understanding of your local prospects. Afterwards, tools like SEO PowerSuite, SEMrush and

Raven Tools will provide you with more in-depth information, allowing you to build the profiles of your prospects.

EmailScraperChief.com

I once attended a webinar run by a black hat marketer who was trying to sell a seriously overpriced tool. Instinctively I agreed with one point during the webinar, which was that you should avoid reliance on third parties when building your business model. One example that comes to mind is over-reliance on pay per click as a mean of generating leads; it will most often result in increased costs over time, lower margins, and pressure on your business. This marketer emphasized the importance of keeping control of your business, and that building assets such as targeted email lists was essential. You may not fully grasp the importance of this powerful insight; however, recently Facebook and Instagram have forced out of business several high-profile social growth automation companies including Instagress and Mass Planner. Many users who had been building their business model around these tools were hard hit when this happened. Hence, back to email lists: several strategies are available to support you in building your lists, and one involves a tool called EmailScraperChief. Like many tools in the field, this one focuses on functionality rather than on look and feel.

What does it do?

In a nutshell, the tool scrapes the Internet for email addresses. You can scrape selected websites, specific search engines, or the entire Web. Furthermore, you can scrape the Web according to specified keywords, eliminate keywords, or scrape only websites including specific keywords. Finally, you can export your list in Excel, remove duplicates, filter your list, and prepare your list for launch. Official Lead Grabber and Email Findr are two other tools you might use for email scraping purposes; they provide very similar functionality as does EmailScraperChief. If you are looking for market leading email-finder tools, then Hunter.io and VoilaNorbert are by far the most popular tools available. Of course, do remember our conversation on the process of engaging people and decide case by case whether this approach is worthwhile. Think of this as a cold-call approach.

SMS Leads Puller

SMS Leads Puller is a tool offering the same capability as the email-scraping tools we have been discussing, with the difference that it scrapes the Web for phone numbers. An option is also provided to upload your own lists of phone numbers. Furthermore, you can set up and run SMS campaigns. For example, you may send SMS messages to all the phone numbers on a list.

Bananatag

We have spoken about the different tools and platforms you can use to manage email marketing campaigns. All these tools include comprehensive analytics of metrics, such as number of emails opened, opening rates, and click-through rates. But what if you are not running a standard email marketing campaign? What if, for whatever reason, you need to email people personally? These people may include your boss, your colleagues, your clients, your friends, or your business partners. How will you track their responses to your emails, and how will you determine your follow-up action? Should you call them, or should you allow them more time to read the email you sent two days ago? As an example, consider the following scenario. You send an email to your boss and await a reply. Your boss might open your email but not get back to you. If you were aware of the situation, you might give him a call or send him a follow-up email. However, an alternative is that your boss has yet to open the original email, in which case you might decide to allow more time before following up. This is where Bananatag comes in; it provides you with the ability to track what happens with your emails after you have sent them, generates in-depth metrics and reports, and sends you reminders and notifications. Another tool providing similar functionality is Mailtrack.io.

Boomerang for Gmail

Boomerang for Gmail provides similar functionality to Bananatag and Mailtrack.io, but it is its email-writing feature that really distinguishes it. Simply start writing your email title or body and a set of heat map bars provides you with information on whether your title or word count is too long, the reading level, and the number of questions. Boomerang also provides an advanced feature indicating the levels of positivity, politeness, and subjectivity of an email.

Sales Navigator for Gmail

Sales Navigator for Gmail is a very useful widget plugin displaying information about your contacts right inside your inbox. The information includes: image of the person you are emailing, where the person is based, where they work, and their position. All info is collected by accessing your contacts' LinkedIn profile details and social media information.

Yet another essential aspect of your email marketing campaign is the delivery percentage of your emails. You will want to ensure that as many of your emails as possible are delivered to the inboxes, rather than to the spam folders of your target audience.

Unlock The Inbox

Many marketers and business owners fail to understand, or disregard the importance of, tools such as Unlock The Inbox. The tool provides a complete solution to monitoring the health of your email marketing campaign.

How does it look in practice?

You work hard and create great content, amplify it, and grow your email list. You are now ready to start your email marketing campaign. However, before launching your campaign you should consider the number of emails that will bounce back for reasons such as the email address not being valid anymore, or your email being blacklisted by an addressee for whatever reason. How many emails will be delivered to the spam folders of you audience? If you are like most people, you will probably consider these metrics only after you have begun your campaign, when it is probably too late to fully optimize its delivery rates. To explain the importance of this step, let me draw a parallel with Google's ranking factors and signals on determining the relevancy of a website. Email providers also use algorithms for ranking the relevance of the email sender. Have too many emails bouncing back marked as spam, invalid, or blacklisted, and your emails will likely be delivered to the spam box. And all that great content, amplification, and list-building effort will have been wasted. To sum up: you should think about the optimization of your email campaigns in the same way you will ensure that your website is technically optimized. Let's call this step "Technical Email Marketing." Of course, all major email marketing providers like Mailchimp, Aweber or SendinBlue have this facility inbuilt.

VerifyEmailAddress.org

You can use the VerifyEmailAddress tool to verify that all emails on your list are valid before commencing your email marketing campaign, thus improving your Email "spam score."

CHAPTER 19.
COMPETITOR BENCHMARKING

Competitor benchmarking in its current form is outdated in many businesses I have been a consultant for. Remember the traditional hotel benchmarking tool in the form of car park walks with your sales manager, making notes about the clients of your competitor? This is still in operation in most hotel businesses. On reflection, how many times has this competitor benchmarking action brought you a lead or a client? Instinctively, you know it does not work and yet you continue to do it; after all, you need to show your boss and his boss what you do, and the more of it you do, the better. Right? The next sections will teach you how to benchmark your competition using tools and practices you have already been learning about in the previous chapters. In this section I will not introduce new tools, as all the tools have been presented already, or will be presented later in the book. In fact, benchmarking your competitors is nothing other than applying the same thorough growth-hacking processes, practices, and tools you have been applying to your website. Using competitor benchmarking practices to complement your existing growth-hacking strategy will place you well ahead of most of your competitors. You will gain a far better understanding of their strategies, services, suppliers, clients, and more.

Social Media Benchmarking

Stay up to date with your competitors' social activity, products, promotions and mentions by setting up automatic reports on their social media posts. Things competitor analysis often reveals: current performance; trends within their social media activity; spikes and lows in engagement rates; publishing trends, days and times; various performance metrics; demographics; and comparison with other businesses. You will get answers to many questions that will help you close the gap between you and your competition. What channels are my competitors leveraging? What content strategies do they have in force? How effective are their social campaigns and channels? How do their strategy and performance compare with mine, and what could I do better? What type of content engages their followers and how often? Am I missing out? You may notice a spike in engagement rates on your competitors' social media channels. Investigate, and discover a niche you have not considered yet. You could also notice that your content publishing pattern is different to theirs. However, they are getting more engagement and more followers; maybe you should test different delivery times, as well. The truth is that the possibilities are endless.

Competitor keyword analysis

A competitor keyword analysis will provide valuable insights into the strategies of your competitors. Some questions you may ask are: what keywords are they ranking for? What search volumes? And how is your website performing by comparison? How are their digital marketing campaigns performing over a period of time? How do they compare to your performance, and what are the reasons? How is the website traffic of your competitors performing locally or nationally? How about yours? You could notice a significant increase in traffic on some of your competitors' keywords, investigate further, and discover that they have introduced a new product or have been running a successful social media campaign. Or you could discover one niche that your competitor dominates but you haven't thought of; or even a keyword with a high traffic and conversion potential.

Competitor brand monitoring

Competitor brand monitoring is an extension of the social media benchmarking exercise. Various options are available for gaining visibility of digital mentions of your competitors. A client posts a blog item introducing its partnership with your competitor? You will know it. Or maybe they featured in an industry publication? You may want to get in there as well. How about a press release about a new product or acquisition? Setting up notifications to finding out when your competitor is mentioned in relation to a certain keyword, product, or service is also an option.

Competitor backlink analysis

My all-time favorite competitor benchmarking process is the backlink analysis of competitor websites. When I managed several branded hotels, I would always challenge my sales manager to improve both lead generation and conversion. He or she would always bring me a list of actions with competitor car park walks close to the top. It did not work, and I cannot recall one instance where this traditional exercise delivered any meaningful results. And yet, take part in any commercial meeting and you will most often be presented with numerous similar sales-related actions. By contrast, we generated just one lead via a backlink analysis. It delivered 200k and that account become the top revenue performer in two consecutive years.

In another situation, a backlink analysis discovered a university linking to a competitor hotel website. On investigation, it transpired that the university was recommending most direct competitor websites to their students and delegates. Needless to say, the hotel manager contacted the university and got his website linked to that page, too.

How does it look in practice?

You conduct a backlink analysis of your competitor hotel's website and discover that a training company is recommending your competitor on their website. After investigating, you find that this company is building offices in preparation for moving into your town. You get in touch, convince them to give you a try, over-deliver, and gain the contract from your competitor.

CHAPTER 20.
AFFILIATE MARKETING

You now have great content and lots of traffic to your website. You are passionate; indeed you love what you do. Why not monetize your traffic? There are several opportunities available to you. If you are a blogger looking for an idea to monetize your blog, without much effort on your part, then the obvious option is Google AdSense. By signing up to Google AdSense you become part of Google's Display Network, allowing Google to place contextual ads for its remarketing or display campaigns. The "contextual" part is particularly important, as Google crawls your page content and serves ads matching the theme of your page. By doing so, your brand identity is not affected, and as most ads are relevant to your content they will in fact add value to your users.

If you are looking for more-traditional ways of monetizing your blog, then three of the best popular platforms are Click Bank, CJ (Commission Junction), and ShareASale. If you are looking to discover new, innovative tools to support your growth-hacking efforts then you must give JVZoo and WhiteHatBox a try.

VigLink

VigLink is an affiliate program that will enable you to monetize your blog with very little effort on your part. It takes a maximum of five minutes to create an account, get a snippet of code, add it to your website, and forget it exists. VigLink works in partnership with thousands of businesses that are paying commission to the platform for any purchases via the platform. As soon as you have added the code on your website, VigLink scans your website, identifies any products or contextual words, mentions, links, or names of their affiliate partners, and automatically adds affiliate links to the partner websites. You now earn commission when people purchase a product via your automatically created affiliate link. And all it takes is five minutes to set up and forget.

How does it look in practice?

You are a translator providing your CV on your website. You specify skills and tools you have been using; Trados would be an example. Assume that VigLink has forged a partnership with Trados. As soon as you install the VigLink code on your website, VigLink scans and discovers the word Trados in your CV and automatically adds a link to the Trados website. Next time someone reads your CV, notices the link to Trados, gets curious to find out more, clicks the link and decides to purchase Trados or another product through that link, you earn a commission.

Thirsty Affiliates

One plugin you can use for all your affiliate-link-related needs is Thirsty Affiliates. This plugin prepares your links and makes them look pretty for sharing purposes. Great functionality and various add-ons are available to help you manage affiliate links like a pro.

When doing your online research, you will discover many blog posts reviewing the 10 best affiliate plugins. The interesting part is that the writers have never actually used these plugins, and yet they write reviews and recommend them. You will know by now that many recommendations are simply driven by the highest commission earned rather than by actual performance. Do not let yourself be drawn into this; the options below are probably the best available.

So what does the Thirsty Affiliates plugin do?

You write many articles, and most of the time the URLs are quite long and don't look great when shared on social media, guest blogs, or other mainstream channels. With Thirsty Affiliates you can customize your link, make it look professional, clean, and tidy, while also carrying the affiliate benefit. You may argue that you can simply change the URL of the article. However, remember that you will also be looking to optimize your URL for SEO. With Thirsty Affiliates you can have the best of both worlds: the URL is optimized and you can customize the link you share on various blogs. In practice, you may customize a link to appear as seoconsultant-london.com/translators-tools when sharing on a specific translators' forum, and as seoconsultant-london.com/hotel-management-tools when sharing the tool on a hotel-related website. And all this with no changes to your original article URL. You can also use Thirsty Affiliates for your affiliate marketing links. Affiliate links are generally ugly and include various parameters, which makes customizing your links quite important. Other features include great statistics, an automated link creation throughout your website, based on keywords, and automatic Google event tracking.

Affiliate Traffic Lab

There are many affiliate marketing platforms that make searching for the best products and selling them online extremely easy. One platform I have come across recently is Affiliate Traffic Lab. This platform currently works with JVZoo, ClickBank and WarriorPlus. From the dashboard, you can start by searching for and choosing affiliate products you would like to promote. Next, the tool has a really cool feature that allows you to search for videos and customize them to the point where you can make them your own. You can change fonts, images, and text; add audio, add your affiliate links, and deploy the videos to YouTube. I like this software, as it is intuitive and, in line with the theme of this book, makes it very easy for affiliate marketers who do not have enough time, budget, or interest to create their own videos. Imagine you have seen a very good training tutorial on YouTube and have decided to promote the product, but you have no video editing or coding skills. Simply find the product in Affiliate Traffic Lab, get the YouTube tutorial, customize it and deploy it.

Alterzon

Another great affiliate marketing tool is a WordPress plugin called Alterzon. It works on any website that is running WooCommerce, and it allows fast set-up of affiliate marketing websites. Its simplicity is its most powerful feature, and it offers a wide variety of sellers you can choose products from: Amazon, Best Buy, eBay, Walmart, AliExpress, and others. Simply choose a seller and the category of products you are looking for, then review all the products that will be listed on your dashboard. Choose the ones you like and import them into your store. The product page itself is very professional; it is customizable, and you can add several images of the product. Moreover, the zoom technology when hovering over the product image gives this plugin an edge. Price comparison with other websites is available on the product page, as well, which serves as social proof that your audience gets the best possible deal. People can sign up to price drop alerts, thus providing you with their contact details, as well. The idea is that these details can be used later for such as remarketing and email marketing. Price drop alerts are fully customizable. Wish lists, keyword information on user queries about your shop, social media syndication, and great filter capabilities are just a few of the many powerful features this plugin displays.

CHAPTER 21.
CONCLUSION

Having done my share of reading over the years, I am quite familiar with most approaches taken by writers in concluding their work. Most often, a comprehensive and clever review of the main concepts is provided, and plenty of advice is offered, encouraging readers to follow up with actions. I am hoping that you will not be disappointed to learn that I will do neither of those things. After reading my two books, you should have a reasonable understanding of the trends shaping the future of digital marketing. So let me try to keep it short and sweet.

In the section on the future of my book HACKING DIGITAL GROWTH 2025: Exploiting Human Biases, Tools of the Trade & The Disturbing Future of Digital Marketing I argued that SEO is dying a slow death. It is only a matter of time until algorithms like Google's RankBrain dismiss all SEO ranking factors other than great content. I have also argued that professional services such as SEO, Content Writing, Website Design and Paid Search are already on track to becoming commodities. It is only a matter of time until clients like the small business owner or entrepreneur will finally realize that it is quite possible for them to run their own digital marketing campaigns, to build their own website or outsource it at far better rates than they might have thought. My arguments have implications that apply well beyond the digital marketing industry, and extend to every industry or profession you can think of. Automatic checkout points take over manned stations in supermarkets, both improving efficiency and reducing costs such as salaries and wages. Hotels are introducing self-check-in points, reducing the need for qualified front desk staff and lowering the hotels' wage bills in the process. Platforms like Copify, Freelancer, Alibaba, Fiverr, SEOClerks and PeoplePerHour have been shifting the balance of power from professional workers, who now have a choice between joining these platforms on lower fees, or losing their business altogether. Driverless cars will replace the need for professional drivers, or require less-qualified drivers to complement the algorithms. Google's Translate service has already made great advancements in the accuracy of its translations, as its performance on language combinations like Portuguese–English demonstrates. Moreover—to contradict the arguments of many professional translators—most companies will find the standard of Google's translations adequate to their needs, thus eliminating completely, or reducing the need for, professional translators. The examples could be continued. As a worker, you may or may not accept my arguments. If you don't, then I have very little doubt that there will be a time when you will be left behind. You may, however, concede that you will have no other choice than to work for less money while increasing the number of hours you work. However, as I have shown, "services as commodities" is only a step away from automation, therefore you must avoid getting too comfortable with this scenario. So what should you do? The truth is that I do not have clear answers to these challenges; the world moves faster and faster, and technologies improve and situations change sometimes faster than humans are able to cope with. That being said, you do have a choice between throwing in the towel and continuously upgrading your skills. The most important skill you will need for the future is the ability to change your career as often as needed. I would not be surprised if entire professions and skills became obsolete or were taken over by machines as frequently as every one or two years in the future. Most likely, the ability to shift direction involves developing the grit and determination to leave your comfort zone probably more than once, with the courage to leap into the unknown. Only you can decide your next step, and I refuse to patronize by providing specific advice or industries that you should consider next; this is personal to every individual and their skills and circumstances. As a personal example, I am fully committed to walking the walk and, after graduating with an MBA and an MA in Marketing and Innovation, and having worked in three different industries, I have currently enrolled myself on a third Masters in Data Science, taking courses on statistics, mathematics, analytics, and machine learning. There are troubled times ahead, and I encourage you to acknowledge that you can either act, or be acted upon.

In the section on Psychology, I argued that a deep understanding of the principles underlying human behavior is paramount to the success of your digital marketing efforts. I drew various connections between the more traditional psychology studies and their applications to online behavior. On occasions, I provided examples of, or reflected on, the impact of these principles on the behavior of website visitors. However, most times I have preferred to draw attention to the principles and allowed your imagination to make the necessary connections. I hope you enjoyed the conversation, though you must remember that any information that is not driving action is useless.

In the chapter on the tools of the trade, I introduced various tools and concepts aimed at enabling you to perform most digital marketing tasks for yourself. Alternatively, you can now better challenge your digital marketing consultant or agency. Most important, my hope is that I have managed to instill some confidence that a DIY approach is well within your capabilities, if you choose to follow that route. Many of these tools I have used myself, many have been recommended to me by colleagues or other marketers. In the end, it is for you to discover what works best for you, and you should now be in a far better position to understand the variety of tasks you can perform. Given the nature of the digital marketing field, I expect that many of these tools will be upgraded and improved and that some of them will even disappear in the near or not-too-distant future. For example, since I started writing this book new Google AdWords and Google Search Console interfaces have been launched, SEMrush has added several new features, such as a Social Media Auto-posting option, and 300 new tools were marketed to me on JVZoo. The best advice I can provide you with is: stay up to date with the new features, and remember that too many tools can lead to decision paralysis—sometimes less is more. In the words of Kevin Kelly, "No matter how long you have been using a tool, endless upgrades make you a newbie—the new user often seen as clueless. In this era of "becoming," everyone becomes a newbie. Worse, we will be newbies forever. That should keep us humble." Kelly (2014, p. 10)

These are great times, if we consider that not too long time ago, brands dominated the digital marketing space simply by having the budgets to do so. Nowadays, savvy SMEs and individuals can match the marketing efforts of many of these brands, empowered by the diversity and ease-of-use of digital marketing tools. As entrepreneur Daniel Priestley has pointed out, "to be in business today requires you to have a laptop, a phone and an idea." (Priestley, 2014, p. 25) So...be bold, be courageous, never stop learning, and most of all, never allow yourself to become a commodity.

REFERENCES

1. Anderson, Chris (2009). The Longer Tail. How Endless choice is creating unlimited demand, GB : Random House Business Books

2. Ariely, Dan (2012). The (Honest) Truth about Dishonesty, UK: Harper Collins Publishers

3. Ariely, Dan (2009). Predictably Irrational. The Hidden Forces that Shape Our Decisions, UK: Harper

4. Ash, Tim. Ginty, Maura. Page, Rich (2012). Landing Page Optimization: The Definitive Guide to Testing and Tuning for Conversions, 2nd Edition, US : John Wiley & Sons

5. Baron-Cohen, Simon (2012). Zero Degrees of Empathy. A New Theory Of Human Cruelty And Kindness, GB: Penguin Books

6. Baumeister, Roy F & Tierney, John (2012). Willpower. Rediscovering Our Greatest Strength, UK: Allen Lane

7. Bernazzani, Sophia (2017). The Decline of Organic Facebook Reach & How to Outsmart the Algorithm, Retrieved from https://blog.hubspot.com/marketing/facebook-declining-organic-reach

8. Bloom, Paul (2011). How Pleasure Works. Why we like what we like, GB : Vintage Books

9. Brafman, Ori & Brafman, Rom (2011). Click. The Power Of Instant Connections, GB: Virgin Books

10. Brooks, David (2012). The Social Animal. A Story of How Success Happens, GB : Short Books

11. Cabane, Olivia Fox (2012). The Charisma Myth. How Anyone Can Master the Art and Science of Personal Magnetism, GB: Penguin Group

12. Caldwell, Leigh (2012). The psychology of price. How to use price to increase demand, profit and customer satisfaction, GB: Crimson Publishing Ltd

13. Carnagie, Dale (2006). How to Win Friends and Influence People, GB: Vermilion

14. Chabris, Christopher & Simons, Daniel (2010). The Invisible Gorilla And Other Ways Our Intuition Deceives Us, GB: Harper Collins Publishers

15. Christensen, Clayton M (2013). The Innovator's Dilemma. When New Technologies Cause Great Firms To Fail, US: Harvard Business Review Press

16. Christakis, Nicholas & Fowler, James (2011). Connected. The Amazing Power of Social Networks and How They Shape Our Lives, UK: Harper Collins Publishers

17. Cialdini, Robert B (2007). Influence. The Psychology of Persuasion, US: Collins Business Essentials

18. Dolan, Paul (2015). Happiness by Design. Finding Pleasure and purpose in everyday life, GB: Penguin Books

19. Domingos, Pedro (2017). The Master Algorithm. How The Quest For The Ultimate Learning Machine Will Remake Our World, UK: Penguin Books

20. Duhigg, Charles (2012). The Power of Habit. Why we do what we do and how to change, UK: Random House

21. Dweck, Carol S. (2008). Mindset. The New Psychology of Success. How We Can learn To Fulfill Our Potential, US: Ballantine Books

22. Enge, Eric. Spencer, Stephan. Stricchiola, Jessie & Fishkin, Rand (2013). The Art of SEO. Mastering Search Engine Optimization, US: O'Reilly

23. Gardner, Dan (2009). Risk. The Science and Politics of Fear, GB: Virgin Books

24. Gilbert, Daniel (2007). Stumbling on Happiness, GB: Harper Perennial

25. Gladwell, Malcolm (2001). The Tipping Point. How little things can make a big difference, GB : Abacus

26. Gladwell, Malcolm (2006). Blink. The Power of Thinking without Thinking, GB: Penguin Books

27. Godin, Seth (2005). Purple Cow. Transform Your Business by Being Remarkable, UK: Penguin Business

28. Godin, Seth (2012). All Marketers Are Liars, US: Penguin Books

29. Harari, Yuval Noah (2015). Homo Deus. A Brief History of Tomorrow, GB: Harvill Secker

30. Heath, Chip & Heath, Dan (2008). Made to Stick. Why some ideas take hold and others come unstuck, GB: Arrow Books

31. Hood, Bruce (2009). Supersense. From Superstition to Religion- the Brain Science of Belief, GB: Constable

32. Johnson, Spencer (1999). Who Moved My Cheese?, GB: Vermillion

33. Jones, Graham (2014). Click.ology. What works in online shopping and how your business can use consumer psychology to succeed, GB: Nicholas Brealey Publishing

34. Klein, Gary (1999). Sources of Power. How People make Decisions, US : MIT Press

35. Laham, Simon (2012). The Joy Of Sin, GB: Constable

36. Kahneman, Daniel (2011). Thinking, fast and slow, GB: Allen Lane

37. Kahneman, Daniel & Deaton, Angus (2010), High income improves evaluation of life but not emotional well-being, Retrieved from https://www.ncbi.nlm.nih.gov/pmc/articles/PMC2944762/

38. Kelly, Kevin (2016). The Inevitable. Understanding the 12 Technological Forces That Will Shape Our Future, US: Viking

39. Kim, Larry (2018). 10 Remarketing Facts that Will Make You Rethink PPC, Retrieved at http://www.wordstream.com/blog/ws/2015/10/01/remarketing-facts

40. Krug, Steve (2014). Don't Make Me Think. A common Sense Approach To Web and Mobile Usability, US: New Riders

41. Marr, Bernard (2016). Big Data in Practice. How 45 Successful Companied Used Big Data Analytics To Deliver Extraordinary Results, GB: Wiley

42. Marr, Bernard (2015). Big Data. Using Smart Big Data Analytics And Metrics To Make Better Decisions And Improve Performance, GB: Wiley

43. Milgram, Stanley (2010). Obedience to Authority, GB: Pinter and Martin

44. Pink, Daniel H. (2011). Drive. The Surprising Truth About What Motivates Us, GB: Cannon Gate

45. Pink, Daniel H. (2013). To Sell Is Human. The Surprising Truth About Persuading, Convincing And Influencing Others, GB : Canongate Books

46. Pink, Daniel H. (2008). A Whole New Mind. Why Right-Brainers Will Rule the Future, GB : Marshall Cavendish International

47. Pinker, Steven (2003). The Blank Slate. The modern denial of human nature, GB: Penguin Books

48. Priestley, Dan (2014). Entrepreneur Revolution. How to develop your entrepreneurial mindset and start a business that works, GB: Capstone Publishing

49. Robertson, Ian (2012). The Winner Effect. How Power Affects Your Brain, GB : Bloomsbury

50. Ross, Lee & Nisbett, Richard E. (2011). The Person And The Situation. Perspectives of Social Psychology, GB : Pinter and Martin

51. Schmidt, Eric & Rosenberg, Jonathan (2014). How Google Works, GB: John Murray

52. Searchmetrics (2017), Rebooting Ranking Factors – Google.com, Retrieved at http://pages.searchmetrics.com/rs/656-KWJ-035/images/Searchmetrics-Rebooting-Ranking-Factors-US_whitepaper.PDF?mkt_tok=eyJpIjoiTmpaak9EQTVaV0kzTm1ZMiIsInQiO iJjQVlaZnlCSmtveU5UZWc3NEM2ZlwvbkRMSDRRcnVUWlZRRNFlQNnRlYVR FTEszak5EaHdraDd4eWFGUXhjNmdSOTJVS21BTFwveHVSa2J0dXIzUkZ5V 2Z3SUE4ZHU4cm5uV0JweU8zcW4wRU5SU0hHUjJOOVJoSndianUyenVVZF VYIn0%3D

53. Sharot, Tali (2012), The Optimism Bias. Why we're wired to look on the bright side, GB: Robinson

54. Sharp, Byron (2010). How brands Grow. What marketers don't know, Australia: Oxford University Press

55. Slater, Laura (2005). Opening Skinner's Box, GB: Bloomsbury Publishing

56. Snaptchat (2018), Retrieved at 21/05/2018 from https://forbusiness.snapchat.com/,%2022%20Sept/

57. Sutherland, Stuart (2007). Irrationality, GB: Pinter and Martin Ltd

58. Steele, Claude M. (2011). Whistling Vivaldi. How stereotypes affect us and what we can do, US: W. W. Norton

59. Stone, Brad (2013). The Everything Store, GB: Transworld Publishers

60. Taleb, Nassim Nicholas (2007). Fooled by Randomness. The Hidden Role of Chance in Life and in the Markets, US : Penguin Books

61. Tapscott, Don & Williams, Anthony D. (2006). Wikinomics, How Mass Collaboration Changes Everything, US : Portfolio

62. Tavris, Carol & Aronson, Elliot (2008). Mistakes Were Made (but not by me). Why we justify foolish beliefs, bad decisions and hurtful acts, GB: Pinter and Martin

63. Totham, Isabel (2017).10 Online Dating Statistics You Should Know, Retrieved from https://www.eharmony.com/online-dating-statistics/

64. Trivers, Robert (2011). Deceit and Self-Deception. Fooling Yourself the Better to Fool Others, GB: Allen Lane

65. Trotman, Andrew (2014), Facebook's Mark Zuckerberg: Why I wear the same T-shirt every day, Retrieved from https://www.telegraph.co.uk/technology/facebook/11217273/Facebooks -Mark-Zuckerberg-Why-I-wear-the-same-T-shirt-every-day.html

66. Walton, Sam & Huey, John (1993). Made In America, US : Bantam

67. Weinberg, Gabriel & Mares, Justin (2015). Traction. How Any Startup Can Achieve Explosive Customer Growth, UK: Portfolio Penguin

68. Wiseman, Richard (2010). :59 Seconds. Think a little, Change a lot, GB: Pan Books

69. Wiseman, Richard (2007). Quirkology. The Curious Science Of Everyday Lives, GB: Macmillan

70. Wilson, D. Timothy (2011), Redirect. The Surprising New Science of Psychological Change, GB : Allen Lane

71. Wilson, D. Timothy (2002), Strangers to Ourselves. Discovering the adaptive unconscious, GB: The Belknap Press of Harvard University Press

72. York, Alex (2018). 61 Social Media Statistics to Bookmark for 2018. Retrieved at https://sproutsocial.com/insights/social-media-statistics/

73. Zimbardo, Philip (2009). The Lucifer Effect. How Good People Turn Evil, GB: Rider

Made in the USA
Middletown, DE
25 August 2018